Contributions to Economics

For further volumes:
http://www.springer.com/series/1262

Diana Sonntag

AIDS and Aid

A Public Good Approach

Physica-Verlag

Dr. Diana Sonntag
Vienna University of Economics and Business
Institute for Social Policy
Nordbergstraße 15
1090 Wien, Austria
diana.sonntag@wu.ac.at

Accepted as a dissertation at Chemnitz University of Technology under the title: "Financing International Health-Promoting Public Goods Against AIDS - A Supply-Side Approach".

ISSN 1431-1933
ISBN 978-3-7908-2418-6 e-ISBN 978-3-7908-2419-3
DOI 10.1007/978-3-7908-2419-3
Springer Heidelberg Dordrecht London New York

Library of Congress Control Number: 2009943061

Cover design: SPi Publisher Services

Printed on acid-free paper

Physica-Verlag is a brand of Springer-Verlag Berlin Heidelberg
Springer-Verlag is a part of Springer Science+Business Media (www.springer.com)

Contents

List of Figures

List of Tables

Abbreviations and Acronyms

AAH	Action Against Hunger
AEL	Aid Effectiveness Literature
AIDS	Acquired Immune Deficiency Syndrome
ART	Antiretroviral Therapy
AVAC	AIDS Vaccine Advocacy Coalition
CD4	Cluster of Differentiation 4
CDC	Center for Disease Control and Prevention
CEACAM1	Carcinoembryonic Antigen-Related Cell Adhesion Molecule 1
CES	Constant Elasticity of Substitution
CGIAR	Consultative Group on International Agriculture Research
CIA	Central Intelligence Agency
CMH	Commission on Macroeconomics and Health
CRS	Credit Reporting System
DALY	Disability-Adjusted Life Year
DFID	Department for International Development
DHAP	Division of HIV/AIDS Prevention
DOTS	Directly Observed Treatment Short-Course
ECR	Expanded and Comprehensive Response
ed(s).	editor(s)
e.g.	exempli gratia
EGDI	Expert Group on Development Issues
et al.	et alii
etc.	et cetera
EU	European Union
EuroHIV	European Centre For Epidemiological Monitoring of HIV/AIDS
Eurostat	Statistical Office of the European Communities
FANRPAN	Food, Agriculture and Natural Resources Policy Analysis Network
FANTA	Food and Nutrition Technical Assistance
FAO	Food and Agriculture Organization
FCCC	Framework Convention on Climate Change
ff.	and the following
FHI	Family Health International
GDP	Gross Domestic Product
GEF	Global Environmental Facility
GNI	Gross National Income
GRID	Gay-Related Immunodeficiency Disease
G7	Group of Seven industrially advanced nations
HIV	Human Immunodeficiency Virus

HIV-1	Human Immunodeficiency Virus Type 1
HM Treasury	Her Majesty's Treasury
HPA	Health Protection Agency
IAVI	International AIDS Vaccine Initiative
ICP	International Comparison Program
IDB	Inter-American Development Bank
IDS	Institute of Development Studies
i.e.	id est
IFF	International Finance Facility
IFPRI	International Food Policy Research Institute
Impact	Implementing AIDS Prevention and Care Project
IOM	International Organization for Migration
LDB	Life Database
MC_i	Country *i*'s Marginal Costs
MDG	Millennium Development Goals
MRS_i	Country *i*'s Marginal Rate of Substitution
NAM	National AIDS Manual
NGO	Non-Governmental Organisation
NIAID	U.S. National Institute of Allergy and Infectious Diseases
No.	Number
ODA	Official Development Assistance
OECD	Organisation for Economic Co-operation and Development
OI	Opportunistics Infections
OPEC	Organization of the Petroleum Exporting Countries
p.	page
pp.	pages
PCP	Pneumocystis Carinii Pneumonia
PEPFAR	The President's Emergency Plan for AIDS Relief
PNEAR	National Rural Drinking Water Supply and Sanitation Programme
PPP	Purchasing Power Parity
PRB	Population Reference Bureau
R&D	Research and Development
SADC	Southern African Development Community
STD	Sexually Transmitted Disease
STI	Sexually Transmitted Infection
TB	Tuberculosis
U.S.	United States
UK	United Kingdom
UN	United Nations
UNAIDS	The Joint United Nations Programme on HIV/AIDS
UNDP	United Nations Development Programme
UNEP	United Nations Environment Programme
UNESCO	United Nations Educational, Scientific And Cultural Organization
UNFPA	United Nations Population Fund
UNGASS	United Nations General Assembly Special Session
UNICEF	United Nations Children's Fund
USAID	U.S. Agency for International Development
VCT	Voluntery Counselling and Testing
WDI	World Development Indicators
WFP	World Food Programme
WHO	World Health Organization
YLD	Years Lived With a Disability
YLL	Years of Life Lost

Chapter 1
Introduction

The unfolding tragedy of the AIDS epidemic is an instance where a disease with local origins has created consequences worldwide.
Todd Sandler (2001a)

Health concerns are firmly embedded in the developing world. Conditions of poverty like inadequate health infrastructures and sanitation, limited access to treatment of diseases etc. have increased the susceptibility to diseases. However, there is an increasing awareness that health problems of the poor cross national borders and, hence, affect the well-being of people globally. Of all the health crises originating from the developing world the HIV/AIDS epidemic does not only seem to be the largest humanitarian concern but also possesses major economic, demographical and social consequences. AIDS could cause even bigger consequences in the future if the spread of HIV is not stopped.

The international community has recognised this necessity by determining the fight against AIDS as one of the eight Millennium Development Goals (MDGs[1]). The MDGs which range from halving poverty to achieving universal primary education represent a global commitment given by 189 nations at the Millennium Summit in 2000 (UN 2000). Goal 6 elevates anti-HIV efforts to one of the highest development priorities in the world. Governments have committed themselves to halt the spread of HIV by 2015 and to begin to reverse it. Currently countries are not on track on achieving this target (UN Millennium Project 2005, p. 15). The World Health Organization (WHO) and other big health lenders have responded by calling for an increase in funds. Many institutions and funding mechanisms like the Global Fund to Fight AIDS, Tuberculosis and Malaria (GFATM), the International Finance Facility (IFF) and others have been established to collect additional financial resources (HM Treasury and DFID 2004, p. 2; Global Fund 2007, p. 9). However, while an increased supply of anti-HIV programmes requires an enhanced funding, experiences of the past indicates that scaling up budgets cannot ensure a higher

[1]The MDGs and interdependencies between them are discussed by John and Ruebbelke (2007, pp. 5–10).

D. Sonntag, *AIDS and Aid*, Contributions to Economics,
DOI 10.1007/978-3-7908-2419-3_1,

effectiveness (UNAIDS 2008, p. 27; Riddell 2007, p. 188; Lewis 2005); a general discussion about aid effectiveness can be found in Killick (2005).

Against this background, this book aims at analysing whether or not MDG 6 can be achieved through an increased quantity of funding.[2] Or, which policies exist to increase the effectiveness of international financing mechanisms? For example, should international assistance be targeted to regions like Sub-Saharan Africa to prevent further cross-bordering transmissions of HIV? Since governments of developing countries can often not utilise financial support, under which circumstances are in-kind transfers preferable to lump-sum transfers? Finally, which policy options would facilitate the own provision efforts of recipients?

In contrast to the academic literature on AIDS that evaluates national consequences of anti-HIV programmes and its financial implications, this book discusses these political questions from an international point of view. Because this analysis will focus on the transnational scope of the HIV/AIDS crisis and its consequences for interventions, the effectiveness of financing policies can be evaluated from an international perspective. Thus, it will be shown that targeting international support to countries that bear the highest financial burden of AIDS can be nationally effective but is even counterproductive globally. The analysis will focus on three key interventions developing an AIDS vaccine, prevention of tuberculosis and knowledge transfers.

We use the analytical framework of international public goods. This concept seems to be crucial since HIV/AIDS has become an international issue with wide-ranging economic, social and biological spillovers. International organisations like the United Nations Development Programme (UNDP) and others have acknowledged the importance of international public goods to achieve MDG 6 (Commission of the European Communities 2007, p. 52; International Bank for Reconstruction and Development and World Bank 2004, p. 25). However, little attention is paid to policies to finance health-promoting public goods. Exceptions are Teixeira (2006) and Kaul (2005) arguing that underprovision can be solved by an increased quantity of funding. In contrast to our analysis, their argument focuses on the demand side. Thus, causes of underprovision are attributed to missing incentives of governments to implement anti-HIV programmes. Supply-side characteristics as the public supply aggregation are not explicitly considered. The public supply aggregation (henceforth, aggregation technology) seems essential since national efforts of governments do not correspond to a global response. In order to define the overall effect, it has to be clarified how individual contributions are combined to the transnational provision level. For example, one can assume that national contributions to prevent HIV-transmission are added up to determine the global level of prevention. Or, one can suppose that the ability to stop further transmissions worldwide is defined by the government that provides the smallest amount of health measures. In the latter case, the global success of

[2]Our discussion is primarily related to Target 7 aiming to halt and to begin to reverse the spread of HIV by 2015.

anti-HIV activities corresponds to the government that delivers the smallest contribution. This brief presentation already indicates the variety of aggregation technologies.

In contrast to the standard approach of the academic literature on AIDS that derives policy recommendations from the demand side, this book introduces an additional perspective to evaluate the provision of health-promoting public goods and the consequences for international assistance. The explicit consideration of the aggregation technology as a main focus in this book gives a new insight into the effectiveness of international policies. Thus, international assistance can be allocated in a more effective way than recommended today. In addition, the consideration of supply-side characteristics casts new light on the public goods literature. The choice of the optimal policy, in-kind or income transfers is unresolved in the debate on developing an AIDS vaccine. The standard approach in economic theory, which assumes an additive aggregation of individual contributions to a public good, shows that these transfer mechanisms result in the same equilibrium allocation. However, our analysis indicates that in-kind transfers are preferable to financial support only if recipients are more cost-efficient than donors. It follows that targeting resources to research institutions in developing countries is not an effective policy even if it is justified from the epidemiology of HIV since high infection rates would decline.

The analysis proceeds as follows: Chapter 2 starts with basic information about the level and the distribution of HIV. Afterwards, national and transnational impacts of AIDS are outlined. Following a short presentation of the most obvious consequences of AIDS on health and life expectancy, the financial burden of AIDS is quantified. Then, biological spillovers of health problems in the developing world, how they interact with HIV/AIDS and yield transnational consequences are discussed. The chapter proceeds by identifying the main focus of the anti-HIV programmes at the moment. Following the distinctions of the epidemiology of HIV, current anti-HIV strategies are presented. By taking the cross-bordering impacts of HIV into account, the subsequent section explains why the concept of international public goods seems crucial. By reviewing the characteristics of public goods on the demand and supply side, this chapter points out the importance of the variety of aggregation technologies, and its implications for both providing and financing policies; those are analysed in Chapters 3 and 4.

Chapter 3 addresses the issue whether or not the problem of suboptimality is inherent if health-promoting public goods against AIDS are provided. Therefore, the impact of various aggregation technologies on efficiency is analysed to determine the status quo of provision levels. The investigation starts with a benchmark case that replicates the standard argument stating that international public goods are underprovided because of insufficient incentives. Afterwards, this analysis is extended by explicitly considering the variety of aggregation technologies and its implications on provision policies. The consideration of diverse aggregation technologies does not only identify further causes of suboptimality. Based on these results it also indicates how international assistance should be allocated to solve shortcomings.

In Chapter 4 the resulting implications for international transfers are worked out in detail. It is analysed under which circumstances unconditional income transfers are an efficient tool to increase the voluntary provision of health-promoting public goods against AIDS. In addition, it is shown that there are cases where a financial support of the poor is unlikely to ensure transnationally efficient provision levels. It is also demonstrated why it may even be counterproductive. Because financial assistance can be utilised for private consumption instead for providing a public good, the chapter then turns from unconditional support to transfers in kind. Following an analysis on the efficiency of these two transfer mechanisms, a third kind of international support, subsidy schemes, is highlighted. Based on the limits of effectiveness of a subsidy, an alternative financing mechanism that can achieve efficient provision levels is developed.

Chapter 5 shows why effective responses to HIV/AIDS also require solutions addressing regional constraints like missing access to clean water, inadequate sanitary facilities and malnutrition. Therefore, the impacts of these regional concerns on the AIDS crisis are outlined. Because these analyses refer to the importance of official development assistance (ODA), the linkage between ODA and international transfers is discussed thereafter. Additionally, institutional considerations as the roles of non-governmental and multilateral organisations are outlined.

The final Chapter summarises the main results, gives some policy implications and presents some scope for further research.

Chapter 2
The Challenge: A Transnational Response to HIV/AIDS

Fighting AIDS is really a global public good.
Peter Piot (2005)

Since the appearance of the human immunodeficiency virus (HIV) more than 25 years ago the virus has been spread all over the world, but unevenly. The concentration of HIV in developing countries is worrying because their governments are often reluctant to intervene. Those governments are faced with other important demands as addressing malnutrition which are competitive for scarce financial resources. Hence, their willingness to establish anti-AIDS programmes is little. The epidemiological, political and social consequences do not only become visible within developing countries, but also globally. This cross-country health interdependency has to be reflected in a worldwide response because isolated interventions do not seem to be effective in the long run. The concept of international public goods was suggested in the academic literature on AIDS to solve international concerns. Several governments and international organisations like the World Bank or the WHO have followed this recommendation by setting this topic on their agendas (World Bank 2000, pp. 2, 6; Engqvist 2001, p. 3). The WHO and the Joint United Nations Programme on HIV/AIDS (UNAIDS), for example, refer to the provision of HIV prevention as a classic public good intervention in their annual report about the AIDS epidemic in 2005 (UNAIDS and WHO 2005, p. 7). However, it seems that the provision of international public goods does not meet the requirement to result in effective policy responses in the fight against HIV/AIDS. Cross-country benefit and cost spillovers and the resulting difficulties in determining the corresponding prices imply that the control of HIV/AIDS tends to be suboptimal. In contrast to national health-promoting public goods as maintaining hospitals, there is no government that can intervene either by using taxes for financing or by direct provision (Smith et al. 2004, p. 272). This chapter shows why a consideration of international public goods with respect to the global AIDS epidemic is still justified.

Our analysis proceeds as follows: Starting with an overview about the AIDS epidemics in industrialised and developing countries, national and transnational

D. Sonntag, *AIDS and Aid,* Contributions to Economics,
DOI 10.1007/978-3-7908-2419-3_2, © Springer-Verlag Berlin Heidelberg 2010

impacts of AIDS are described. The consequences of AIDS for health and the resulting financial burden of governments are analysed in detail. We then turn to epidemiological spillovers of AIDS. Giving the line of reasoning why AIDS has become a global concern, we proceed by introducing the concept of international public goods. After outlining the conceptual background, different types of health-promoting public goods are presented. The chapter concludes with a short summary.

2.1 The Epidemiology of HIV

The earliest known case of a HIV infection was reported in 1959 (Zhu et al. 1998, p. 594). It was found in a preserved blood sample of a Bantu man from Leopoldville, Belgian Congo – today Kinshasa in the Democratic Republic of the Congo. However, the official date of the onset of the AIDS epidemic is nearly 22 years later. The United States Centers for Disease Control and Prevention (CDC) reported five young gay men in Los Angeles who suffered from a relatively rare form of pneumonia (CDC 1981, p. 1). Since additional pneumonia cases occurred among young gay men within the next seven months throughout the United States, the immune disorder was initially designated as GRID for "Gay-Related Immunodeficiency Disease" (Altman 1982). However, as the same infections also emerged among heterosexual Haitian males (CDC 1982a, p. 353) and heterosexual hemophilia patients (CDC 1982b, p. 365), the CDC applied the more general name Acquired Immune Deficiency Syndrome (AIDS) (Marx 1982; CDC 1982c, p. 507).

Since the CDC's first warning about AIDS more than 60 million people have been infected all over the world. Nowadays, the estimated number of people living with HIV is approximately 33 million (UNAIDS and WHO 2007, p. 3). This is a reduction of 16% compared to the estimations in 2006 (UNAIDS and WHO 2006, p. 2). This decline results from a major revision in November 2007. The WHO and UNAIDS released updated estimations based on refinements in methodology and an increased data availability (The Kaiser Family Foundation 2008). A reduced number of people living with HIV results from revisions of India's and Sub-Saharan Africa's HIV data. By comparing the adjusted estimate for 2006 (32 million instead of 39 million) with data for 2007, the number of HIV-positive individuals has increased. Several factors like continuing HIV infections, growing populations and people living longer after getting infected yield an increased amount of HIV-infected people (The Kaiser Family Foundation 2008). A prolonged life as a result of strengthened treatment services also implies a current decline in deaths due to AIDS. AIDS deaths have diminished from roughly three million in 2005 to 2.1 million in 2007 (UNAIDS and WHO 2007, p. 1). However, HIV remains one of the leading causes of death worldwide (The Kaiser Family Foundation 2007a).

In sum, these current global trends characterise HIV/AIDS as an expanding epidemic. Yet, regional situations can differ from the described global snapshot. Governments face different stages of epidemics in their countries. The main causes are differences in the occurrence of the first HIV cases, in the pattern of epidemics and in the willingness of governments to respond (Ainsworth and Over 1999, p. 86). Thus, in some areas like in Sub-Saharan Africa the number of people living with HIV has stabilised or shows signs of declining due to having reached a level of saturation while that in Eastern Europe is growing (The Kaiser Family Foundation 2007a). We proceed by presenting a typology to classify HIV/AIDS epidemics. Then, these criteria are applied to characterise epidemics in industrialised and developing countries.

2.1.1 A Typology for Classifying AIDS Epidemics

AIDS epidemics are varying from country to country as well as from subpopulation to subpopulation within a country. There is no unique or best approach to classify AIDS epidemics. Taxonomies can differ depending on the purposes for which they are intended, e.g. identifying differences in the pattern of HIV transmission or determining the distribution and the level of HIV infections. Regarding the aim of this section to give an overview about recent regional trends, it is useful to classify AIDS epidemics according to three criteria: first, the number of annual new infections per million inhabitants, second, the main pattern of HIV transmission and third, the extent of an epidemic.

Current levels of HIV infections can be measured by the HIV prevalence. The HIV prevalence expresses the cumulative number of HIV infections (Ainsworth and Over 1999, p. 55). We have to distinguish this concept from that of HIV incidence as demonstrated in Box 2.1. HIV prevalence is estimated for frequently monitored subpopulations, e.g. commercial sex workers or injecting drug users, and for groups with low risk, e.g. pregnant women attending antenatal clinics (Ainsworth and Over 1999, p. 86).[1] Samples of the population are applied because not all HIV infections are reported and, hence, an exact determination of the extent of epidemics from documented cases is impossible. However, collecting data on prevalence among these groups is subject to some methodological limitations. It is difficult to identify a representative sample of sex workers and injecting drug users. Additional problems are reaching subpopulations engaging in high-risk behaviour[2] and collecting information about their sexual behaviour like condom use or partner change. As a result, the development of an epidemic cannot be predicted with accuracy.

---

[1]Data of pregnant women are available because antenatal clinics are well-attended.

[2]High risk behaviour means unprotected sexual intercourse with many partners or sharing injecting equipment like unsterilised needles and syringes (Ainsworth and Over 1999, p. xxiv).

Box 2.1: HIV Incidence versus HIV Prevalence

HIV incidence refers to the number of new HIV cases that occur during a defined time interval, e.g. a year. If the incidence has increased during the last 12 months, more people are infected. Thus, it measures the rate of the spread of HIV. By contrast, HIV prevalence refers to the current number of people who are infected with HIV at a given point of time. Hence, the total number of HIV infections is measured.

Even though incidence and prevalence are different criteria, they are affiliated with each other. In the early years of an epidemic, few people are newly infected per year and, hence, the incidence is low. The prevalence of HIV increases rapidly because more and more people become infected and few are dying. Yet, prevalence cannot rise endlessly. Over the years, the number of AIDS deaths also rises. If the number of deaths is greater than the number of new infections, the growth of the HIV prevalence decelerates until a peak is reached. The number of deaths equals the number of new infections. It depends on the ratio between deaths and new infections whether HIV prevalence is then stable, declining or reaches another peak. Thus, a diminished prevalence does not indicate an ending epidemic. Declining HIV prevalences are associated with a lower number of new infections than of deaths. New infections can nevertheless be at a high level.

Notwithstanding these weaknesses, data on HIV prevalence can be used to characterise current levels of AIDS epidemics. According to the wide spread of HIV, the extent of an epidemic can be subdivided into three different stages (Ainsworth and Over 1999, p. 87; USAID 2002, p. 7):

- *Nascent epidemics*: HIV prevalence is less than 5% in all known subpopulations practising high-risk behaviour.
- *Concentrated epidemics*: HIV prevalence is higher than 5% in one or more subpopulations. However, HIV prevalence among pregnant women attending urban antenatal clinics is less than 5%.
- *Generalised epidemics*[3]: HIV has spread far beyond groups engaging in high-risk behaviour and, hence, begins to disseminate within the general population. Prevalence of HIV among pregnant women is higher than 5%.

In the Sects 2.1.2 and 2.1.3, the HIV/AIDS epidemics in the developed and developing world are outlined. After characterising the distribution of HIV in high-income countries, epidemics in low and middle-income countries are analysed.

---

[3]USAID (2002, p. 7) further differentiates between so-called high prevalence countries in which more than 5% of people aged between 15 and 49 are infected with HIV and so-called low prevalence countries in which less than 5% of these people are HIV-positive.

2.1.2 HIV/AIDS in High-Income Countries

HIV infection rates in countries in North America, Western and Central Europe are increasing. The estimated number of people living with HIV rose from 1.9 million in 2005 to 2.1 million in 2007 (UNAIDS and WHO 2005, p. 65; UNAIDS and WHO 2007, p. 33). However, the level of HIV infections appears to be low particularly in comparison with Sub-Saharan Africa with 22.5 million HIV-positive people (UNAIDS and WHO 2007, p. 15). A smaller extent of HIV/AIDS in industrialised countries is also shown in a small HIV prevalence. While the national HIV prevalence is 5.0% in Sub-Saharan Africa, it is 0.3% in Western and Central Europe (UNAIDS and WHO 2007, p. 7). This results from the fact that the epidemics in industrialised countries are primarily concentrated within original subpopulations. Sex between men and injecting drug use remain the prominent routes for HIV transmission. In detail, unsafe homosexual behaviour is the most common reason for the spread of HIV in Denmark, Germany, the United Kingdom and the United States. In the United States 53% of all new infections are caused by this mode of transmission (UNAIDS and WHO 2007, p. 33). Injecting drug use is furthermore an important mode of HIV distribution in some high-income countries like Canada, the United States or the Netherlands. However, HIV diagnoses among injecting drug users are declining as a result of implemented programmes like needle exchange (UNAIDS and WHO 2007, p. 34). In the Netherlands, for example, new infections (17 cases) fell from 182 cases in 2002 to 17 cases in 2006 (EuroHIV et al. 2007, p. 19). However, the patterns of HIV transmission are changing. An increasing share of people is infected by unsafe heterosexual intercourse. This indicates that the epidemics begin to spread beyond subpopulations with high-risk behaviour. In several Western European countries like Belgium, Norway and the United Kingdom this kind of transmission is already the most common mode of new infections. For example, approximately 55% of HIV diagnoses have been found among heterosexuals in the United Kingdom (Health Protection Agency 2008).

In sum, HIV/AIDS epidemics in high-income countries are characterised by similar stages of transmission of HIV. A concentration of HIV can be observed in specific subpopulations. Furthermore, there are signs that HIV does not only spread among people with risky behaviour, but also in other parts of a population. This development is observed in many countries in the developing world as discussed below.

2.1.3 HIV/AIDS in Low and Middle-Income Countries

In contrast to the epidemics in high-income countries, the stages of transmission of HIV are highly diverse. Whereas in some countries like Algeria and Mauritania rates of HIV infections are low, HIV is rapidly spreading in countries like Zambia and Lesotho. In order to take these differences into account explicitly, we classify epidemics according to their different stages, nascent, concentrated and generalised, which were defined earlier.

2.1.3.1 Nascent Epidemics

AIDS epidemics in early stages can be found in the Middle East and in the North of Africa, e.g. in Algeria and Morocco (WHO et al. 2006).[4] The epidemics' extent is also low in some countries in Central America, such as Costa Rica or Nicaragua, and in a few Asian countries, e.g. Bangladesh, Lao PDR and the Philippines (WHO et al. 2006). These epidemics have in common that HIV is primarily concentrated among subpopulations with high-risk behaviour and thus, the epidemics have not started to spread into the general population. AIDS epidemics in some countries in Southeast Asia are primarily driven by heterosexual transmission (UNAIDS and WHO 2005, pp. 31, 43–44). In Bangladesh, in the Philippines and in Lao PDR, for example, risky behaviour among sex workers has mainly caused new HIV infections. By contrast, sex between men is an important factor for the epidemics in Central America (UNAIDS and WHO 2007, p. 32). In Costa Rica, for example, more than two thirds of all AIDS cases are caused by unsafe homosexual intercourse (UNAIDS and WHO 2005, p. 63).

2.1.3.2 Concentrated Epidemics

Most Asian epidemics and more than half of the countries in Latin America have reached concentrated stages, i.e. HIV prevalence is higher than 5% in some subpopulations, either countrywide or at least in some regions (UNAIDS and WHO 2007). In Pakistan and Malaysia, for example, there is a high concentration of transmission in specific subpopulations like injecting drug users. This phenomenon is not restricted to certain geographic areas but can be found countrywide. The same holds for Argentina, Columbia, Venezuela and the most populous countries in Latin America, Brazil and Mexico. The Brazilian and Mexican epidemics have penetrated all regions and, hence, are spread countrywide as well. However, concentrated AIDS epidemics can also be located exclusively within specific regions of a country. The epidemics of China and India, for example, are at a concentrated stage in some provinces like Yunnan and Henan in China or Karnataka and Maharashtra in the South of India while the remaining regions of the two countries are at a nascent stage (UNAIDS 2006a; UNAIDS and WHO 2007, pp. 21 ff; UNAIDS 2007a). Those regional epidemics are a result of the proximity to international heroin areas.

The existence of different stages of HIV epidemics in densely populated countries like China and India indicates that varying HIV prevalences cannot only be traced back to differences between national health policies. There have to

[4]Epidemiological fact sheets are available for each country on the WHO Website: [http://www.who.int/globalatlas/default.asp].

be further determinates of HIV like region-specific biological, cultural and social factors influencing the effectiveness of implemented health programmes and finally the stage of an epidemic. This observation bears important policy implications since interventions primarily focussed on addressing HIV/AIDS seem to fail.[5]

Irrespective of whether epidemics have reached concentrated levels, either countrywide or at least in some parts, they possess some similarities. The pattern of epidemics is changing. HIV starts to spread not only between people having a risky shift but also into other parts of the population. Consequently, heterosexual activity increasingly becomes the main method of spreading. For example, HIV has been established in networks of injecting drug users in Southern and Western China, particularly in Yunnan (Ministry of Health China 2006, p. 4). Prevalence rates beyond 50% are caused by the proximity to international heroin routes and to the Golden Triangle which is located between Lao PDR, Myanmar and Thailand (Ministry of Health China 2006, p. 5; Ainsworth and Over 1999, p. 96). Meanwhile, first signs for the spread of HIV beyond these subpopulations can also be found in Yunnan. HIV prevalence is larger than 1% among pregnant women who do not engage in high-risk behaviour (WHO et al. 2006). Consequently, these epidemics of Chinese provinces are on the verge of a generalised stage.

2.1.3.3 Generalised Epidemics

Most countries that have reached generalised epidemics, i.e. a spread of HIV into the general population, can be found in the Southern and Eastern areas of Africa. This is due to the fact that HIV has first erupted in Sub-Saharan African regions along the Great Rift Valley, some of the poorest regions of the world. More than 68% of all HIV-infected people live there, yet Sub-Saharan Africa's population only accounts for 12% of the world (UNAIDS and WHO 2007, p. 15; Population Reference Bureau 2007a, p. 7). Hence, it is the most affected region worldwide. Particularly, the poorest countries like Lesotho (23.2%), Zimbabwe (15.3%) and Zambia (15.2%) have diagnosed the highest HIV prevalence rates in 2007 (UNAIDS 2008, p. 215).

Generalised epidemics can also be found outside of Sub-Saharan Africa, e.g. in the Caribbean and in some Asian countries like Thailand, Cambodia and Myanmar. The Caribbean with a national HIV prevalence of 1.0% is the second highest affected region after Sub-Saharan Africa with 5.0% (UNAIDS and WHO 2007, p. 7; The Kaiser Family Foundation 2007a). Especially Haiti is seriously affected by HIV. It has the largest number of people living with this disease within the Carribbean. In 2007, 190,000[6] HIV-positive people lived in Haiti compared to 230,000 HIV-infected persons living in the whole Caribbean area (WHO et al. 2006;

[5]The impact of regional concerns on HIV/AIDS and its consequences on health policies is discussed in detail in Chap. 5.

[6]Estimate is based on 2005.

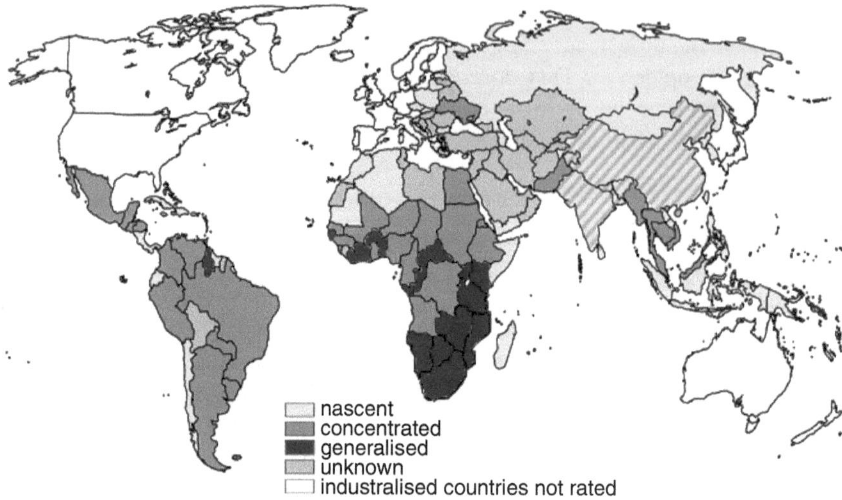

Fig. 2.1 The global HIV/AIDS epidemic
Source: Updated data from Ainsworth and Over (1999, Statistical Appendix, Table 2)

UNAIDS and WHO 2007, p. 29). Hence, more than half of all infected people is diagnosed in Haiti. Poverty and high unemployment have promoted this development (Stillwaggon 2006a, pp. 90, 92, 97). Heterosexual intercourse is the common way of transmission as in Sub-Saharan Africa. Consequently, HIV has not only spread throughout subpopulations at risk, but among people with low-risk behaviour as well. Particularly, women are among those at the largest risk of infection due to their husbands' behaviour (The Kaiser Family Foundation 2007b). HIV prevalence among pregnant Haitians is up to 5% (WHO et al. 2006). Like in other high-prevalence countries or regions, poor and less educated women are most vulnerable to HIV (UNAIDS and WHO 2004, p. 9; UNAIDS and WHO 2005, p. 18; The Kaiser Family Foundation 2007a, p. 2).

The above explanations indicate parallel and concurrent epidemics instead of a single AIDS epidemic. A further striking feature is the uneven spread of HIV. The HIV infections are pooled in the developing world as depicted in Fig. 2.1.

In order to illustrate that a concentration of HIV/AIDS in the developing world is worrying from a national as well as from a transnational point of view, the next section outlines some consequences of AIDS. Following a short overview about national AIDS impacts, we then turn to transnational spillovers.

2.2 National and Transnational Impacts of AIDS

The demographic, economic and social consequences of AIDS are serious and various. Obviously, the HIV-infected people themselves and their families are most affected by HIV. AIDS-related mortality results in a decline of the household income if people of working age are infected with HIV. The loss of earnings is linked with a simultaneous increase of health expenditures, and living standards deteriorate. Yet, the impact of AIDS is not only restricted to the infected families although they are the first ones who are affected by an epidemic. Besides these effects, mortality also influences the production sector. The labour supply declines due to sickness or nursing of infected family members. If the workers are employed in agriculture, smaller plots are farmed, or planting, weeding and harvesting is reduced. As a consequence, food production used for own consumption decreases. If HIV-infected people are not self-employed as smallholders in agriculture, but working in the private sector, the impacts of an epidemic are serious as well. Companies face higher production costs because the productivity and quality of the workforce declines if less experienced people replace experienced employees. The specific pattern of AIDS seems to be the cause for these major impacts. While other diseases like human influenza are concentrated among old and weak people, adults of working age are most vulnerable to HIV (Ainsworth and Over 1999, p. 25). Consequently, AIDS is the leading cause of mortality among adults aged between 20 and 40 years (WHO 2004a, p. 2).

Since the most obvious impact of AIDS concerns health, especially life expectancies, this issue is subsequently discussed more in-depth (USAID and U.S. Department of Commerce 1998, p. 62). The demographic consequences are exemplified by Botswana, Haiti, Namibia, Nigeria, Tanzania and Uganda. These countries are selected because their epidemics have reached the generalised stage and, hence, the effects of AIDS are obvious. Moreover, a huge number of estimates is available as they belong to the focus countries of the President's Emergency Plan for AIDS Relief (PEPFAR).[7]

2.2.1 Demographic Impacts of AIDS

Life expectancies in developing countries have always been low because of high infant mortality. However, implemented initiatives, e.g. providing vaccines and antibiotics or improving food production, have resulted in increased lifespans between 1970 and 1990 (WHO 2004a, p. 6). These gains were diminished or even reversed in large part due to the HIV/AIDS epidemic (Population Reference Bureau 2007b, p. 6).[8] Nowadays, life expectancy in e.g. Southern Africa dropped from 61 to 49 years over the last two decades (Population Reference Bureau 2007b, p. 7).

[7]PEPFAR which was announced in 2003 is a five-year initiative to address HIV/AIDS, tuberculosis and malaria by providing prevention, treatment and care (The Kaiser Family Foundation 2005, p. 8). On July 30, 2008, PEPFAR was renewed by law H.R. 5501, the Tom Lantos and Henry J. Hyde United States global leadership against HIV/AIDS, tuberculosis, and malaria reauthorization act (Congress of the United States of America, 2008).

[8]Other factors include endemic diseases like tuberculosis or malaria, armed conflicts or economic stagnation.

In order to demonstrate the extent of HIV/AIDS on lifespans more in detail, expected lifespans in the selected countries are compared in Fig. 2.2. The black bars represent what would have happened in 2007 if a country had not been affected by AIDS. These series of data are hypothetical figures because HIV/AIDS has affected each country. By contrast, the grey bars show what has de facto happened in each of the selected countries in 2007. Figure 2.2 reveals that the largest impacts of AIDS can be found in Botswana and Namibia. In Botswana, for example, the lifespan has diminished by approximately 18 years (from 68 years without AIDS to 50 years with AIDS). Thus, life expectancy has declined by almost 30%.

In the academic literature on AIDS, it is criticised that estimations of lifespans without AIDS are not representative since AIDS has become a global concern (Loewenson and Whiteside 2002, p. 3). Therefore it is useful to illustrate demographic impacts by comparing life expectancies in 2007 with a projection of

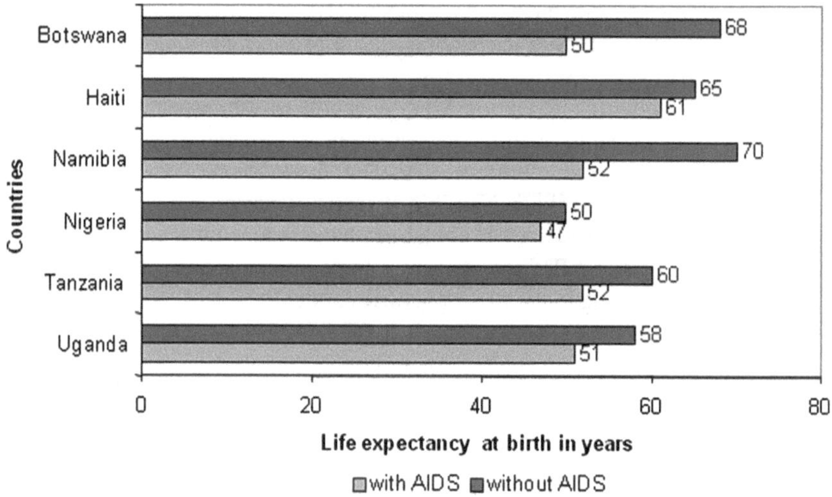

Fig. 2.2 Life expectancies for selected countries with and without AIDS: 2007
Source: UN, Department of Economic and Social Affairs, Population Division (2007a)

Table 2.1 Life expectancies with AIDS: 2007 and 2020

Country	Life expectancies with AIDS	
	2007 (status quo)	2020 (projection based on 2006)
Botswana	50.0	54.5
Haiti	61.0	64.4
Namibia	52.0	54.5
Nigeria	47.0	50.4
Tanzania	52.0	56.2
Uganda	51.0	56.6

Source: UN, Department of Economic and Social Affairs, Population Division (2007a, b)

possible ones in 2020 which is based on the year 2006 (UN, Department of Economic and Social Affairs, Population Division 2007b, pp. 83–84). The results are summarised in Table 2.1.

Table 2.1 shows that lifespans with AIDS in 2007 are nearly equal to or even lower than the life expectancies estimated for 2020. In Uganda, for example, the life expectancy was 51 years in 2007. This is 5.6 years less than the estimated lifespan for 2020. Thus, HIV/AIDS has been more destructing than predicted in the year 2006.

Additionally, a decline of life expectancies has consequences for population structures. The lower the lifespan, the larger will be a deficit of young adults, particularly women. Females are especially affected because they face cultural and social disadvantages increasing their vulnerability to HIV. A lower status of women is the main cause why they cannot choose to reject sexual intercourse or insist on safer sex. In addition, limited access to education results in a lower literacy and thus, they have restricted access to preventive information on the one hand. On the other hand, a low economic status increases the financial dependence on men. Furthermore, violence against women in the form of rape is a well-known concern.

As a consequence of diminished life spans, population structures are altered. The pyramid shape – few old people at the top and a large amount of young people at the bottom – changes to the form of an urn (USAID and U.S. Department of Commerce 2002, p. 78). The shape of an urn can be characterised as follows: Starting from a bulbous bottom of the urn, the shape becomes a taper as people have reached working age. In contrast to the pyramid shape, reductions in population size are smaller. Since the impact of AIDS on life expectancy is particularly strong in Botswana, changes in the population structure are exemplified by this country. The current estimated and the projected size of Botswana's male and female population for 2005 and 2025 are depicted Fig. 2.3.

Figure 2.3 shows a pyramid shape in 2005 at the left side. By contrast, the right side illustrates a reduction of people in all age groups 25 years later. Obviously,

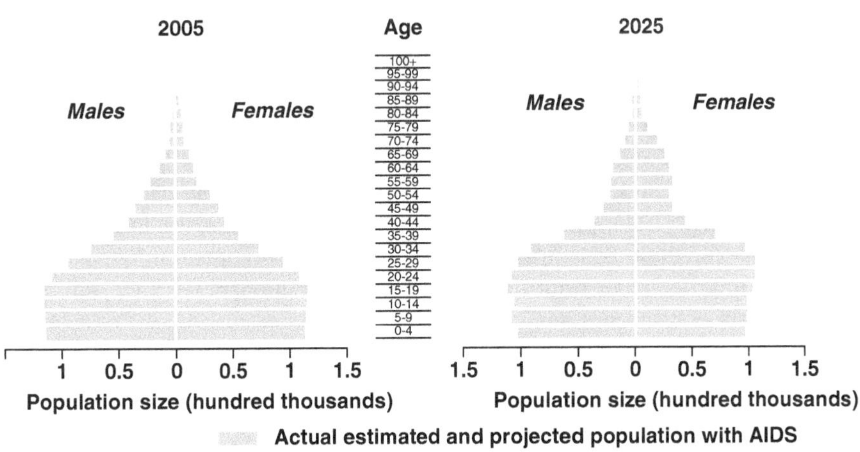

Fig. 2.3 Changes in the population structure in Botswana: 2005 and 2025
Source: UN, Department of Economic and Social Affairs, Population Division (2007b)

people aged between 35 and 50 are most influenced by AIDS. Therefore, subpopulations of working age are particularly affected.

In short, the outlined consequences of AIDS on life expectancies and the resulting changes in population size indicate a large burden, e.g. to governments. However, our analysis only considers mortality effects. In order to determine the costs of AIDS comprehensively, we have to take account of people's suffering during sickness. A concept including both the costs of reduced life expectancies and the costs resulting from suffering is the so-called "Disability-Adjusted Life Year" (henceforth, DALY). It can therefore be applied to measure the overall burden of AIDS.

2.2.2 The Burden of AIDS

The DALY concept was first presented by the World Development Report in 1993. It was introduced to assess the global burden of diseases. DALYs for a disease are calculated as the sum of healthy life years lost by premature mortality and the loss of life years due to disability in a particular year (World Bank 1993, p. 26). Therefore, one DALY measures the loss of 1 year of full health. It can be expressed as:

$$DALY = YLL + YLD, \tag{2.1}$$

where YLL represents the loss of life years due to mortality and YLD quantifies the lost years resulting from suffering.

These terms can be further subdivided. The first expression on the right-hand side of (2.1) considers the difference between the actual age of death and the life expectancy. This life expectancy is 82.5 years for women while 80.0 years are assumed for men referring to Murray (1996, p. 18). The difference of 2.5 years between the genders represents a biological disparity (World Bank 1993, p. 213; Murray 1996, p. 18). The second term on the right-hand side of (2.1) expresses the product of the expected duration of disability and a weight measuring the severity of the disease.[9] Following (2.1) and summing up the annual mortality and disability losses, this sum is discounted at 3% because future years of healthy life are evaluated lower than a year of healthy life in the present. The choice of 3% is arbitrary. Murray (1996, p. 54) argues as follows: "[...] 3% is the lower limit of acceptability for those economists who are persuaded by opportunity cost arguments and it is the upper limit for public health practitioners who are willing to accept a positive discount rate [...]".

In order to quantify the financial burden of AIDS for the selected low and middle-income countries, the DALY concept is subsequently applied. Therefore,

[9]The severity of a disease is measured on a scale from 0 representing perfect health to 1 implying death. More detailed information about severity weights can be found in the World Development Report 1993, pp. 26 ff.

Table 2.2 The burden of AIDS: 2008

Country	DALY in thousands	Total population in millions	Economic loss in percent of GNI
Low and middle-income countries			
Botswana	954	1.8	53
Haiti	739	9.0	8
Nigeria	9,207	144.4	6
Namibia	436	2.1	21
South Africa	10,422	47.9	22
Tanzania	4,869	38.7	13
Uganda	2,708	28.5	10
High-income countries			
Germany	16	82.3	0.02
United Kingdom	8	61.0	0.01
United States	58	302.2	0.02

Source: Mathers et al. (2005), Population Reference Bureau (2007a), author's calculation

the loss of life years expressed by DALYs has to be transformed into units of money by using the human capital or the willingness-to-pay approach (Mills and Shillcutt 2004, p. 70). According to the human capital approach, the present value of an individual's future earnings is an equivalent monetary value of his lost life years. The willingness-to-pay approach assumes that an individual's preferences are reflected in the amounts that he is willing to pay preventing losses in life years. Estimates of these values often rely on opinions of experts like the Commission on Macroeconomics and Health (CMH) recommending that each DALY is valued at a multiple of annual income (CMH 2001, p. 31). This suggestion is based on the idea that one DALY does not only represent the loss of 1 year of working, but also reflects the value of leisure time and the suffering associated with illness.

Subsequently, we follow the proposal, valuing DALYs at annual incomes because statistics about the annual per capita Gross National Income (GNI) are available for low and middle-income countries. In detail, we assume that each DALY is valued at the GNI per capita. If we relate this loss of income to a country's population, we will receive the loss in percent which represents the burden of AIDS. The economic losses in 2008 are summarised in Table 2.2. In addition, the burden borne by governments of some high-income countries are calculated to allow a comparison.[10]

Table 2.2 shows a multiple burden that is faced by governments of low and middle-income countries compared to high-income countries. While the economic loss is valued at approximately 0.02% in high-income countries, it varies between 6 and 53% in low and middle-income countries in the example above. Particularly, governments of Botswana, Namibia and South Africa bear the largest burden because of the highest national HIV prevalence rates among adults: 24.1% in

[10]The DALY data are taken from Mathers et al. (2005). Mathers et al. updated the original global burden of disease study carried out by Murray and Lopez (1996) for the year 1990.

Botswana, 19.6% in Namibia and 18.8% in South Africa are reported (UNAIDS 2006c). In Botswana, for example, more than half (53%) of the GNI is lost due to AIDS.

We have to recall that these results are determined by certain assumptions. Hence, the costs of AIDS can differ from our calculation. It can straightforward be seen that a higher (lower) discount rate reduces (increases) the economic loss. The assessment of DALYs with the annual income per capita is an additional methodological weakness. A value based on the GNI per capita seems too low if healthy life years are appreciated higher than the annual earnings of an individual (Evans 2004, p. 119).[11] Furthermore, the application of the GNI per capita assigns a lower economic value to saving one life year in low and middle-income countries than in high-income countries and therefore leads to ethical problems (Evans 2004, p. 121).[12] This follows from a smaller GNI per capita in low and middle-income than in high-income countries.

The estimates indicate substantial cost savings through effective interventions against HIV/AIDS. This aspect is strengthened by considering that AIDS requires an increasing share of resources which could be spent on pre-existing health problems. Other sexually transmitted infections (STIs), tuberculosis, malnutrition, parasite diseases etc. have repercussions on the AIDS epidemics themselves. Since these biological interrelationships extend the burden of AIDS, yet are not included in DALYs, they are discussed in the next section.

2.2.3 Biological Spillovers of AIDS

In the academic literature on AIDS, there is a growing attention paid to the interaction of HIV with pre-existing health problems (Corbett et al. 2002, p. 2177; WHO 2004a, p. 7). Endemic diseases can increase the likelihood of acquiring and transmitting HIV while HIV weakens the human immune system and thus enhances the infectiousness with other diseases like tuberculosis or other STIs. In addition, HIV possesses the potential to drive the transmission of these HIV-associated infections. Consequently, people become prone for illness irrespective of their HIV-status and thus, other infectious diseases can be disseminated. Figure 2.4 illustrates these bidirectional interrelationships.

The remainder of this section describes these biological effects in detail. We focus on two major kinds of diseases, tuberculosis and other STIs. Our explanations are restricted to these communicable infections because tuberculosis is the leading cause of deaths among HIV-positive individuals (WHO 2003a, p. 11, 2003b, p. 7). STIs are a widely recognised cofactor of HIV because both diseases are sexually transmitted (Stillwaggon 2006a, pp. 45–46).

---

[11]Then, the question which multiple value of the GNI per capita is justified arises.

[12]In addition, an evaluation based on the GNI per capita indicates a higher priority for diseases in industrialised than in developing countries (Evans 2004, p. 121).

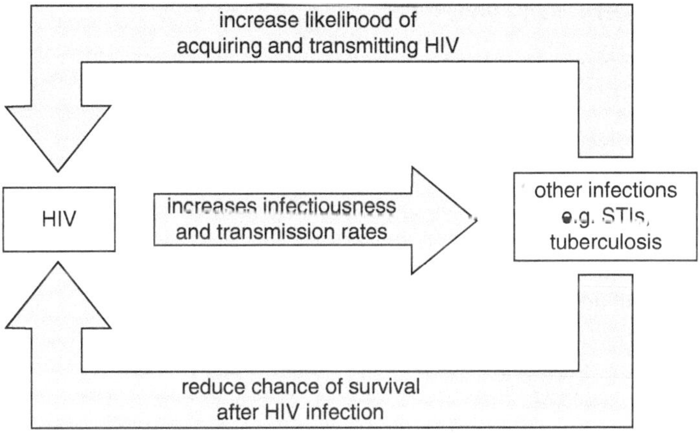

Fig. 2.4 Interrelations between HIV and other infectious diseases

2.2.3.1 HIV/AIDS and Tuberculosis

Tuberculosis has been an endemic disease in the developing world before the first HIV infections were documented (Pallangyo 2001, p. 488). The number of tuberculosis cases has increased by a multiple as the transmission of HIV rose.[13] HIV promotes the reactivation of latent tuberculosis infections (Corbett et al. 2002, p. 2182). Nowadays, 50% of new tuberculosis cases are coinfected with HIV (The Forum for Collaborative HIV research and TB/HIV working group 2007, p. 11). Moreover, tuberculosis-HIV coinfections increase the progression of latent to active tuberculosis when latent tuberculosis infections have not been treated (Corbett et al. 2002, p. 2182). As a result, the transmission of tuberculosis is driven and, hence, the risk of people to become infected rises (Corbett et al. 2003, p. 1016).

It is still uncertain whether a larger tuberculosis epidemic can also intensify the spread of HIV (Stillwaggon 2006a, p. 61). Even if tuberculosis does not have the potential to increase HIV rates to the same extent as HIV rises tuberculosis rates, a high tuberculosis prevalence could have serious implications on the extent of HIV/AIDS epidemics. This impact would particularly be worrying for countries facing a large tuberculosis burden while AIDS epidemics are at the nascent level. The Philippines, for example, have a large tuberculosis prevalence (450 cases per 100,000 people in 2005) whereas the HIV/AIDS epidemic is at an early stage (UNDP 2007a, p. 258). The same holds for some African countries like Mauritania (590 cases per 100,000 inhabitants), Senegal (466 cases per 100,000 people) and Eritrea (515 cases per 100,000 individuals) (UNDP 2007a, p. 259).

[13]Further causes are changes in population size and structures, urbanisation and poverty (Pallangyo 2001, p. 488).

2.2.3.2 HIV/AIDS and Other STIs

There is an epidemiological synergy between other STIs and HIV/AIDS (Wasserheit 1992, p. 61). On the one hand, individuals who are infected with other STIs are at least two to five times more likely to get infected with HIV than non-infected people. On the other hand, HIV infections increase the prevalence of some STIs like genital ulcers. A weakened immune system makes people more vulnerable for these infections. In addition, coinfected individuals are more likely to transmit HIV. Consequently, other STIs can increase the susceptibility to and the infectiousness of HIV (Fleming and Wasserheit 1999, p. 4).

Susceptibility to HIV can be raised in two ways. First, ulcerative STIs like syphilis and herpes cause sores, ulcers or breaks in the vaginal mucosa and thus, mucosal barriers are weakened (Corbett et al. 2002, p. 2179; Fleming and Wasserheit 1999, p. 4). Genital ulcers which are caused by syphilis bleed frequently and, hence, facilitate an entry for HIV during sexual intercourse. Second, non-ulcerative STIs like chlamydia or gonorrhea cause genital inflammations which weaken the mucosal integrity and thus, susceptibility to HIV rises (Corbett et al. 2002, p. 2179). The same holds if cells, e.g. CD4+ cells,[14] are located in the genital tract and thus, serve as targets for HIV. In addition, gonorrhea has a suppressive effect on the immune response by inhibiting the activation and proliferation of CD4+ cells (Boulton and Gray-Owen 2002, p. 234). This delay can increase the likelihood of infections, e.g. chlamydia or HIV.

Studies have shown that STIs are conducive to the shedding of the human immunodeficiency virus in the genital tract and thus, enhance the infectiousness of HIV. Wasserheit (1992), for example, examines 163 studies investigating the relationship between HIV and other STIs. Fifteen studies reveal a three to five times increased risk of an HIV infection if other STIs are prevalent (Wasserheit 1992, pp. 61, 70). Further evidence of an enhanced HIV transmission can be found in Rotchford et al. (2000). By reviewing cross-sectional and cohort studies analysing the effects of genital infections on HIV, they indicate that HIV is detected more frequently in individuals infected with gonorrhea than in uninfected people.

In sum, endemic health problems convey HIV/AIDS epidemics. This impact may be particularly large in regions with weak functional health systems like Sub-Saharan Africa because other diseases remain uncured and hence infectious for a long time. Moreover, policy-makers have to recognise that the HIV/AIDS epidemics in low and middle-income countries can lead to increased negative externalities in high-income countries. Missing interventions do not only forster the transmission of HIV in developing countries but may also have negative spillovers in industrialised countries. Therefore, cross-bordering consequences of AIDS and their implications for anti-AIDS policies are discussed subsequently.

[14]CD4+ or Tcells are white blood cells which protect a human´s body from an infection (Divisions of HIV/AIDS Prevention 2005, p. 3).

2.2.4 Transnational Impacts of AIDS

In the age of globalisation national borders become less effective to prevent spillovers of AIDS from other countries. Globalisation has led to an increased cross-border mobility in the second half of the twentieth century (Oberender and Fleckenstein 2004, p. 3). Nearly 190 million lived outside their country of citizenship in 2005 compared to 175 million people in 2003 (UN 2006).[15] Moreover, approximately 60% of these people move to industrialised countries (UN 2006). This development becomes worrying as the vulnerability of migrants for HIV increases. Poor life conditions, e.g. missing access to education and health services, sex with multiple partners or sex workers etc. put them at risk for an HIV infection. Because of their mobility the virus can spread beyond national borders. This indicates that epidemics in the developing and the developed world are linked with each other.

Subsequently, transnational impacts of AIDS are discussed more in-depth. They are exemplified by the United Kingdom (UK) reporting the second highest net immigration worldwide (CIA 2008).[16] A striking aspect of the epidemic in the UK is a concentration of HIV among people originating from countries with generalised epidemics, particularly Sub-Saharan Africa (UNAIDS and WHO 2005, pp. 68, 69).[17] This is due to the fact that the UK has close traditional links to its former colonies in Eastern and Southern Africa which are worst affected by AIDS (Nicoll and Godfrey-Faussett 1999, p. 1086). As a result, more than 70% of all heterosexual HIV infections that were diagnosed in the UK during 2006 were most likely acquired in countries with generalised epidemics (Health Protection Agency 2007, p. 80). A more detailed description can be found in Fig. 2.5.

Figure 2.5 shows the number of HIV cases acquired in several African regions and which have been diagnosed in the UK between 1995 and 2005. A striking feature is that the majority of HIV-positive people have been infected in Eastern Africa, especially in Uganda, from 1995 until 1999. However, there has been a substantial rise in HIV infections among people originating from South Eastern Africa, particularly Zimbabwe, in recent years (Sinka et al. 2003, p. 1686). This development is a result of several factors. First, due to Uganda's anti-AIDS programmes, new HIV diagnoses have decreased. As a consequence, the national HIV prevalence has dropped from around 18% in the early 1990s to 6.7% in 2005 (Uganda AIDS Commission 2003, p. 4; USAID 2005; Office of the United States Global AIDS Coordinator 2007, p. 2). The prevalence of HIV has declined by more than 60%. A reduced total number of HIV infections may have an inferior impact

---

[15]Data are taken from the 2005 revision population data base and from the report of the International Organization for Migration (IOM 2008, p. 505).

[16]A consideration of the U.S. which has the highest number of immigrants is not possible. Even though HIV data among their population by race and ethnicity like American Indians, African Americans and Latinos are captured, there is no differentiation between foreign-born and U.S.-born people.

[17]Data for the European Union (EU) can be found in Hamers et al. (2006).

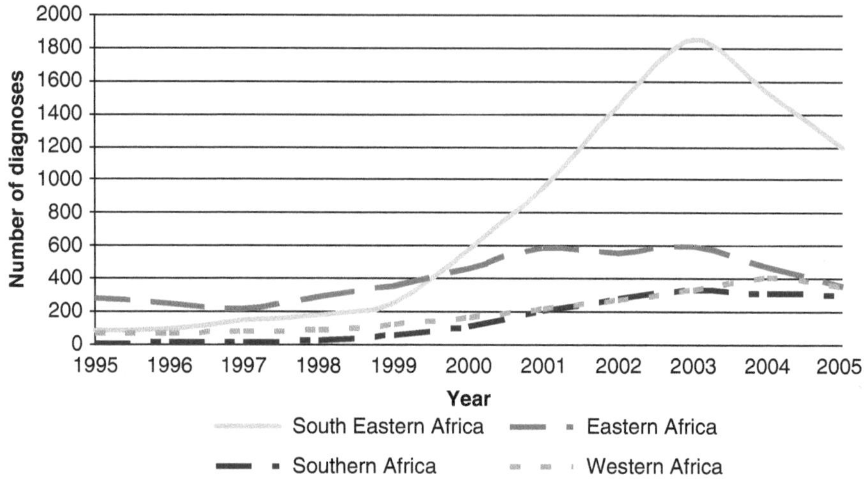

Fig. 2.5 The impact of African epidemics on HIV infections within the UK
Source: Health Protection Agency (2006, p. 79)

on the epidemic in the UK. Second, the largest number of asylum seekers comes from Zimbabwe which has nearly the highest HIV prevalence (20.1%) compared to the rest of the world (UNAIDS 2006b). As a result, there were more Zimbabweans infected with HIV in the UK than UK-born people in 2002 (NAM 2002).[18] In 2005, 68% (821) of the HIV infections acquired in South Eastern Africa were diagnosed among Zimbabweans living in the UK (Health Protection Agency 2006, p. 79).

This sketchy overview demonstrates that the spread of HIV/AIDS in the developing world is mirrored in epidemics within the developed world. However, policy-makers also have to take account of the reverse flow. Short-term visits as tourists or as business people have been responsible for the spread of HIV from high to middle and low-income countries. For example, the European demand for sex tourism has spread the virus backwards to Asia, Africa and Latin America. In addition, labour migration from the United States has driven the epidemics in the Caribbean and in South America. These interrelations indicate that AIDS is no longer exclusively a public health concern in developing countries. AIDS has become an international issue and thus requires international solutions. Consequently, the effectiveness of implemented anti-HIV programmes has to be evaluated from a transnational instead of a national perspective. It follows that policies which are implemented in low- and middle-income countries can be optimal from a national point of view, yet they do not seem optimal for those prefering higher health standards.[19]

[18]In recent years, the number of Zimbabwean entrants has declined due to the introduction of visa requirements (NAM 2002).

[19]For a detailed discussion of allocative consequences of national health interventions see Chap. 3.

2.3 Responding to AIDS

In this section, we look at responses to HIV/AIDS, where priorities are and where they should be to address the AIDS crisis in the long run. We argue first that the implementation of national interventions based on the epidemiology of HIV is plausible against the background of various AIDS epidemics differing with respect to their epidemiological stages. This follows from the fact that no health measure on its own is suitable to alleviate the consequences of HIV for individuals. A continuum of preventive and curative health measures is necessary. Then, we explore that the increasing importance of AIDS as an international issue requires more than national mechanisms. The concept of international public goods which has become more and more relevant in the debate of combating global crises is discussed.

2.3.1 The Prevention, Treatment and Care Continuum

The impact of the epidemiology on the choice of interventions against HIV is recognised. For example, UNAIDS, the Department for International Development (DFID), the U.S. Agency for International Development (USAID) and the United Nations Population Fund (UNFPA) call for health activities adapted to the different stages of an epidemic (UNAIDS 2001; DFID 2001, pp. 6, 16; USAID 1998, p. 6; UNFPA 2002). In detail, prevention among high-risk groups is the key to stop HIV when its transmission is in early stages. When HIV begins to spread beyond these subpopulations and more and more individuals get infected, treatment and care have to be provided additionally. In order to develop a prevention, treatment and care continuum we closely follow the recommendations of the organisations mentioned above. Our explanations remain on a general level because each AIDS epidemic has its own pattern of transmission.

2.3.1.1 Nascent Epidemics

Countries with nascent epidemics face the challenge to avert a development to concentrated or even generalised stages. Prophylactic health measures have to be targeted to people who are most likely to get infected and transmit HIV to others. It seems useful to focus interventions on injecting drug users or commercial sex workers because HIV is concentrated among these subpopulations in early stages. Therefore, access to sterilised needles, syringes and other injecting equipment should be ensured to prevent a direct infection by blood exchanges. This can be achieved by implementing needle or syringe exchange programmes. Regarding sexual transmission of HIV, the likelihood that infected sex workers transmit HIV to their clients and finally their partners can be reduced by the use of latex condoms. Moreover, condoms can reduce the risk of an infection with other STIs like gonorrhea or syphilis. Being aware of the interrelation between STIs and HIV, controlling STIs is therefore a necessary intervention in the fight against AIDS. Yet, biomedical interventions as distributing condoms or implementing needle and syringe exchange programmes cannot increase condom use and reduce sharing needles if individuals do not change their risky behaviour. Particularly, people in developing countries have a low level of HIV awareness and, hence, low incentives to behave safely (Brown et al. 2001, p. 6). Since the consequences of an epidemic are less visible in early stages, individuals may think that HIV is not present at every level and that they are not at risk. Consequently, behaviour-changing interventions as educating people about HIV, its transmission and methods to prevent an infection have to be supplemented. In addition, an AIDS vaccine is effective to stop the transmission of HIV in the long run when preventive health measures as distribution of condoms or the provision of clean needles have failed (Working Group 5 of the Commission on Macroeconomics and Health 2002, p. 45). In developing countries a vaccine would be particularly effective because new HIV infections are a multiple of the rates in industrialised countries as mentioned earlier. However, a vaccine has not been developed by today.

2.3.1.2 Concentrated Epidemics

In order to address concentrated epidemics, a package of prevention and treatment to target those who are most likely to spread HIV is necessary (Mills and Shillcutt 2004, p. 92). In addition, care activities have to be implemented (USAID 2002, p. 33; DFID 2001, p. 16). As more and more people become infected and live with HIV, interventions to reduce their suffering must be carried out. Antiretroviral therapy (ART), for example, can improve physical as well as mental health of HIV-positive patients. ART directly acts on HIV by blocking its reproduction. As a consequence, the development of full-blown AIDS will be delayed and, hence, life can be prolonged (USAID 2004, p. 30). Moreover, the quality of life is improved and HIV-infected people may return to school or to work. Yet, access to ART is either missing or restricted for HIV-positive patients in developing countries. One reason is a missing health infrastructure. Thus, the provision of curative health measures cannot be ensured. Even if therapies can be supplied, the accessibility to treatment is constrained by high prices compared to the annual GNI per capita. For example, approximately US $ 94 per year have to be paid for the most frequently prescribed drugs compared to a GNI of US $ 905 or less in low-income countries and between US $ 906 and US $ 3.600 in middle-income countries in 2007 (WHO 2007a; World Bank 2007). Problems can also arise since patients often interrupt their therapy when they feel better whereas a therapy can only be successful if anti-HIV drugs are regularly taken. If this is the case, HIV can multiply more easily and, hence, the likelihood of the development of resistant HIV clades will be higher. Treatment then becomes less effective. As a consequence, a combination of at least three anti-HIV drugs is required to delay the occurrence of resistance (WHO 2005a, p. 5).[20]

[20]Drug resistance is a natural biological phenomenon and cannot be circumvented.

Even though AIDS treatment is an essential intervention to address concentrated epidemics, governments should also take account of prophylactic health measures (The Economist 2005, p. 68). Prevention can entirely stop the spread of HIV. The "100% condom programme" in Thailand is the most famous example for effective prophylaxis in concentrated stages. Initially estabilished among sex workers and their clients in Ratchaburi province in 1989, the programme was extended country wide 1 year later (Rojanapithayakorn and Hanenberg 1996). Condoms were distributed for free among brothels and massage parlours. Prostitutes and their clients are ordered to use them. Brothels failing to comply are closed. In addition, mass media campaigns are implemented to reach clients of sex workers and educate them about the consequences of their risky sexual behaviour. As a result of the Thai's expanded response, the national HIV prevalence which had steadily increased in the early 1990s up to 4% stabilised below 2% in the following years. In 2006, HIV prevalence dropped to its lowest level ever (1.4%) and there are signs of a further decline in 2007 (UNAIDS 2006b, Annex 1; UNAIDS 2007b).

2.3.1.3 Generalised Epidemics

Prevention remains the key intervention even if epidemics have reached a generalised stage. Thus, prophylactic health measures have to be focussed on subpopulations with high-risk behaviour because HIV is highly concentrated among those groups. In addition, governments have to consider the spread of HIV beyond these vulnerable groups towards the general population. Consequently, the package of services needs to be expanded to those with lower risk (Ainsworth and Over 1999, pp. 291–292). An implementation on a wider scale can be achieved by TV and radio campaigns to increase awareness and understanding of HIV country-wide.

As HIV spreads, preventive health measures need to be complemented by care activities. Voluntary counselling and testing (VCT) is, besides home-based care,[21] an essential component of any package of care (DFID 2001, p. 8). VCT includes pre-test counselling, HIV testing and post-test counselling (UNAIDS 2000). If people are aware of their HIV status, they can benefit from earlier treatment and, hence, their suffering can be mitigated. Thus, VCT presents itself as an entry point to anti-HIV programmes. Care also includes controlling so-called opportunistic infections (OIs) (CMH 2001, p. 172). OIs are caused due to a weak immune system of HIV-infected individuals. They can occur in the brain as Cryptococcal Meningitis, in the lungs as Pneumocystis Carinii Pneumonia (PCP), on the skin as Herpes Simplex etc. (UNAIDS 1998). The most serious HIV-related opportunistic infection is tuberculosis because of its biological synergy to HIV as we know from Sect. 2.2.3.

[21]Home-based care aims at providing comprehensive health and social services, e.g. supporting family members' care activities, transporting patients to hospitals, providing resources like soap, etc. (Lamptey et al. 2001, p. 39).

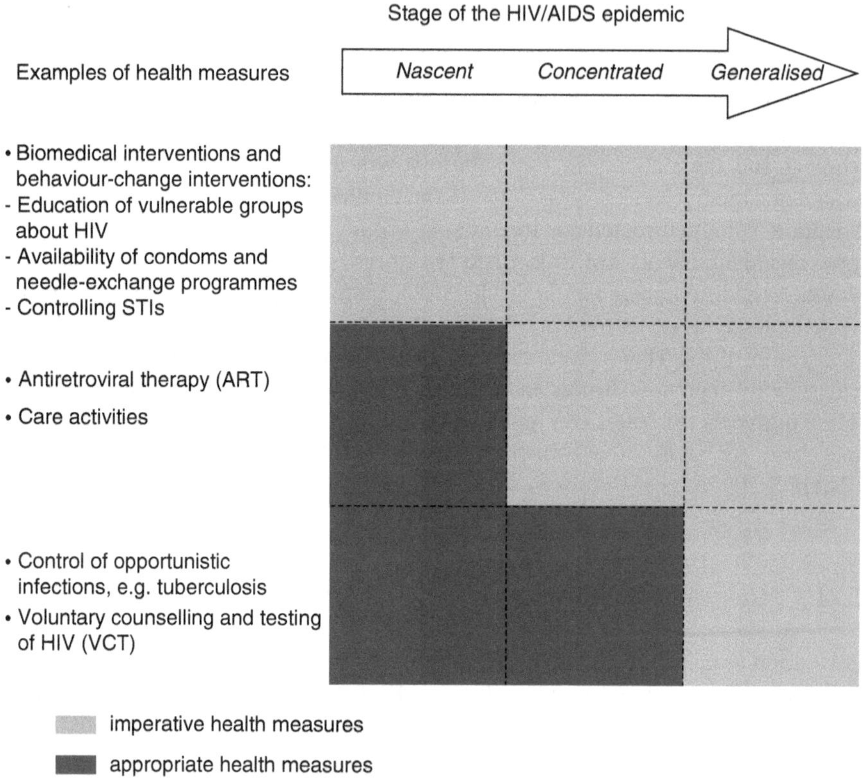

Fig. 2.6 A prevention, treatment and care continuum
Source: Modified illustration of UNAIDS' prevention, treatment and care continuum (1998, p. 6)

The sketched prevention, treatment and care continuum demonstrates the influence of the epidemiology of HIV on a governments' priorities to implement health measures. Figure 2.6 summarises the discussed interventions according to the stage of an epidemic. We differentiate between imperative and appropriate health measures. Imperative interventions should be implemented no later than at this stage of the epidemic. For example, education programmes need to be established at the nascent level. By contrast, appropriate health activities can be provided at this epidemic's stage. This holds for care activities if HIV is concentrated among subpopulations and thus, an epidemic is at a nascent stage.

In sum, setting priorities according to a continuum of prevention, treatment and care seems plausible because the specific characteristics of each stage of HIV/AIDS can be taken into account. However, our description of AIDS epidemics and their cross-country consequences indicates that interventions which are only based on an epidemiological reasoning can be ineffective in an international context. A further characteristic of the HIV/AIDS epidemic, its international extent, has received little attention in health programmes. National mechanisms are not effective to avert a transnational crisis like HIV/AIDS. In order to reform implemented interventions, an increasing reference to the debate on international public goods[22] can be found in the literature (Kaul et al. 1999; Smith et al. 2003).

2.3.2 The Conceptual Background of International Health-Promoting Public Goods

The addressing of transnational crises with international public goods has been suggested by Sandler (1997). He recommends to apply this concept for responding to transnational economic, environmental and political problems. The application of this new paradigm was brought into an international focus by a UNDP monograph published by Kaul et al. in 1999. The authors describe the influence of the public good perspective on the effectiveness of transnational cooperation in sectors like international peace and security, environment, equity etc. The application of the concept to health is discussed as one out of many issues. A more detailed consideration of public goods with respect to health has developed in the following years. Kaul and Faust (2001), for example, discuss from a public good perspective how the sustainability of health initiatives to control AIDS, malaria and tuberculosis can be improved. Following the UNDP, a lot of international organisations have recognised the importance of the concept for their activities. For example, the CMH mentioned the supply of international public goods as a means to improve the health of the poorest (CMH 2001). Noteworthy within the debate on health-promoting public goods is the monograph published by Smith et al. (2003) exploring the application of the concept to a number of health fields, e.g. polio eradication, control of tuberculosis, containment of antimicrobial resistance etc. In addition, they discuss several questions, e.g. whether health can be per se classified as an international public good and which interventions may serve as public goods for health which has not been debated heretofore.

Since the importance of AIDS as a transnational issue becomes prevalent, the relevance of the concept of international public goods in the field of HIV/AIDS is increasing. The cross-border effects of the AIDS epidemics are a further rationale why public goods are crucial. Therefore, the international linkage between countries becomes more intense and thus, country-specific interventions like strengthening national health systems or public infrastructures may not be effective. Even if these health interventions can generate transnational externalities, spillovers are small compared to national benefits. Consequently, international public goods can be provided to internalise these externalities[23] (Arce and Sandler 2002a, p. 1; Kanbur et al. 1999, p. 5; Chen et al. 1999, p. 285). In addition, the disparity between the extent

[22]As usual, the term "public" does not refer to the kind of provision. It characterises the degree of non-rivalry of consumption and non-excludability of consumers.

[23]An externality exists if an agent does not take the full marginal consequences of his action on other individuals into account.

of the AIDS crisis and the mechanisms to address it is another reason to implement international public goods (Chen et al. 1999, p. 289; Mills 2001, p. 4; Woodward and Smith 2003, p. 3; Arhin-Tenkorang and Conceicão 2003, p. 488). While global cooperation going beyond the capability of a single country has to be carried out to address the international health crisis, the responsibility for providing health services remains national (Chen et al. 1999, p. 287; Jamison et al. 1998, pp. 514–515).

Despite the acknowledgement that the concept of international public goods is crucial in the field of HIV/AIDS, little attention is paid to its application, notably to financing mechanisms. The majority of the academic literature on AIDS focusses on discussing whether or not preventive and curative health interventions represent international public goods (Archibugi and Bizzarri 2004, pp. 1663–1664; Smith and MacKellar 2007). They intensively dispute to what extent health measures like ART and AIDS prevention in the form of condom distribution, VCT and others satisfy the characteristics of public goods, non-rivalry and non-excludability. Building on these results, their provision status is determined. The main strand of literature follows the standard argument of the public goods literature that public goods are underprovided (Samuelson 1954). Since international health-promoting public goods generate benefits for many countries, each country has an incentive to act as a free rider and gains from the anti-HIV programmes financed by other countries' governments (Kremer 1998, p. 74).

Policies to finance international health-promoting public goods are briefly considered in the academic literature on AIDS. Exceptions are Smith and MacKellar (2007), Jacquet and Marniesse (2006) and Teixeira (2006). While Smith and McKellar argue that underprovision cannot be overcome by an additional financing since other sources of funding are crowded out, Teixeira, Jacquet and Marniesse recommend an increased quantity of financial resources. Given the transnational scope of spillovers of AIDS, incentives of donors increase in order to provide more financial means reducing budgetary limitations in developing countries (Teixeira 2006, p. 4). By contrast, this book will discuss means to increase the effectiveness of implemented international financing mechanisms.

2.3.3 *Definitions*

In the literature, public goods have traditionally been defined by two demand-side characteristics: Non-rivalry and non-excludability of consumption. Characteristics on the supply side were not explicitly considered at first (Musgrave et al. 1994, pp. 68 ff; Hirshleifer 1983, p. 372). In the recent years, an increasing reference has been made to supply-side characteristics. The aggregation technology is applied to define the supply side of a public good. We start with a presentation of demand-side characteristics and then turn to the supply-side.

The first demand-side characteristic of a public good is non-rivalry, i.e. the benefits of an activity for one agent do not diminish the benefits that are available for others. For example, the discovery of an AIDS vaccine yields non-rival benefits (Sandler 2004, p. 15). Applying a vaccine procedure to patients in one country does not detract the benefits which can occur in other countries from its application (Kanbur et al. 1999, p. 55). This is not true for curative health measures like antiretroviral therapy (Smith and MacKellar 2007). Since anti-retroviral medicaments can become less effective as a result of resistant HIV clades, rival benefits may occur in the long run (Sandler 1978). Future generations will not gain from treatment since HIV acquires immunity.

The second demand-side characteristic, non-excludability, implies that benefits can be received both by providers and by non-providers once a public good has been supplied. This is based on the inability to exclude others from the benefits of the provided activity. Limiting the transmission of infectious diseases like HIV/AIDS and tuberculosis are examples of non-excludable public goods (UNAIDS 2004, p. 142). All people benefit from these preventive health interventions regardless of whether their government has provided prevention or not. The risk to acquire an infection is thereby reduced. The same line of reasoning holds for discovering an AIDS vaccine. By contrast, treating patients with anti-retroviral medicaments is subject to exclusion (Smith and MacKellar 2007).

The description of the characteristics of a public good indicates that health measures can vary according to their degree of publicness. Treatment, for example, is a private good because a patient who has been treated with medicaments mostly benefits (Ainsworth and Over 1999, p. 291). This is not true for health interventions like developing an AIDS vaccine or prophylactic health measures against tuberculosis which are examples for pure health-promoting public goods. It is important to remember that (non)rivalry and (non)excludability represent extreme characteristics of a public good. In-between classes of public goods can be detected by allowing partial rivalry of benefits or partial excludability of non-payers.[24] These types of goods are not mentioned here specifically. We focus on the supply-side characteristic of public goods: the aggregation technology.

The aggregation technology determines the manner in which individual provision efforts are combined to the overall provision level of a public good (Sandler and Sargent 1995, p. 152). Since there is no global government providing health-promoting public goods, it cannot be assumed that the sum of individual efforts at the national level equals a global effort. Thus, interventions which are optimal from a national government's point of view may be suboptimal from a global perspective. Therefore, an evaluation whether or not implemented national interventions are effective in an international context requires their aggregation.

2.3.4 The Concept of Aggregation Technology

It is traditionally assumed in the literature that the total amount of a public good equals the sum of all individual contributions. Thus, the so-called summation

[24]A detailed description of further classes of impure public goods can be found in Sandler and Arce (2002).

technology was used. If the aggregation technology is additive, each agent's provision is perfectly substitutable for the provision of others (Sandler and Arce 2002, p. 207). This follows from the fact that each contributed unit is equally added to the overall provision level. Curative health measures like treatment and care are examples for the application of additive technologies. The overall level of treatment of HIV-positive patients depends on the sum of people who have been treated. Similarly, the aggregated knowledge about HIV/AIDS accumulates with the amount of implemented anti-AIDS programmes (Jacquet and Marniesse 2006, p. 81). The more educational actions are carried out, the more people are educated about HIV and its transmission. Therefore, the stock of knowledge will grow.

Hirshleifer (1983, 1985), as well as Cornes and Sandler (1984a) were the first ones pointing out that this assumption of the literature is a special case.[25] Other aggregation technologies than the summation technology arise by considering only a single contribution to a public good. Hirshleifer differentiates between the "weakest-link case" and the "best-shot case". For the "weakest-link technology" the overall provision level is determined by the smallest contribution whereas for the "best-shot technology" it is determined by the largest effort. For a better understanding of these alternative approaches, Hirshleifer gives two intuitive explanations (Hirshleifer 1983, pp. 371, 373).

Hirshleifer's motivation for the weakest-link case is the Anarchia metaphor. Anarchia is a circular island which shall be protected against the flood. Each citizen owns a wedge-shaped slice. Since there is no government, everyone is responsible to construct and to maintain a dyke along its coast himself. However, the security of each habitant does not depend on his own contribution but on the smallest effort to build an embankment. In times of a flood, the sea will penetrate where the lowest dyke is built or at the worst maintained part of the dyke. If this is the case, the whole island will be flooded because of Anarchia's topography. Higher or better maintained embankments cannot compensate lower or worse ones because the height or the quality of the least maintained dyke determines the security of the island. Thus, the amount of flood protection does not equal the sum of the individual preventive efforts. It is determined by the lowest embankment – the weakest link.

Additionally, Hirshleifer gives the following best-shot example. A city is surrounded by a number of anti-missile batteries which are firing at a single incoming nuclear-armed missile. If the enemy breaks through the defence, the whole town will be destroyed. In this situation, not the average accuracy of the shots is crucial but whether or not the best defensive shot is sufficient to destroy the enemy. Then, further shots are redundant. Thus, the defence of the city does not depend on the sum of the shots, but on the best shot.

Following these general examples of the weakest-link and best-shot technology, we proceed by turning back to the health sector and analysing the aggregation

[25]Hirshleifer himself did not use the term "aggregation technology". He defines it as social composition function (Hirshleifer 1983, p. 372). The expression "technology of public supply aggregation" is coined by Cornes and Sandler. See also Sandler and Sargent (1995, p. 152). Arce (2001, p. 115) labels it as contribution aggregator.

technologies of some health-promoting public goods provided to address HIV/AIDS. As the lowest dyke determines the security of an island, the overall success in limiting the domain of a disease like tuberculosis depends on the country providing the lowest amount of prevention (Barrett 2006, p. 14). Larger initiatives to provide prophylactic health measures in other countries cannot finally prevent further disseminations. A disease is persistent until the virus is eradicated in the region where the smallest interventions are carried out. Hence, prevention is an example for a weakest-link public good. By contrast, the discovery of a cure or a vaccine is most likely where the largest financial means exist.[26] However, if research teams are equally equipped, success is stochastic.

Considering Hirshleifer's idea, a variety of alternative aggregation technologies can be determined beyond the weakest-link and the best-shot technology. Further aggregation technologies include e.g. the weaker link and the better shot.[27] Both are less extreme cases than the weakest link and the best shot as their names imply. For weaker-link (better-shot) public goods the smallest (largest) contribution possesses the largest marginal impact on the overall public good provision level followed by the second smallest (largest) effort and so on (Cornes 1993, p. 261; Arce and Sandler 2001, p. 495). However, weaker-link and better-shot aggregation technologies with respect to health are rarely considered. A noteworthy exception is the publication by Sandler and Arce (2002) exploring their relevance for health activities. Examples are collecting data for transnational health statistics or developing new anti-retroviral medicaments against HIV. R&D in second-drug lines is necessary because of the emerging resistance of HIV to currently applied therapies as discussed earlier. Therefore, additional efforts to find further methods to prevent the replication of HIV add marginal benefits. The same line of reasoning holds in a stochastic model where research teams having equal likelihoods of finding an AIDS vaccine compete with each other for a discovery. Even if a vaccine is found, additional benefits are reached by the discovery of further effective vaccines. Table 2.3 summarises definitions and some examples with respect to health for each aggregation technology.

The variety of aggregation technologies implies that health-promoting public goods do not only differ according to their characteristics non-rivalry and non-excludability, as primarily recognised by parts of the academic literature on AIDS. Health interventions displaying the same demand-side properties can be determined by various aggregation technologies. For example, prophylactic health measures to limit the domain of tuberculosis and the discovery of an AIDS vaccine both yield

[26]However, if the interests of pharmaceutical companies to find a vaccine are low since purchasing power is lacking in low-and middle-income countries, the best-shot argument does not hold.

[27]There are further aggregation technologies like threshold or weighted sum. A threshold international public good is characterised by surpassing a threshold to receive benefits (Sandler 2001b, footnote 10). The weighted sum aggregation technology is a generalisation of the summation technology. In contrast to an additive technology, each contributor's effort can have a different additive impact on the overall provision level.

Table 2.3 Alternative aggregation technologies

Aggregation technology	Characterisation	Examples with respect to health
Summation	The sum of individual efforts determines the overall public good provision level.	Knowledge about HIV treatment
Weakest-link	Only the smallest effort determines the overall public good provision level.	Preventive measures, e.g. limiting tuberculosis
Best-shot	Only the largest effort determines the overall public good provision level.	Developing an AIDS vaccine or a cure
Weaker-link	The smallest effort possesses the largest marginal impact on the overall public good provision level, followed by the second smallest and so on.	Collecting data for transnational health statistics
Better-shot	The largest effort possesses the largest marginal impact on the overall public good provision level, followed by the second largest and so on.	Discovering second-drug lines against HIV

non-rival and non-excludable benefits. Yet, if these public goods are further subdivided according to their third characteristic, Table 2.3 reveals different aggregation technologies. The former intervention is an example for a weakest-link while the latter is a best-shot public good. Thus, a simple merging of preventive and curative health interventions into health-promoting public goods as practised today is misleading since the variety of aggregation technologies is not taken into account. Moreover, the description of several types of supply-side characteristics, ranging between a minimum and a maximum aggregation technology, indicates varying allocative consequences and finally the requirement of different financing policies to ensure effective interventions. For example, the transmission of tuberculosis can only be transnationally stopped if health programmes implemented by the country supplying the lowest amount of prophylactic have been scaled up as a result of international assistance. In contrast, extending educational campaigns a country which is at least involved in educational actions does not influence the aggregated knowledge about HIV/AIDS accumulating with the amount of implemented anti-HIV programmes.

2.4 Conclusions

In order to illustrate the importance of HIV/AIDS and the necessity to give effective policy responses, the chapter provides basic information about the various HIV/AIDS epidemics and their consequences within and beyond national borders. Our analysis reveals that anti-HIV interventions are already justified from a national perspective. The calculated financial burden faced by governments in low and middle-income countries, shows that AIDS wastes a large part of aggregate human capital. Pre-existing health concerns in the developing world like tuberculosis and other STIs add to the costs of AIDS. The demand for a response is strengthened if transnational AIDS spillovers are taken into account. The overview about cross-border consequences has indicated epidemiological impacts of AIDS in developing countries on the developed world and vice versa.

Given the line of reasoning why transnational policies are useful, this chapter refers to the importance of international public goods with respect to AIDS. In addition, we have shown that health-promoting public goods involve several characteristics: Non-rivalry, non-excludability and the aggregation technology. Health interventions which do not differ from the demand side can vary according to their aggregation technology on the supply side. Particularly, this third characteristic influences whether or not national efforts are efficient from a global perspective. It follows that the concept of aggregation technology seems useful to identify the status quo of provision and subsequently an effective aid mechanism. In order to confirm this assumption more in-depth, Chap. 3 analyses the allocative implications of various aggregation technologies.

Chapter 3
Profiling the Provision Status of Health-Promoting Public Goods Against AIDS

Many of today's crises have their roots in the serious underprovision of global public goods.
Inge Kaul et al. (1999)
HIV/AIDS control is underprovided.
Inge Kaul (2002)

It is well-known that the private provision of public goods results generally in collective underprovision. The same situation seems plausible in the case of combating HIV/AIDS. The desire to intervene effectively has been addressed by a lot of international negotiations. A landmark in international efforts is the Declaration of Commitment on HIV/AIDS (UN 2001). It was adopted at the United Nations General Assembly Special Session in June 2001 (Department of HIV/AIDS Family and Community Health 2003, p. 10). For the first time governments from 189 states gathered to discuss a specific health problem. The Declaration describes the HIV/AIDS epidemic and its effects as well as desired interventions. Basic priorities are educating people, especially the youth; stopping mother-child-transmission; providing treatment to all those who are infected; developing an AIDS vaccine or a cure and alleviating the impacts of HIV/AIDS. Although specific time-bound targets exist for each of those aims, these agreements are not legally binding. Governments cannot be compelled to keep their promises since an enforcing authority is missing. Since autonomous governments primarily consider their national benefits, they fail to take positive cross-border effects into account. As a consequence, an efficient transnational provision level of health measures cannot be provided (Kremer 2006, p. 26; Kaul 2002, p. 27).[1] However, this conclusion is based on the very strong assumption that the sum of individual efforts at the national level equals the global effort. The condition of a summation technology is not valid for every health-promoting public good as we know from Chap. 2.

Against this background, the chapter aims at investigating whether the problem of underprovision is inherent if health-promoting public goods against AIDS are

[1] A more general description of suboptimality based on insufficient incentives can be found in Olsen (1965).

D. Sonntag, *AIDS and Aid,* Contributions to Economics,
DOI 10.1007/978-3-7908-2419-3_3, © Springer-Verlag Berlin Heidelberg 2010

supplied or not. Therefore, we analyse how various aggregation technologies influence the provision level of international public goods. In detail, we investigate how countries behave when they decide to provide these health-promoting public goods and discuss the efficiency of the resulting allocations.[2] These allocative implications are exemplified by three health measures which are essential in the fight against AIDS – "knowledge about HIV", "limiting the domain of tuberculosis" and "developing an AIDS vaccine". The restriction on these health-promoting public goods is justified from the epidemiology of HIV because they are crucial to prevent further transmissions of HIV.[3]

Our analyses are given within a static non-cooperative game. Of course, a static investigation is subject to some criticism. It is less likely that anti-HIV programmes are supplied single-shot, e.g. by governments. Providers often interact repeatedly. Such repeated interactions allow them to study and to learn the reactions of others. If this is the case, agents can match the others' decisions over time.[4] Although such dynamic considerations can mitigate collective action problems because agents cannot gain from being non-providers in the long run, the causes of allocative shortcomings do not vanish. However, the different causes of a suboptimal provision level need to be taken into account to tailor international transfers. The effects on welfare are analysed by the criterion of Pareto-optimality. An allocation is Pareto-efficient if it is not possible to raise one individual's well-being without diminishing the well-being of at least one other individual (Pareto 1906). This definition possesses some drawbacks. For example, different Pareto-optimal allocations cannot be compared since this decision depends on individual preferences. In spite of the criticism, it remains a normative standard to evaluate the outcomes of the behaviour of several agents.

The analysis continues as follows: After outlining the importance of the three key health measures we proceed by depicting the benchmark case "knowledge about HIV" at first. It replicates the argument of the academic literature on AIDS where the aggregation technology is additive. Then, we turn to the other cases "limiting the domain of tuberculosis" and "developing an AIDS vaccine". We take account of non-additive aggregation technologies and analyse their allocative consequences. Finally, this chapter closes with a summary of the main results.

---

[2]For concreteness, governments act on behalf of their citizens.

[3]The subsequent analyses concentrate on these three health interventions and thus measures like collecting data for transnational health statistics and developing second-drug lines against HIV also mentioned in Chap. 2 will not be discussed. We explain in Sect. 3.1 why we focus on the three key health-promoting public goods.

[4]A simple but successful strategy is Tit-for-Tat which has got attention after the publications of Axelrod (1980a, b). Axelrod invited game theorists to design strategies which do not fail in repeated games. To identify the most successful proposal, a computer competition was simulated in which each submission was tested. Tit-for-Tat which was submitted by Rapoport won. The idea is to cooperate in the first round if the choices of the other are unknown. In the subsequent rounds, previous cooperation is rewarded by cooperation and opportunistic behaviour is answered by becoming opportunistic.

3.1 Key Health-Promoting Public Goods

In this section, we discuss why our further analyses concentrate on the health-promoting public goods mentioned above. The key in the fight against AIDS is to stop the transmission of the virus because in this way further HIV infections can be prevented. This can primarily be attained by providing sex education about sexual intercourse, STIs and how to avoid them. Preventive health measures to limit the transmission of tuberculosis are still a prior intervention. Because of the biological synergies with HIV, these infections are mutually exacerbating. Tuberculosis accelerates HIV replication while HIV increases the risk of both activation of a latent tuberculosis infection and the risk of diseases afterwards (Corbett et al. 2002, p. 2182). The new outbreak of drug-resistant tuberculosis in South Africa strengthens this argument (Wines 2007). Fifty-two out of 53 infected patients who died had suffered from AIDS. Moreover, it seems that it has spread to neighbouring countries as Lesotho, Swaziland and Mozambique. This reinforces the need for prophylaxis. A further reason to focus our attention on preventing tuberculosis is noted by Stillwaggon (2006a, p. 61). She points out that its effect on HIV transmission is neglected in the literature. Such an impact can be very serious in regions with high prevalence of tuberculosis, but low HIV prevalence. If tuberculosis increases the susceptibility to HIV because of a weakened immune system, the transmission of HIV may worsen in these regions.

Preventive health measures should be supported by the development of an AIDS vaccine because prophylaxis as condom distribution or needle exchange can slow down the spread of the virus, but cannot stop it. The final end of the HIV/AIDS epidemic can only be attained by developing an effective and accessible vaccine. Even those with a low effectiveness can substantially change the spread of the virus (CMH 2001, p. 49). Thus, vaccine-related efforts are an important priority in the fight against AIDS. Nevertheless, the five big pharmaceutical companies, GlaxoSmithKline, Merck, Novartis, Sanofi-Aventis and Wyeth are hardly involved in AIDS vaccine research (IAVI 2008). Incentives to search for an AIDS vaccine are low because its discovery is an international public good (Kremer 2006, p. 33). Thus, many individuals would gain from such a vaccine. However, investors cannot internalise all national and international benefits. If R&D results cannot be patented, private companies will have little incentives to fund HIV vaccine research. Further reasons are the high costs of R&D while finding an AIDS vaccine is sketchy. Even in the case of a successful discovery, there is no guarantee that costs will be amortised. The need for a vaccine is greatest among people in Sub-Saharan Africa where purchasing power is lacking.[5] In addition, an AIDS vaccine would be administered once and thus, it is less profitable than medications to control cholesterol or asthma which need to be taken daily over long periods

[5]Kremer (2006, pp. 34–37) suggests the implementation of a large-scale purchase commitment programme financed by the World Bank to encourage R&D in vaccine research.

Table 3.1 Annual investments in HIV vaccine research (US $ million): 2004–2007

Sectors	2004	2005	2006	2007
Public sector	603	672	776	789
U.S.	516	574	654	659
Europe (include funding from the EU)	57	69	82	79
Other apart from U.S. and Europe	28	27	38	49
Multilaterals	2	2	2	2
Philanthropic Sector	12	12	78	88
Total non-commercial Sector	615	684	854	877
Commercial Sector	68	75	79	84
Total global investment	683	759	933	961

Source: HIV Vaccines and Microbicides Resource Tracking Working Group (2008, p. 12)

of time. Consequently, the public sector dominates HIV vaccine research.[6] Data about the annual funding for HIV vaccines between 2004 and 2007 reinforce this observation.

Table 3.1 reveals that public agencies and institutions continue to dominate investments in HIV vaccine research. In 2007, they funded US $ 789 million or about 82% of R&D. The private industry invested about US $ 84 million into AIDS vaccines. Its funding constitutes about 8% of the US $ 961 million spent on research. The same holds for the philanthropic sector that finances 9% of the total investment in AIDS vaccines. The highest philanthropic vaccine funder is the Bill & Melinda Gates Foundation that provided more than US $ 80 million in 2007 (HIV Vaccines and Microbicides Resource Tracking Working Group 2008, p. 15).

The public sector also dominates the supply of prophylactic health measures like raising the knowledge about HIV and limiting the domain of tuberculosis. Even if the private sector is affected by HIV/AIDS due to sickness and death of workers and thus has to be interested in reducing costs through the implementation of preventive programmes, initiatives to disseminate knowledge about HIV are primarily implemented by the public sector (Ramachandran et al. 2006). As knowledge is a global public good and thus, non-payers cannot be excluded, private firms would have no incentive to supply educational campaigns (Stiglitz 1999). The same argument holds for programmes that prevent further transmissions of tuberculosis. According to the WHO (2008 p. 66), governments of high-burden countries like India and the Russian Federation fund US $ 1,656 million into tuberculosis control in 2008. These investments meet about 73% of the total costs of tuberculosis control, US $ 2,280 million. The remaining costs of national tuberculosis programmes are covered by grants (WHO 2008, p. 5).

In sum, the non-commercial sector dominates the provision of health measures like "knowledge about HIV", "limiting the domain of tuberculosis" and "developing a vaccine against AIDS" even if all sources - governments, private industry and

[6] If private firms do not compete in HIV vaccine research, patent-race games seem less appropriate. Multiple firms spend resources on R&D until one of them makes a discovery. The firm that innovates first will obtain a patent while all other firms will gain nothing.

Table 3.2 Aggregation technologies of key health-promoting public goods

Key health-promoting public good	Aggregation technology
Knowledge about HIV	Summation
Limiting the domain of tuberculosis	Weakest-link
Developing a vaccine against AIDS	Best-shot

foundations – are involved. Although all three interventions are supplied mainly by the public sector, we have to analyse the behaviour of governments and their implications on welfare for each case separately. This is due to the fact that each of these health-promoting public goods is characterised by a different aggregation technology as depicted in Table 3.2.

Table 3.2 indicates that these public goods represent extreme cases of aggregation technologies. Particularly, the assumption of the weakest-link technology that there are perfect complements is very strong. Perfect complements are inputs, like country i's contribution to a public good, which are used in a fixed proportion. If country i raises its own contribution without an increase of the others' efforts, the minimum public good provision cannot be raised. In contrast, enhancing all contributions to a health-promoting public good in the best-shot case cannot result in a higher provision level. Only the agent with the largest effort determines the overall success. Nevertheless, there are reasons why we focus on these three cases. It is not necessary to discuss the implications of each possible aggregation technology when the impact of several aggregation technologies on providing and financing policies has to be analysed. The results of less extreme cases as weaker-link and better-shot are comparable but extenuated to that in weakest-link and best-shot situation (Sandler 2003, p. 136). Consequently, in order to illustrate the tendencies of provision and income policies, a restriction on extreme cases as a minimum or a maximum technology seems sufficient. They can be interpreted as reference scenarios.

In order to analyse these technologies, it is helpful to construct them as special cases of a general aggregator function. We follow Cornes and Sandler (1996, p. 185) and interpret the aggregation technologies as a production function where the individual contributions g_i determine the overall public good provision G just like production factors contribute to the output. Various types of aggregation technologies can be expressed by

$$G = \alpha \left[\left(\frac{1}{n} \right) \sum_{i=1}^{n} {g_i}^{v} \right]^{\frac{1}{v}} \quad \text{for } i = 1, 2, ..., n, \tag{3.1}$$

where α and v are exogenous parameters. The parameter α can be interpreted as a distribution parameter measuring the share of agents who can influence the overall provision level G. The aggregation parameter v can be determined by $\frac{1}{1-v} = \sigma$ where σ represents the elasticity of substitution.

Equation (3.1) is a symmetric constant elasticity of substitution (CES) production function. It can straightforward be seen that summation, weakest-link and best-shot cases can be derived by choosing specific values for α and v. For example, by setting $\alpha = n$ and $v = 1$ we obtain the summation technology:

$$G = \sum_{i=1}^{n} q_i. \tag{3.2}$$

Equation (3.2) reveals that the individual contributions g_i are prefect substitutes because from $v = 1$ follows $\sigma = \infty$ which represents the case of pure substitutes.

If we set $\alpha = 1$ and $v \to -\infty$, (3.1) turns into

$$G = \min\{g_1, g_2, ..., g_n\}, \tag{3.3}$$

which represents the weakest-link case where the smallest contribution g_i determines the overall public good provision level G.

By inserting $\alpha = 1$ and $v \to +\infty$ we obtain the best-shot case

$$G = \max\{g_1, g_2, ..., g_n\}, \tag{3.4}$$

where the largest contribution g_i determines the overall public good provision level G.

Following this characterisation of health-promoting public goods, we proceed by analysing the summation case which represents the basis for further analyses. Allocative consequences of an additive technology are widely discussed in the public goods literature. In order to give a short overview about the impact of a summation technology on efficiency, we replicate the results of the literature by closely following the analysis of Cornes and Sandler (1996 pp. 144–147) and Hirshleifer (1983).

3.2 The Benchmark Case

We consider a country whose preferences are defined by two commodities: a pure private good y_i which is used as the numeraire and the health-promoting public good "knowledge about HIV" G. The utility function[7] $U_i(y_i, G)$ is continuous, strictly increasing, strictly quasi-concave and twice differentiable with respect to its arguments.[8] Each country is endowed with the exogenous income I_i. Income can

[7]For simplicity the utility function does not include externalities caused by implemented health interventions. For example, the discovery and supply of an HIV vaccine could reduce the provision of curative health activities like treatment with antiretroviral drugs since an infection with HIV could be prevented.

[8]For concreteness, a country cannot receive benefits. We suppose that countries possess benevolent governments that act on behalf of their citizens who gain from health measures. Because we have assumed identical individuals, the utility function of a representative individual is represented.

be used either for private consumption or to provide the public good. The supply price of the public good equals a constant uniform price p. Thus, the budget constraint can be written as:

$$y_i + pg_i = I_i \quad \text{for } i = 1, 2, ..., n. \tag{3.5}$$

Country i maximises its utility subject to its budget constraint:

$$\begin{aligned} &\max_{y_i, g_i} U_i(y_i, g_i + G_{-i}) = U_i(y_i, G) \\ &\text{s.t.} \\ &y_i + pg_i = I_i, \quad \text{for } i = 1, 2, ..., n, \end{aligned} \tag{3.6}$$

where the expression $G = g_i + G_{-i}$ results from the summation technology. The public good provision level G is determined by the sum of country i's individual contribution g_i and the efforts of the other countries G_{-i}.

The Lagrangian function can be expressed as:

$$L = U_i(y_i, G) - \lambda(y_i + pg_i - I_i), \tag{3.7}$$

where λ is the Lagrange multiplier. For an interior solution, the first-order conditions are:

$$\begin{aligned} \frac{\partial L}{\partial y_i} &= \frac{\partial U_i}{\partial y_i} - \lambda = 0 \\ \frac{\partial L}{\partial G} &= \frac{\partial U_i}{\partial G} - \lambda p = 0 \\ \frac{\partial L}{\partial \lambda} &= y_i + pg_i - I_i = 0, \end{aligned}$$

where the last derivative with respect to λ is country i's budget constraint. Dividing the second equation by the first, we obtain the following first-order condition which is valid for every country i:

$$\begin{aligned} &\frac{\partial U_i / \partial G}{\partial U_i / \partial y_i} = p \\ &\text{or} \\ &MRS_i = p, \end{aligned} \tag{3.8}$$

where MRS_i is country i's marginal rate of substitution between the public and the private good. Country i provides education programmes up to the level where MRS_i equals p which coincides with the marginal rate of transformation MRT_i (see also Cornes and Sandler 1985). If condition (3.8) is satisfied, the supply of the public

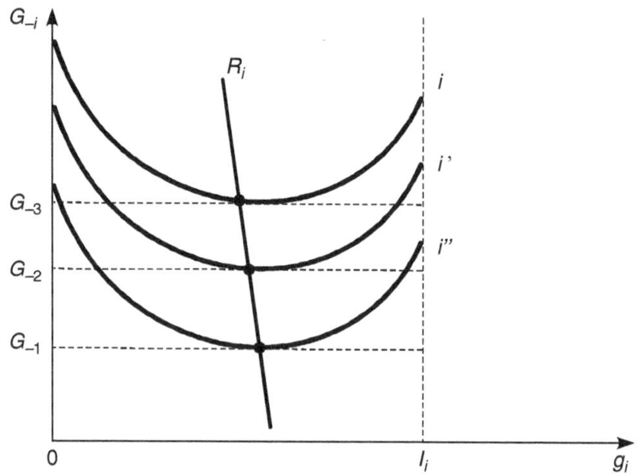

Fig. 3.1 Indifference map in (g_i, G_{-i}) space

good "knowledge about HIV" is optimal for country i. The first-order condition is illustrated in Fig. 3.1.[9]

Country i's contribution to the public good g_i is measured along the horizontal axis while the other countries' efforts G_{-i} are measured along the vertical axis. There is a family of indifference curves which describes country i's preferences. Superior indifference curves imply higher values of bundles of goods. The indifference curves are bounded by a vertical line I_i which describes the value of g if country i's income is completely utilised. Different values of G_{-i} can be illustrated by horizontal dashed lines (G_{-1}, G_{-2}, G_{-3}) since the provision of others is exogenously given.[10] Country i's best response to the other countries' efforts is represented by the point of tangency between its highest attainable indifference curve and these horizontal lines. This can be depicted in the point on the highest attainable indifference curve where its slope becomes zero. Variations of G_{-i} generate i's reaction curve R_i. Consequently, a reaction curve shows country i's best responses for different levels of G_{-i}. It is downward-sloping as illustrated in Fig. 3.1. The higher the aggregate contribution of the others is, the lower country i's own contribution will be.

So far we have investigated how country i behaves when it decides to provide the health-promoting public good. We proceed by analysing the implications on welfare if all countries behave like country i.[11] We consider an economy consisting of two countries ($n = 2$) to allow for an illustration. Since all countries

[9]A similar figure can be found in Cornes and Sandler (1996, p. 146).

[10]This assumption is known as a zero conjecture variation in that sense that each agent regards the behaviour of the other agents as independent of its own (Cornes and Sandler 1984b, p. 371).

[11]An analytical investigation of the existence of a Nash equilibrium can be found in Bergstrom et al. (1986, pp. 32–34).

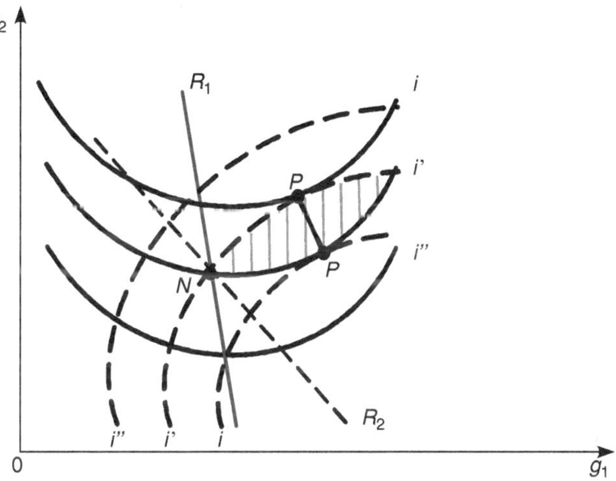

Fig. 3.2 Nash equilibrium in a two-country world (summation case)

act independently and simultaneously, the Nash equilibrium represents the non-cooperative solution. It is illustrated in Fig. 3.2.[12] In a two-country world the contribution of the others G_{-i} equals country 2's contribution g_2 which is measured along the vertical axis. Country 1's contribution g_1 is depicted along the horizontal axis. Additionally there are both countries' indifference curves. Country 1's indifference map is drawn solid while the one of country 2 is dashed. Point *N* represents the Nash equilibrium. It is the intersection between the reaction functions R_1 and R_2. At *N*, each country chooses its optimal contribution to the health-promoting public good "knowledge about HIV" g_i given the other's current contribution.

It can straightforward be seen that the equilibrium *N* is not Pareto-efficient.[13] The shaded area depicts a region of mutual advantage. Pareto-efficient allocations of the health-promoting public good "knowledge about HIV" are located at the curve *PP* which is a part of the contract curve.[14] It passes through the points of tangency between country 1's and country 2's indifference curves, therefore Pareto-efficient allocations are characterised by equal slopes. To express this condition analytically the following observation is useful: Along any indifference curve, country *i*'s utility $U_i(y_i, G) = U_i(I_i - pg_i, g_i + G_{-i})$ does not change and, thus, it holds:

$$-p\frac{\partial U_i}{\partial y_i}dg_i + \frac{\partial U_i}{\partial G}dg_i + \frac{\partial U_i}{\partial G}dG_{-i} = 0. \tag{3.9}$$

---

[12] This depiction follows the figure in Hirshleifer (1983, p. 375).

[13] For the standard result see Hirshleifer (1983, pp. 375–376) as well as Cornes and Sandler (1996, pp. 155–158).

[14] The contract curve represents all Pareto-efficient allocations given the price p and the income levels I_i for $i = 1, 2$.

Hence, the slope of an indifference curve can be expressed as:

$$\left.\frac{dG_{-i}}{dg_i}\right|_{U_i=\overline{U}_i} = p\frac{\partial U_i/\partial y_i}{\partial U_i/\partial G} - 1. \tag{3.10}$$

Applying (3.10) to both indifference curves, we obtain:

$$p\frac{\partial U_1/\partial y_1}{\partial U_1/\partial G} - 1 = \frac{1}{p\frac{\partial U_2/\partial y_2}{\partial U_2/\partial G} - 1}. \tag{3.11}$$

Rearranging yields:

$$\frac{\partial U_1/\partial G}{\partial U_1/\partial y_1} + \frac{\partial U_2/\partial G}{\partial U_2/\partial y_2} = p$$
or
$$MRS_1 + MRS_2 = p, \tag{3.12}$$

which is the Samuelson condition (Samuelson 1954, p. 387, 1955, p. 354) for a world of two countries. People should be educated about HIV, its transmission and possible preventive measures until the sum of the marginal rates of substitution between the public good "knowledge about HIV" and the private good equals p that expresses the marginal rate of transformation.[15]

Comparing the Samuelson condition for n countries $\sum_{i=1}^{n} MRS_i = p$ with (3.8), we see that the Nash equilibrium is suboptimal. The source of inefficiency can be explained as follows: Each country adjusts its own contribution to educate people only up to the level where its private marginal rate of substitution equals the price per unit p. External benefits are not considered. Therefore, the overall provision of the health-promoting public good "knowledge about HIV" is suboptimal.

In order to show that this conclusion is not valid for the weakest-link case "limiting the domain of tuberculosis" and the best-shot case "developing an AIDS vaccine", the impact of alternative aggregation technologies on the overall provision level of international public goods is analysed below.

3.3 Efficient and Equilibrium Allocations: The Weakest-Link Case

Starting with Hirshleifer (1983, 1985), there are some authors in the public goods literature analysing the allocative implications of a weakest-link technology. Among these authors are Ihori (2005) and Vicary (1990), as well as Harrison and

[15]The right-hand side of (3.12) is equivalent to the marginal costs MC which are identical for each country $(MC_1 = MC_2)$.

Hirshleifer (1989). Ihori (2005) and Vicary (1990, pp. 378–379), for example, replicate the analysis of Hirshleifer (1985) by deriving agent i's reaction curve and the Nash equilibria. Moreover, Ihori explains in detail the impact of the weakest-link technology on the shape of an agent i's indifference curve. Based on this result, he also shows graphically how agents equipped with different incomes behave when they decide to provide a public good. In contrast to Hirshleifer, implicitly focussing on homogenous agents, the analyses of Vicary (1990) and Ihori (2005) also include the implications of a minimum technology on efficiency if agents are heterogenous. It follows that the assertion of Hirshleifer (1983, p. 377) that a maximum public good provision level is Pareto-optimal fails in the case of heterogeneity.

In order to give a comprehensive overview about the impact of a weakest-link technology on the voluntary provision of a public good, this section summarises the several analyses mentioned above. In addition, the first-order conditions and the Samuelson condition for a weakest-link public good are discussed more in-depth to allow a comparison with the results of the summation case in Sect. 3.2.

We refer to the model above. Consequently, almost all assumptions can be retained. The technology for providing the public good "limiting the domain of tuberculosis" is defined as

$$G = \min\{g_i\} \quad \text{for } i = 1, 2, ..., n. \tag{3.13}$$

In order to analyse how country i reacts if it decides to supply prophylactic health measures against tuberculosis, we maximise its utility subject to its budget constraint and to (3.13). The second condition is relevant since no country will provide more of the public good than anyone else (Hirshleifer 1983, p. 376). Otherwise, additional expenditures will be wasted without a compensating increase of the public good provision. In addition, if the decisions of others are observable for each agent, it follows

Definition 1. *Each country i must have an expectation regarding* $\min\{g_{-i}\}$ *where* $g_{-i} = (g_1, ..., g_{i-1}, g_{i+1}, ..., g_n)$.[16]

Country i's maximisation problem is as follows:

$$\begin{aligned} &\max_{y_i, g_i} U_i[y_i, \min\{g_1, g_2, ..., g_n\}] = U_i(y_i, G) \\ &\text{s.t.} \\ &y_i + pg_i = I_i. \end{aligned} \tag{3.14}$$

In contrast to the summation case, we cannot derive one first-order condition that is valid for every country i. This results from the fact that contributions to the public good are not perfect substitutes. Therefore, we have to find a set of first-order conditions.

[16] A similar argument can be found in Ihori (2005).

3.3.1 First-Order Condition if i is the Weakest-Link Country

For an interior solution, the first-order condition can be expressed as:

$$\frac{\partial U_i/\partial G}{\partial U_i/\partial y_i} = p, \text{ for some } i \in R,\ R = \{i|g_i \leqslant g_j\},\ j = 1, 2, ..., n$$
$$\text{or}$$
$$MRS_i = p, \tag{3.15}$$

where MRS_i is country i's marginal rate of substitution between the public good "limiting the domain of tuberculosis" and the private good. It will provide prophylactic measures to prevent tuberculosis up to the level where the marginal rate of substitution MRS_i equals p. Hence, the own provision of prevention maximizes the payoff of country i if (3.15) is fulfilled.

3.3.2 First-Order Condition for all Other Countries j

If the weakest-link country is the first one that achieves an equality between MRS_i and p, the decisions of the other countries occur at a higher level of prevention (Hirshleifer 1983, p. 377):

$$\frac{\partial U_j/\partial G}{\partial U_j/\partial y_j} \geqslant p, \text{ for all j} \neq \text{i}, j = 1, 2, ..., n$$
$$\text{or}$$
$$MRS_j \geqslant p, \tag{3.16}$$

where MRS_j is the marginal rate of substitution between the public and the private good of country j. MRS_j is larger than or equals the price of a unit of limiting the domain of tuberculosis because MRS_j has been evaluated at the prevention level of the weakest-link country.

The set of first-order conditions can be illustrated as follows.[17] Firstly, we consider i's decision problem as depicted in Fig. 3.3. To ensure a better understanding, we are going to explain the shape of its indifferences curves more in detail at first. Figure 3.3 shows that country i's graph possesses the usual curvature. In contrast to the summation case, the dashed part of each indifference curve becomes irrelevant. This can be explained as follows: Suppose country i is located in point A. If it supplies less than $\min\{g_{-i}\}$, which is illustrated by a horizontal dashed line, the overall provision level reduces by the same amount as country i's effort

[17]We closely follow Ihori (2005). Figure 3.3 is similar to the depiction in Ihori (2005).

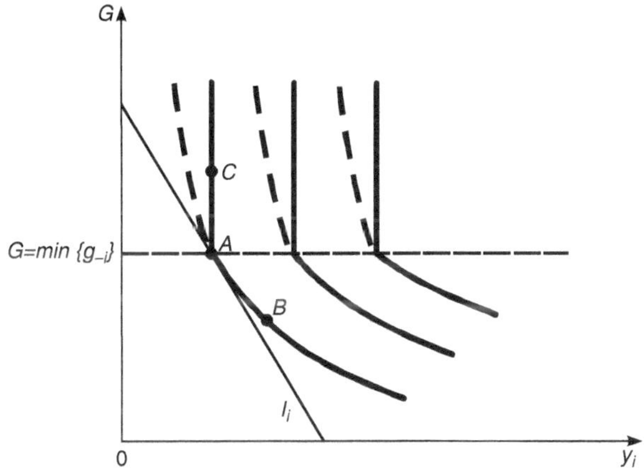

Fig. 3.3 Indifference map in a (y_i, G) space and country i's decision problem

diminishes. This follows from the fact that the public good provision is determined by the smallest effort. Hence, country i requires an increased private consumption to compensate its loss. In this case, country i moves from point A to point B. Yet, the overall level of health measures cannot be raised above $\min\{g_{-i}\}$ if other countries increase their contributions. Supplying more of the health-promoting public good than anyone else does not lead to any additional utility. Therefore, the vertical portion of country i's indifference curve becomes relevant.

Equipped with these observations, it can straightforward be seen that country i's best response to the other's contribution is represented at point A. It matches the contribution of the others in point A since it is located on the dashed horizontal line $\min\{g_{-i}\}$. Thus, the condition $G = \min\{g_1, g_2, ..., g_n\}$ is satisfied. In addition, point A is the tangency point where its highest attainable indifference curve touches its budget line I_i. Hence, the budget constraint is also fulfilled. Yet, point A does not seem optimal for those who prefer a higher amount of the health-promoting public good "limiting the domain of tuberculosis" than country i. In order to analyse this aspect, we closely follow the analysis of Ihori (2005). To allow for an illustration, a two-country world ($n = 2$) as depicted in Fig. 3.4 is assumed.

The total effort of limiting tuberculosis G is measured on the vertical axis while the amount of private consumption y_i is depicted along the horizontal axis. The preferences of the countries are represented by a family of indifference curves. In addition, country 1's (2's) budget constraint I_1 (I_2) is depicted. We assume that $I_1 < I_2$ holds. Our analysis starts with country 1. From the analysis above we know that country 1 chooses point A since the highest attainable indifference curve touches its budget constraint. If $G = \min\{g_1, g_2\}$ is also fulfilled, point A represents country 1's optimal amount of prophylactic health measures g_1^*.[18] Hence, the

[18]This is due to the fact that the second constraint also needs to be fulfilled.

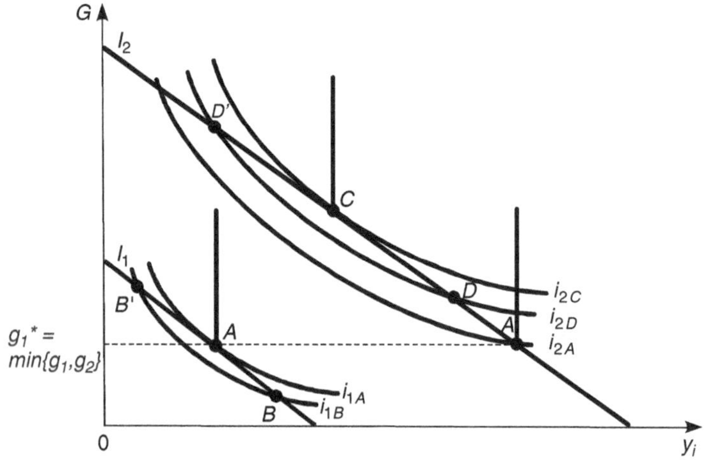

Fig. 3.4 Set of first-order conditions

overall provision level G is determined by $G = g_1^*$. By contrast, preventing tuberculosis is optimal for country 2 at point C. There its highest attainable indifference curve i_{2C} touches its budget constraint I_2. However, due to the weakest-link technology, country 2 will not provide more prophylactic health measures than the weakest-link country (here: country 1). Hence, country 2 will choose an allocation such as point A where $MRS_2 > p$.

The analysis of Fig. 3.4 can additionally be used to derive both countries' reaction curves which are illustrated in Fig. 3.5.[19] Firstly, we consider country 1's reaction curve which can be derived by variations of $\min\{g_1, g_2\}$.[20] By assuming that the minimum public good supply ($g_1^* = \min\{g_1, g_2\}$) occurs in point B instead of point A, country 1 would choose point B as its optimal point because both constraints, the budget constraint and the condition $g_1^* = \min\{g_1, g_2\}$, are satisfied (Ihori 2005). However, if we suppose that the minimal provision level occurs in point B', the amount of the produced health-promoting public good is again represented by point A. Country 1 can do better by moving to point A because a higher indifference curve can be reached.[21] Hence, all points from country 1's budget line at $G = 0$ to point A and the vertical line upwards from point A belong to its reaction curve.

[19] In order to derive country i's reaction curves we follow Hirshleifer (1985, p. 221) and Ihori (2005). Similar figures can be found in Vicary (1990, p. 379), Hirshleifer (1985, p. 222); as well as Ihori (2005).

[20] Reaction curves can be derived as in the benchmark case. However, in the previous analysis we have modified G_{-i} to receive a reaction curve.

[21] Country 1 can reduce its contribution to the public good and can utilise an increasing part of income for private consumption in point A compared to B'.

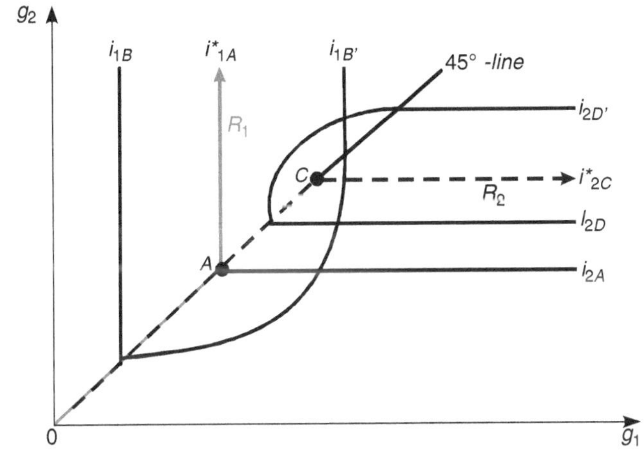

Fig. 3.5 Nash equilibria in a two-country world (weakest-link case)

This is depicted in Fig. 3.5 as the line R_1 between the point of origin and point A on the 45°-line[22] and country 1's vertical indifference curve i^*_{1A} at point A. Country 2's reaction curve R_2 is drawn dashed and can be derived similarly. As we know from Fig. 3.4, point C represents country 2's maximum effort to limit tuberculosis that it is willing to contribute regardless of the action of the other country. Consequently, R_2 moves along the 45°-line up to point C and then along on the horizontal indifference curve i^*_{2C}.

The intersection points along the 45°-line between R_1 and R_2 are Nash equilibria. In contrast to the summation case, there is a range of non-cooperative solutions where countries match one another's efforts. Hirshleifer (1985, p. 221) claimed that a maximum public good level G exists. The final equilibrium is located at the upper limit of the range at point A because moving upwards the 45°-line up to point A improves the welfare of both countries. The line AC is a locus of Pareto-optimal allocations. This indicates that point A itself is Pareto-optimal (Hirshleifer 1985, p. 221). However, this conclusion does not seem generally valid. Vicary (1990, p. 379) and Ihori (2005) referred to a case in which the health-promoting public good is underprovided. This can be shown by determining the constraint for Pareto-optimal allocations. In contrast to the summation case, the Samuelson condition cannot be derived by setting both countries' indifference curves equal because their slopes differ. The slope of country 1's vertical indifference curve is infinite while country 2's is zero. Thus, the condition of Pareto optimality can be obtained by maximising one country's utility function subject to the following constraints: fixed utility levels of the other country, the aggregate budget constraint for both countries

[22]As noted by Hirshleifer (1983, p. 376), the 45°-line where $g_1 = g_2$ plays an important role. Country 1 (2) will never provide prophylactic health measures outside of the range $g_1 \leqslant g_2 (g_2 \leqslant g_1)$. This results from the weakest-link technology.

and the requirement that $g_i = \min\{g_{-i}\}$ is true (Sandler 1992, p. 15). Thus, choosing $(U_2 = \bar{U})$ for country 2 and maximising 1's utility function yields:

$$L = U_1(y_1, G) - \lambda[U_2(y_2, G) - \overline{U}] - \mu(y_1 + y_2 + pg_1 + pg_2 - I_1 - I_2), \quad (3.17)$$

where λ is the Lagrange multiplier on the utility constraint and μ on the budget constraints. Since $g_1 = g_2 = G$ is true at any Pareto-optimal allocation, the Lagrangian function can be expressed as:

$$L = U_1(y_1, G) - \lambda[U_2(y_2, G) - \overline{U}] - \mu(y_1 + y_2 + 2pG - I_1 - I_2). \quad (3.18)$$

For an interior solution the first-order conditions are:

$$\frac{\partial L}{\partial y_1} = \frac{\partial U_1}{\partial y_1} - \mu = 0$$
$$\frac{\partial L}{\partial y_2} = -\lambda\frac{\partial U_2}{\partial y_2} - \mu = 0$$
$$\frac{\partial L}{\partial G} = \frac{\partial U_1}{\partial G} - \lambda\frac{\partial U_2}{\partial G} - 2p\mu = 0.$$

Dividing the third equation by μ yields:

$$\frac{1}{\mu}\frac{\partial U_1}{\partial G} - \frac{\lambda}{\mu}\frac{\partial U_2}{\partial G} - 2p = 0.$$

Then, the first and the second condition are inserted into the third expression to obtain:

$$\frac{\partial U_1/\partial G}{\partial U_1/y_1} + \frac{\partial U_2/\partial G}{\partial U_2/y_2} = 2p$$
$$\text{or} \quad (3.19)$$
$$MRS_1 + MRS_2 = 2p.$$

Equation (3.19) represents the Samuelson condition for the weakest-link health-promoting public good "limiting the domain of tuberculosis". It indicates that prophylactic health measures should be provided until the sum of the marginal rates of substitution between the public and the private good equals two times the price per unit (Harrison and Hirshleifer 1989, p. 210).[23]

Comparing the Samuelson condition for a world consisting of n countries $\sum_{i=1}^{n} MRS_i = np$ with (3.15) and (3.16), we see that the Nash equilibrium is

[23] The right-hand side of (3.19) is equivalent to the sum of both countries' marginal costs $MC_1 + MC_2$.

suboptimal if countries are heterogenous in endowment (see also Vicary (1990, p. 379)). This case is depicted in point A in Fig. 3.5. If both countries are homogeneous, suboptimality is less of concern as each country desires the same public good provision level. It follows $MRS_i = MRS_j = p$. This situation can be illustrated if point A equals point C in Fig. 3.5. Then, point A represents country 2's optimal amount of preventing tuberculosis because both the budget constraint and (3.13) would be satisfied. Its reaction curve R_2 would move along the 45°-line up to point A and then along the horizontal indifference curve i_{2A}. If this is the case, (3.19) will be fulfilled and hence, point A itself will be Pareto-efficient.[24]

3.4 Efficient and Equilibrium Allocations: The Best-Shot Case

Little attention is paid to the impact of a best-shot technology on the voluntary provision of public goods. Exceptions are Hirshleifer (1983) and Conybeare et al. (1994) outlining the implications on the equilibrium allocation if the overall public good provision level is determined by the largest contribution.[25] Hirshleifer (1983), for example, shows that the Nash equilibrium is characterised by one providing agent while the other agents act as free riders. He concludes that even if the agent who is most cost-efficient in producing the best-shot public good becomes the single provider, the overall provision of best-shot public goods is suboptimal. This is because the single provider only produces up to the level where his individual marginal rate of substitution between the public and the private good equals his marginal cost (Hirshleifer 1983, p. 381).

The subsequent analysis, based on the model in Sonntag (2009a), contributes to this strand of literature. In addition to these cases in which an agent that is most able to provide a public good is the sole supplier, we also discuss the issue that the agent with the largest effort is a non-provider and thus gives the whole responsibility to others. Particularly with regard to asymmetries of R&D interests between industrialised and developing countries, this second case seems to be a necessary extension of existing models. We proceed by first applying the analysis of Hirshleifer to the case "developing an AIDS vaccine" and then extending it by considering the allocative consequences of asymmetric interests in vaccine research.

[24] This is the case which is explained by Hirshleifer (1983).

[25] An alternative way of analysing allocative implications of a best-shot aggregation technology can be found in Cornes and Hartley (2007a, pp. 1701–1704). In contrast to the approach of a best response function, they use a replacement function expressing an agent i's best response as a function of the overall public good provision level G and not of the sum of the best replies of all other agents. For a further characterisation of individual and aggregated replacement functions see Cornes and Hartley (2006) as well as Cornes and Hartley (2007b).

3.4.1 Applying Hirshleifer's Analysis to the Case "Developing a Vaccine"

Given that the overall public good provision level G is determined by

$$G = \max\{g_i\} \quad \text{for } i = 1, 2, ..., n, \tag{3.20}$$

country i's maximisation problem modifies to:

$$\begin{aligned} &\max_{y_i, g_i} U_i[y_i, \max\{g_i\}] = U_i(y_i, G) \\ &\text{s.t.} \\ &y_i + pg_i = I_i \quad \text{for } i = 1, 2, ..., n. \end{aligned} \tag{3.21}$$

Solving yields the following set of first-order conditions:

$$\begin{aligned} &\frac{\partial U_i/\partial G}{\partial U_i/\partial y_i} = p \text{ for some } i \in S,\ S = \{i|g_i > \max\{g_j\}\},\ i \neq j,\ j = 1, 2, ..., n \\ &\text{or} \\ &MRS_i(\widehat{g}_i) = p \\ &\text{and} \\ &g_j = 0, \end{aligned} \tag{3.22}$$

where $\widehat{g}_i$ is the greatest effort to find an AIDS vaccine (Conybeare et al. 1994, p. 530). Country i searches for a vaccine up to the level where the marginal rate of substitution between the public and the private good $MRS_i(\widehat{g}_i)$ equals p at the highest level $\widehat{g}_i$. If country i is the first whose marginal rate of substitution equals the price of a unit of the public good, the efforts of the others will drop down to zero $g_j = 0$. This is depicted in Fig. 3.6.

The total effort to develop a vaccine G is depicted on the vertical axis, while private consumption y_i is measured along the horizontal axis. We have illustrated a family of indifference curves and country i's budget constraint. The horizontal dashed line represents $\max\{g_{-i}\}$. Country i will never choose $g_i \leqslant \max\{g_{-i}\}$ because there is no benefit from providing the public good. Thus, it has to provide $g_i > \max\{g_{-i}\}$. Country i's best response to the others' provision is represented by point A because both the budget constraint and the condition $G = \max\{g_1, g_2, ..., g_n\}$ are satisfied. This follows from the fact that point A is a point of tangency. There, country i's highest attainable indifference curve touches its budget line. In addition, point A is located on the horizontal dashed line $\max\{g_{-i}\}$ and thus, the second constraint $G = \max\{g_1, g_2, ..., g_n\}$ also holds.

We proceed by assuming that all countries behave in the same way like country i. In order to analyse such a strategic situation as simply as possible, the following example will be considered.

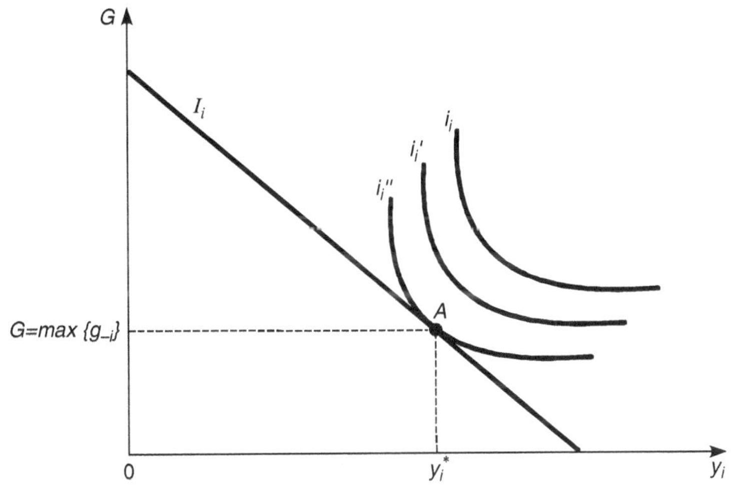

Fig. 3.6 Country i's decision problem

Example 1. It is assumed that country i's utility function can be expressed as:

$$U_i = \alpha \ln y_i + (1-\alpha) \ln G, \tag{3.23}$$

where α determines country i's preferences for private consumption and, hence, $0<\alpha<1$. In addition, we set $G = \max\{g_1, g_2\}$ and $i = 1, 2$. Our analysis will be restricted to two countries $(n = 2)$ to allow for an illustration. It can straightforward be seen that $G = g_i = (1-\alpha)I_i$ and $y_i = \alpha I_i$ if country i chooses to be a contributor. Inserting these results into country i's utility function from (3.23) yields:

$$U_i = \alpha \ln \alpha I_i + (1-\alpha) \ln(1-\alpha) I_i. \tag{3.24}$$

However, if country i decides being a non-contributing country, we obtain $g_i = 0$ and $y_i = I_i$. Its full income is utilised for private consumption. Its utility function is as follows:

$$U_i = \alpha \ln I_i + (1-\alpha) \ln(1-\alpha) I_{-i}, \tag{3.25}$$

where I_{-i} is the income of the others.

We know that country 1 will be the only researching country if country 2 does not search for an AIDS vaccine and vice versa. To express these two cases, the following observation is necessary. Country 2 will choose to be a provider $(g_2 = (1-\alpha)I_2)$ if the received benefit is larger than the benefit if its whole income is utilised for private consumption. Otherwise, country 2 decides to be a non-provider $(g_2 = 0)$. This can be expressed as:

$$\alpha \ln \alpha I_2 + (1-\alpha) \ln(1-\alpha) I_2 > \alpha \ln I_2 + (1-\alpha) \ln(1-\alpha) I_1, \tag{3.26}$$

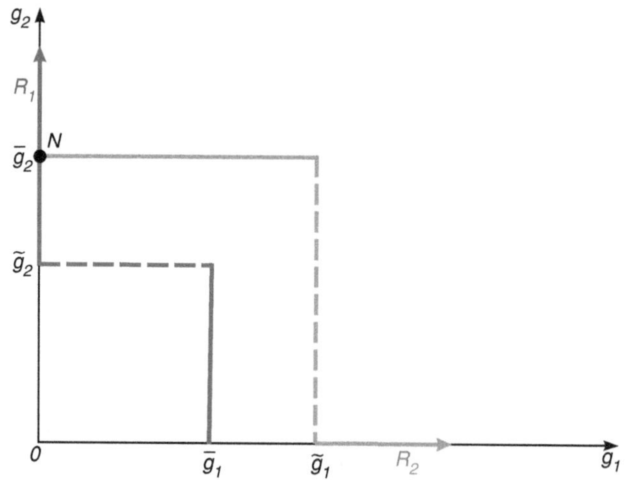

Fig. 3.7 Nash equilibrium in a two-country world (best-shot case)

if country 2 searches for a vaccine. Or, equivalently

$$\frac{1}{\alpha^{\frac{\alpha}{1-\alpha}}} < \frac{g_2}{g_1}, \tag{3.27}$$

where $1/\alpha^{\alpha/1-\alpha}$ is larger than unity due to the definition of α $(0 < \alpha < 1)$. Rearranging yields:

$$\frac{g_1}{\alpha^{\frac{\alpha}{1-\alpha}}} < g_2. \tag{3.28}$$

Condition (3.28) reveals that country 2 will provide the public good if its contribution to the public good is larger than a threshold $\tilde{g}_1$:

$$\tilde{g}_1 = \frac{g_1}{\alpha^{\frac{\alpha}{1-\alpha}}}.$$

However, if its contribution to the public good g_2 is less or equal to a threshold $\tilde{g}_1$, country 2 is a nonprovider and $g_2 = 0$:

$$\tilde{g}_1 = \frac{g_1}{\alpha^{\frac{\alpha}{1-\alpha}}} \geqslant g_2. \tag{3.29}$$

Conditions (3.28) and (3.29) can be used to derive country 2's reaction curve which is depicted in Fig. 3.7.[26] Country 1's reaction curve can be derived in a similar way.

[26]This depiction follows the figure in Sonntag (2009a).

In Fig. 3.7, country 1's effort to develop a vaccine g_1 is depicted on the horizontal axis, while country 2's effort g_2 is measured along the vertical axis. We suppose that country 2 is an industrialised country and has better chances to develop a vaccine than the developing country 1. In case $\bar{g}_1$ is the amount that 1 provides if $g_2 = 0$, and $\bar{g}_2$ is the amount that country 2 supplies if $g_1 = 0$, then $\bar{g}_2 > \bar{g}_1$. This is due to the assumption that country 2 is more likely to find a vaccine.

At first, we want to derive the reaction curve of country 2 (R_2). Condition (3.28) indicates that variations of 1's contribution g_1 do not influence country 2's contribution as long as $g_2 > \tilde{g}_1$. Consequently, country 2's reaction curve runs horizontally from $\bar{g}_2$ to $\tilde{g}_1$. However, if 1's contribution g_1 exceeds $\tilde{g}_1$ country 2's effort to develop a vaccine will drop down to zero. If, for example, country 1 makes the discovery first, then further R&D efforts will not add any benefit. As a result, country 2's reaction curve R_2 runs along the horizontal axis. Similarly, R_1 can be obtained. The Nash equilibrium is located in point N on the vertical axis. In the depicted case country 2 contributes the entire amount of the health-promoting public good while country 1 acts as a free rider. Thus, only the country with the largest effort provides the public good.

Problems arise if the single provider is less interested in supplying the health-promoting public good. This can result in shortcomings (Sandler 2006, p. 171). For example, the private industry is more interested in research for uncommunicable diseases like cancer or heart attacks or new therapies that prolong the life of HIV-infected people. This results from the fact that R&D expenditures of an AIDS vaccine could not be covered because vaccines need to be supplied at low prices in low and middle-income countries. By contrast, people gain from vaccines that prevent further HIV transmissions because high infection rates would be at least diminished. Such an asymmetry can lead to research-related activities in low and middle-income countries as recommended by the International AIDS Vaccine Initiative (IAVI) (IAVI 2004, p. 28).[27] In order to analyse the implications of asymmetric preferences on the overall provision level, the model of Hirshleifer has to be extended.

3.4.2 An Extension of Hirshleifer's Analysis

The scientific literature pays little attention to cases where the less cost-efficient agent determines the best-shot public good provision level. To our knowledge, only Varian (2004, p. 4) has exemplified this issue. Varian analyses the security of computer systems where administrators design programmes whose reliability is determined by their efforts. He has shown numerically that a second Nash equilibrium can occur if the best-shot agent chooses to be a non-contributor and leaves the whole responsibility to the other agent. Hereinafter, a simple example is considered

[27]IAVI is the world's largest organisation focussing on the development of an AIDS vaccine.

to discuss the consequences of different R&D interests on the equilibrium allocation of the public good "developing an AIDS vaccine".

Example 2. To compare these results with those of example 1, country i's utility function should have the following form again:

$$U_i = \alpha \ln y_i + (1 - \alpha) \ln G, \tag{3.30}$$

where $0<\alpha<1$ and $i = 1, 2$. Yet, in contrast to Example 1, let the identity of the single producer switch from the country with the largest effort to the other.

It can straightforward be seen that $g_i = (1 - \alpha)\ I_i$ or $g_i = 0$ depend on whether country i's utility from contributing is larger or smaller than its utility from non-contributing. In detail, country i will be the single providing country if its contribution to the public good g_i is larger than the threshold $\tilde{g}_{-i}$:

$$\tilde{g}_{-i} < g_i, \tag{3.31}$$

or equivalently,

$$\tilde{g}_{-i} = \frac{g_{-i}}{\alpha^{\frac{\alpha}{1-\alpha}}} < g_i, \tag{3.32}$$

which follows from (3.30). However, country i will become a non-provider ($g_i = 0$) if its contribution to the public good is equal or less than the threshold $\tilde{g}_{-i}$:

$$\tilde{g}_{-i} \geqslant g_i \tag{3.33}$$

Conditions (3.31) and (3.33) can be used to derive both reaction curves. At first, country 2's reaction curve will be derived. Condition (3.31) indicates that variations of country 1's contribution g_1 do not influence 2's efforts as long as $g_2 > \tilde{g}_1$. Consequently, country 2's reaction curve runs horizontally starting from $\bar{g}_2$ as shown in Fig. 3.7. Country 2 is now less interested in providing the public good compared to Example 1 and therefore it has a higher preference for private consumption y_2. As a result, an increasing part of its income is spent for consumption of private goods and less income is used for the public good. This can be expressed analytically by an increasing α which will lead to a reduced threshold $\tilde{g}_i$ for $i = 1$ if one follows condition (3.32). This case is depicted in Fig. 3.8 where the threshold $\tilde{g}_1$ in which country 2's reaction curve drops down to zero is further left compared to Fig. 3.7.[28]

As a result, country 1 becomes the providing country. Therefore, a second Nash equilibrium occurs in point *NN* which is located on the horizontal axis in Fig. 3.8. At this point, country 1 is the one that searches for an AIDS vaccine, while country 2 is a non-provider. If this is the case, the less cost-efficient country (here: country 1) supplies the whole amount of the health-promoting public good "developing a vaccine against AIDS".

[28]Figure 3.8 follows the depiction in Sonntag (2009a).

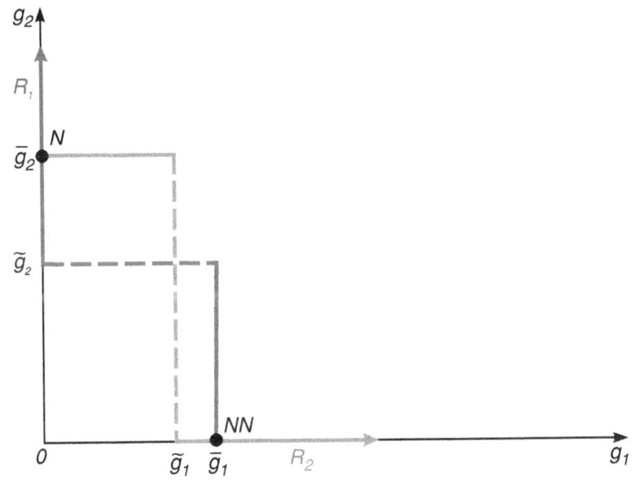

Fig. 3.8 Nash equilibria in a two-country world (best-shot case)

This result bears important policy recommendations. In order to accelerate the development of an AIDS vaccine against the background of asymmetric interests in R&D, HIV-vaccine trials also have to be established in low- and middle-income countries, even if their capacity is currently lower than in industrialised countries. Following this line of argument, our analysis substantiates the recent suggestions of IAVI to implement vaccine trials in the developing world. Moreover, our result has some implications on the design of international transfer mechanisms. It indicates that targeting financial resources to scale up R&D in low and middle-income countries seems an effective policy under certain circumstances.[29]

Following the derivation of Nash equilibria, we investigate whether or not the countries' incentives for R&D are sufficient to provide an efficient overall provision level. The Samuelson condition for a best-shot health-promoting public good can be derived in a similar way like in the weakest-link case. As a consequence, we obtain the following Lagrangian function:

$$L = U_1(y_1, G) - \lambda[U_2(y_2, G) - \overline{U}] - \mu(y_1 + y_2 + pg_1 + pg_2 - I_1 - I_2), \quad (3.34)$$

where λ is the Lagrange multiplier on the utility constraint and μ on the budget constraints. Yet, in contrast to the weakest-link case only one country provides the health-promoting public good. If country 1 is the sole researching country we can substitute g_1 by G and get:

$$L = U_1(y_1, G) - \lambda[U_2(y_2, G) - \overline{U}] - \mu(y_1 + y_2 + pG - I_1 - I_2). \quad (3.35)$$

[29] A detailed discussion under which circumstances financial support has to be given to research institutions in the developing world can be found in Chap. 4.

For an interior solution the first-order conditions are:

$$\frac{\partial L}{\partial y_1} = \frac{\partial U_1}{\partial y_1} - \mu = 0$$
$$\frac{\partial L}{\partial y_2} = -\lambda \frac{\partial U_2}{\partial y_2} - \mu = 0$$
$$\frac{\partial L}{\partial G} = \frac{\partial U_1}{\partial G} - \lambda \frac{\partial U_2}{\partial G} - \mu p = 0.$$

If we divide the third expression by μ, we will obtain:

$$\frac{1}{\mu}\frac{\partial U_1}{\partial G} - \frac{\lambda}{\mu}\frac{\partial U_2}{\partial G} - p = 0.$$

Inserting the first and the second equation into the third term yields:

$$\frac{\partial U_1/\partial G}{\partial U_1/y_1} + \frac{\partial U_2/\partial G}{\partial U_2/y_2} = p$$

or

$$MRS_1 + MRS_2 = p \tag{3.36}$$

and

$$g_2 = 0.$$

This is the Samuelson condition for the best-shot public good "developing a vaccine against AIDS" (Harrison and Hirshleifer 1989, p. 211). It indicates that vaccine-related activities should be provided until the sum of the marginal rates of substitution between the public good "developing a vaccine" and the private good equals p. However, we have to consider that p is country 1's (best-shot country) price of a unit of the public good which is not valid for 2.[30] Country 2 does not search for an AIDS vaccine ($g_2 = 0$).

Comparing the Samuelson condition for a world consisting of n countries $\sum_{i=1}^{n} MRS_i = p$ and $g_j = 0$ with (3.22), we see that suboptimality may be a problem. Country i only produces to the point where its individual marginal rate of substitution equals p. If the overall provision level and not just the discovery matters, the capacity of the provider has to be large enough to supply the public good to all other countries.

3.5 Conclusions

This chapter starts with the argument of the academic literature on AIDS that decisions of governments are unlikely to produce an efficient level of anti-HIV efforts at the transnational level. By contrast, our analysis demonstrates that the

[30]The right-hand side of (3.36) will equal country 1's marginal costs MC_1 if country 2 is a non-contributor. Hence, there is a difference compared with the summation case where $MC_1 = MC_2 = MRS_1 + MRS_2$.

efficiency of provision policies is influenced by the supply-side characteristics of a health-promoting public good. In detail, the main results are as follows:

- Countries' behaviour yields a suboptimal overall provision level in the summation case. Incentives to provide a transnationally efficient level of knowledge about HIV are insufficient because cross-bordering benefits are not taken into account.
- Suboptimality will be less of concern in the weakest-link case "limiting the domain of tuberculosis" if providers are homogenous in endowment. Each country desires the same level of prevention and, hence, matches each other's effort. However, if providers are heterogenous, the overall provision level will be suboptimal if some of them do not have the means to provide the weakest-link public good at an acceptable standard.
- Developing an AIDS vaccine will not lead to suboptimality if the health-promoting public good can be supplied continuously at the transnational level. This will be the case if R&D and production are located in several institutions. Otherwise, capacity can become a concern.[31]

These outcomes indicate that decisions made by individual countries need not result in a transnational suboptimal allocation. Thus, we can conclude that under-provision will not be an inherent problem if international health-promoting public goods are provided. It is important to bear in mind that this conclusion is based on the constructed model. Assumptions like two commodities, identical marginal costs in providing etc. restrict the validity of the results. For example, a transnational efficient provision of anti-tuberculosis programmes is less likely because countries are different in e.g. financial endowment and, hence, the condition of homogeneity is not fulfilled. In addition, cost differences in R&D for vaccines are well-known. By taking different marginal costs into account, the scenario that vaccine research is primarily carried out in low and middle-income countries is not realistic. Thus, it cannot be concluded that the behaviour of autonomous governments yields efficiency at the transnational level as theoretically predicted in some cases. To receive more convincing recommendations, a useful extension of our analysis seems to take account of, e.g. intergenerative spillovers of health-promoting public goods and their evaluation compared to actual benefits by providing countries.[32] Future research in this field is conducive for allocative decisions because not only the present but also future generations can gain from a diminished transmission of HIV or an environment which may even be free of HIV if an effective AIDS vaccine is found.

Moreover, we find out that the causes of shortcomings are not similar if aggregation technologies vary. Insufficient incentives are the reason for the underprovision

---

[31]By contrast, in patent races competition in R&D may lead to excessive expenditures on R&D relative to the social optimum where the marginal social return equals the marginal cost. One rationale may be rent-seeking to secure patent protection ahead of other firms. A detailed analysis of the consequences of R&D competition can be found in Dasgupta and Stiglitz (1980).

[32]A detailed derivation of allocative decisions by taking intergenerative spillovers into account can be found in Sandler (1978).

of public goods with a summation technology while capacity becomes an issue in the case of non-additive aggregation technologies. Moreover, the capacity concerns of weakest-link and best-shot public goods should not be mixed up. Undersupply is determined by the capability of the country with the largest effort in the best-shot case. Therefore, efforts should be pooled to surpass a required threshold. By contrast, if some developing countries do not have the means to provide health-promoting public goods, other countries will be put at high risk in the case of weakest-link. Hence, their capacity needs to be built up equivalently to reach efficiency in the weakest-link case (Arce and Sandler 2002b, p. 29). As a consequence of these different types of capacity problems, a single financing policy, e.g. supporting developing countries, seems insufficient to ensure allocative efficiency if various aggregation technologies are taken into account. If so, the aggregation technology of a health-promoting public good will not only influence the efficiency of providing but it also has implications on financing policies. To analyse this observation, several international transfers are discussed in Chap. 4.

Chapter 4
International Transfers

The global AIDS epidemic brings the greatest pressure to date to solve the undersupply of international public goods.
Sally K. Stansfield et al. (2002)

The recognition of weakest-link international public goods provides a whole new rationale for foreign assistance.
Todd Sandler (2002)

In principle, underprovision of public goods can be overcome by collective action. Against the background of intra-country income inequality, supporting low and middle-income countries seems a plausible policy option to cope with shortcomings. Even if there is no general agreement whether or not inequality has increased in recent years – Sala-i-Martin (2002) finds a decrease while Milanovic (2005) and Dikhanov (2005) estimate an increase – the substantial magnitude of inequality is not in doubt.[1] Calculations using the most recent dataset of the International Comparison Program (ICP)[2] show a significant higher global inequality than previous estimates based on the World Development Indicators (WDI) (Milanovic 2007, p. 4). In contrast to the World Bank which calculated a global Gini coefficient of 0.55 for the year 2005, inequality is now estimated at 0.57 (Milanovic 2007, p. 6). Moreover, this increase is even higher when unequal population sizes between countries are considered. If those are taken into account by weighting each country by its population, latest calculations show that inequality is 0.57 compared to

[1]With respect to the discussion about the direction of change of inequality, there is a growing body of literature where the link between globalisation and inequality is analysed. For example, Dreher and Gaston (2008) find that globalisation has exacerbated inequality.

[2]The ICP is a global statistical initiative which collects data on prices of more than 1,000 goods in 100 economies (World Bank 2008a). The programme of the Statistical Office of the European Communities (Eurostat) and the Organisation for Economic Co-operation and Development (OECD) covers information from 46 countries. These data are used to estimate purchasing power parities (PPPs) benchmarked to the year 2005. The ICP report links the regional results of the ICP programme, conducted by the ICP Global Office within the World Bank and the PPP programme initiated by Eurostat and the OECD, to a global dataset (World Bank and ICP 2008, p. xi).

D. Sonntag, *AIDS and Aid*, Contributions to Economics,
DOI 10.1007/978-3-7908-2419-3_4, © Springer-Verlag Berlin Heidelberg 2010

previous appraisals of 0.51 (Milanovic 2007, p. 6). A large part of this increased diversity results from new estimations of prices and thus of the real per capita gross domestic product (GDP) for China and India, two of the most populous economies worldwide (Milanovic 2007, pp. 1–3). A global Gini coefficient of 0.57 indicates a large inequality when it is compared with, e.g. the Ginis of Brazil (0.57) and South Africa (0.58) which are two of the most unequal countries worldwide (UNDP 2007a, Table 15). In addition, a more intuitive understanding of the extent of inequality can be obtained by comparing the average income received by the top decile, which is ranked by a country's per capita GDP, with that of the bottom decile.[3] Milanovic (2007, p. 6), for example, finds that the top-to-bottom ratio was 39 to 1 in 2005.

Governments, multilateral donors, aid agencies, private foundations, etc. assisted low and middle-income countries. Aid to combat HIV/AIDS increased in recent years.[4] Support totalled US $ 1.0 billion in 2000 of which US $ 772 million were provided bilaterally. It rose steadily to US $ 2.6 billion in 2005 of which US $ 1.86 billion were supplied bilaterally (OECD 2008).[5] However, the expansion of HIV/AIDS indicates that the current practice of increasing the quantity of support which is donated to low and middle-income countries to overcome shortcomings is unlikely to be an effective policy option. Policy-makers who suppose that redistributing income can correct the underprovision of health interventions confine the causes of inadequate policy responses to the developing world. Although the consequences of HIV/AIDS are more serious in these regions, the assumption that increasing anti-HIV efforts in these regions will enhance the overall success is too simple. As demonstrated in Chap. 3, missing capacity is only one rationale for suboptimal provision levels and does not always justify targeting financial resources to low and middle-income countries.[6]

To analyse this observation more in-depth, this chapter aims at investigating bi- and multilateral financing schemes as a means to overcome inefficient provision levels. The chapter proceeds as follows. First, we discuss under which circumstances unconditional income transfers, i.e. transfers that do not depend on the behaviour of recipients, are an effective policy to augment public good provision. We also point to cases in which financial support cannot influence transnational efforts against AIDS or is even counterproductive. Afterwards, the chapter highlights further kinds of international assistance like in-kind transfers and subsidies. They restrict the incentives of transfer-receiving countries to use support for other

[3]A comparison between the top and the bottom decile possesses some weaknesses. It only shows that the gap between the richest and the poorest increases.

[4]Data about financial support of health-promoting public goods in general can be found in te Velde et al. (2002, p. 130).

[5]Data from 2000 to 2002 are collected in a special OECD and UNAIDS report (2004) which includes the first comprehensive overview of aid to HIV/AIDS measures.

[6]Assistance programmes are also motivated by altruism or self-interest to fund anti-HIV programmes in low and middle-income countries.

issues than the donors have intended. Following an analysis whether in-kind or income transfers should be given, the effectiveness of subsidies in an international context is investigated critically.

4.1 Unconditional Income Transfers

In the literature there have been discussions whether or not income policies are suitable policy options to correct suboptimal public good provision levels. An important element within these discussions is the neutrality theorem by Warr (1982, 1983). It states that an equilibrium allocation in a Nash game cannot be altered by an income redistribution among an unchanged set of contributors. Consequently, donors would not be willing to transfer income and thus, underprovision cannot be corrected through transfers. Similar propositions have already been derived by Shibata (1971) and Becker (1974). Shibata depicted a non-cooperative solution in a two-person bargaining triangle (1971, pp. 21–22). This diagram showed that a Nash equilibrium cannot be influenced by an income redistribution if the set of contributors does not change.

Since then, a lot of studies have been published for a better understanding of the application of the neutrality theorem and its limits. For example, Kemp (1984) extended Warr's neutrality result to an economy with several international goods. Ihori (1992, 1996) demonstrated that neutrality does not occur in the case of impure public goods in that sense that a health measure results in an agent-specific private benefit and a public outcome like a reduced health risk beyond the borders of a provider.[7] However, most of these studies cannot answer the question whether or not an income transfer influences the provision levels of the health-promoting public goods "knowledge about HIV", "limiting the domain of tuberculosis" and "developing an AIDS vaccine". This is due to the fact that most of them neglect the variety of aggregation technologies. The vast majority use the summation technology. In the following, this gap will be closed.

The analysis proceeds as follows: At first, we are going to show that the neutrality theorem is valid for the case "knowledge about HIV". Therefore, we set out a model investigating the interaction between countries that provide the health-promoting public good and can transfer income. Thus, we can give a deeper characterisation of the neutrality theorem than heretofore. Then, it is examined under which conditions neutrality does not occur and hence, donors have incentives to redistribute income. Subsequently, we take a closer look at the health-promoting public goods "limiting the domain of tuberculosis" and "developing an AIDS vaccine". Since each of them is characterised by a non-additive aggregation technology, we will examine whether neutrality occurs or not. The final section summarises the main results.

[7]For a detailed characterisation of impure public goods see Sandler and Arce (2002).

4.1.1 The Basic Model

We consider a world of n countries. Referring to the analysis in Chap. 2, we assume that each country consumes two commodities. The first one is a pure private good y_i. It is used as the numeraire. The second commodity is the health-promoting public good "knowledge about HIV" G. The overall public good provision level equals the sum of the individual contributions g_i. Furthermore, we suppose that each country is endowed with income, where, endowments differ. In contrast to the previous chapter, countries have the possibility to provide income transfers. Consequently, they can utilise their endowments for private consumption, contributing to the public good and transferring income. Therefore, the following time structure of actions is considered. At stage 1, countries have to decide simultaneously which part of their endowment they are willing to transfer. The remaining income is freely disposable. Thus, countries have to decide how much they spend on private consumption y_i and on the public good "knowledge about HIV" G at stage 2.

This two-stage game can be solved by backward induction. At first, we examine country i's maximisation problem. Then, the effect of an income transfer on the equilibrium values y_i and G is analysed. Since country i's decision at stage 1 has already been discussed in Chap. 3, we briefly summarise this analysis.

Stage 2: Country *i*'s Maximisation Problem

Country i maximises its utility derived from the private and the public good subject to its budget constraint:

$$\begin{aligned} &\max_{y_i, g_i} U_i(y_i, G) \\ &\text{s.t.} \\ &y_i + pg_i = I_i \qquad \text{for } i = 1, 2, ..., n. \end{aligned} \tag{4.1}$$

Due to the assumption that G_{-i} is exogenously given, g_i can be substituted by $g_i = G - G_{-i}$. Consequently, the budget constraint modifies to $y_i + p(G - G_{-i}) = I_i$. Inserting this condition into country i's utility function, the maximisation problem can be defined equivalently as:

$$\max_{G} U_i(I_i - pG + pG_{-i}, G). \tag{4.2}$$

Differentiating with respect to G and solving leads to:

$$G = f_i(I_i + pG_{-i}, p), \tag{4.3}$$

where f_i is country i's demand function. By subtracting G_{-i} from (4.3) we obtain country i's contribution to the health-promoting public good g_i:

$$g_i = f_i(I_i + pG_{-i}, p) - G_{-i}. \tag{4.4}$$

The argument in f_i implies that country i's effort to provide the public good (g_i) depends on its full income ($I_i + G_{-i}$).[8] The derivative of f_i with respect to full income (f_{iI}) is country i's marginal propensity to provide the health-promoting public good. If both the private and the public good are normal goods, then $0 < f_{iI} < 1$, where I represents country i's full income.

Stage 1: An Analysis of Financial Support

In order to analyse the impact of an income transfer on the overall provision level of the health-promoting public good and private consumption, the assumption of an exogenously given income is abandoned. We assume that a possibility to redistribute income exists, yet, countries cannot redistribute more income than they contribute to the health-promoting public good.[9]

By totally differentiating (4.4) for each country i, the analysis proceeds as follows:[10]

$$\begin{aligned} dg_i &= f_{iI}(dI_i + pdG_{-i}) - dG_{-i} \\ &= f_{iI}dI_i + (pf_{iI} - 1)dG_{-i}. \end{aligned} \tag{4.5}$$

Substituting $dG_{-i} = dG - dg_i$ in (4.5) and rearranging, we obtain:

$$dg_i = \underbrace{\frac{f_{iI}}{f_{iI}}}_{=1} \frac{dI_i}{p} + \frac{pf_{iI} - 1}{pf_{iI}} dG. \tag{4.6}$$

Summing the above equation for all countries i yields:

$$\sum_{i=1}^{n} dG = \sum_{i=1}^{n} \frac{dI_i}{p} + \sum_{i=1}^{n} \frac{pf_{iI}}{pf_{iI}} dG.$$

[8]Becker (1974, pp. 1063, 1067) calls $I_i + pG_{-i}$ the social income. It is the sum of an individual's income and the monetary value of his social environment to him. Hence, the social income represents more than the individual monetary income.

[9]By using this assumption ($g_i \geqslant t_i$) where t_i is country i's cash transfer, corner solutions can be excluded. We take non-interior cases into account in Sect. 4.1.2.

[10]This analysis is a modified version of Andreoni's proof (1990, p. 474). He proved whether or not neutrality exists for an impure public good.

Solving for dG results in:

$$dG = a\sum_{i=1}^{n}\frac{dI_i}{p} \quad \text{for } i = 1, 2, ..., n \text{ and } 0 \leqslant a \leqslant 1, \tag{4.7}$$

with

$$a = \frac{1}{1 - \sum_{i=1}^{n} \frac{pf_{il}-1}{pf_{il}}}.$$

Equation (4.7) reveals neutrality if an income redistribution implies that $\sum_{i=1}^{n} dI_i = 0$ and, hence, $dG = 0$ is true. This is the neutrality theorem where an income redistribution does not alter the overall public good provision level. To explain the term $\sum_{i=1}^{n} dI_i = 0$, the following example has to be considered.

To allow for a simple illustration, our analysis is restricted to two countries ($n = 2$). Country 2 is supposed to be a donor that transfers one unit of its endowment to country 1. The donor reduces its own effort to provide the health-promoting public good by one unit ($\Delta g_2 < 0$) because its income declines. As a result, the overall provision level of the public good diminishes. The recipient can compensate this reduction by an increase of its own contribution. More precisely, it raises its effort by one unit ($\Delta g_1 > 0$) because its income has risen due to the received transfer. Consequently, the distribution of the individual contributions has altered. However, the overall provision level of the public good is unchanged ($\Delta G = 0$). The provision of a public good depends on the full income $I_i + G_{-i}$ which remains constant. The same holds for the consumption of the private good ($\Delta y_1(\Delta y_2) = 0$) (Warr 1983, p. 210). If the overall public good provision level and the private consumption do not change after an income transfer, suboptimality cannot be corrected. Thus, donors do not possess an incentive to redistribute income. The same is true regardless of differences in individual preferences or in marginal propensities to contribute to the public good (Warr 1983, p. 207).

Following this line of reasoning, underprovision of education programmes cannot be overcome by transfers because donors would not be willing to redistribute income. However, heretofore we have neglected two aspects which will be discussed below and which may be crucial for the validity of non-neutrality:

- Some countries have not implemented national programmes to educate people. In such a case, we have to change our assumption that all agents provide the health-promoting public good. It should be differentiated between countries providing programmes to educate people and those who choose to be non-providers.
- Domestic suppliers may have advantages in providing the health-promoting public good compared to foreign suppliers. One can imagine specific cultural needs or different languages as a barrier. Therefore, marginal costs can differ among providers.

4.1.2 Corner Solutions

Bergstrom et al. (1986) show that financial support can overcome suboptimality even if there is a summation technology. The neutrality theorem does not apply if some countries choose to be non-providers. By allowing for corner solutions, the main results from their analysis are:

1. An income redistribution among contributors increases the public good provision level if a donor's transfer (t_i) is larger than the value of its contribution to the public good ($t_i > g_i$).
2. An income transfer from a non-contributor to a contributor increases the overall provision level.

In this section, we follow Bergstrom et al. to determine under which circumstances financial assistance can correct suboptimality of the health-promoting public good "knowledge about HIV". To illustrate these cases, a world of at least two countries such as in Fig. 4.1 is considered.[11] We use a diagrammatic method developed by Buchholz (1990). He derived income expansion paths to depict alternative equilibrium allocations of public goods.[12] An income expansion path illustrates the locus of all utility-maximising bundles of the public and the private good for different levels of income and given relative prices.

In Fig. 4.1 the overall provision level of the health-promoting public good G is measured along the vertical axis. Country 1's private consumption y_1 is on the

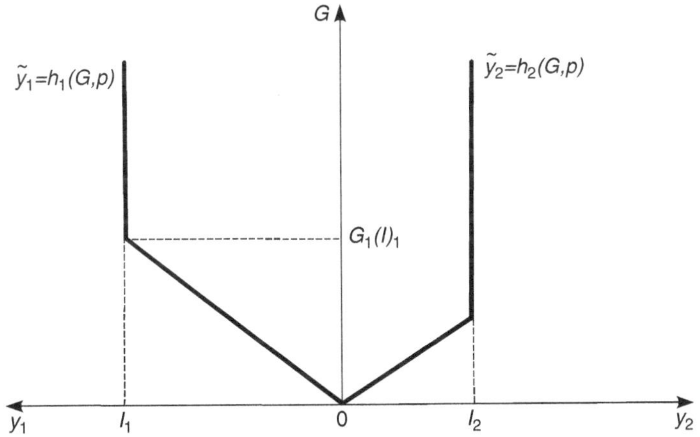

Fig. 4.1 Corner solutions in a two-country world

[11] This depiction closely follows the figure in Buchholz (1990, p. 114).

[12] Buchholz has found a further possibility besides the existing one by Samuelson (1955) or Cornes and Sandler (1985, 1996) to illustrate equilibrium allocations of public goods.

left-hand side on the horizontal axis, while 2's private consumption y_2 is drawn on the right-hand side. Furthermore, country i's income expansion path is illustrated. It is kinked at point $G_i(\bar{I}_i)$ where $\bar{I}_i$ represents the maximum amount of its income which it is willing to spend for the public good. We see that country i's income expansion path is strictly increasing in G until point $G_i(\bar{I}_i)$ is reached. Then, it parallels the vertical axis. This can be explained as follows: Country i is located at the increasing segment of its income expansion path when its endowment is used for the public and the private good. This will be the case if country i is a provider.

However, if it expends $\bar{I}_i$, it will choose to be a non-provider. Then, its total income will be spent on private consumption and the country will be located at the vertical segment of its income expansion path.[13] It follows that country i's income expansion path $\tilde{y}_i = h_i(G, p)$ can be expressed as:

$$\begin{aligned} \tilde{y}_i = h_i(G,p) : &\overset{\wedge}{=} y_i = h_i(G,p) \text{ for all } G \text{ with } y_i(G,p) \leqslant \bar{I}_i \\ &\overset{\wedge}{=} \bar{I}_i \text{ for greater values of } G. \end{aligned} \tag{4.8}$$

The slope of the strictly monotonically increasing segment is determined by the income elasticity, i.e. the responsiveness of demand to a change of income.[14] If the amount of the public and the private good increases proportionally with a rising income, the income elasticity will be unity for both commodities. This would be the case if the slope of the income expansion path was $\alpha = 45°$. However, if country i has a higher preference for private consumption, y_i will rise by a larger portion than its income increases. The income elasticity of private consumption will be less than unity. Therefore, its income expansion path becomes flatter ($\alpha < 45°$) as illustrated by country 2 in Fig. 4.1. By contrast, if country i prefers the public good and, hence, spends an increasing part of its rising income for it, the slope of its income expansion path will be steeper ($\alpha > 45°$) than it would be if the income elasticity was equal to one. Such a case is depicted for country 1.

Equipped with these observations we can analyse two cases: First, both countries contribute to the health-promoting public good "knowledge about HIV". Second, only one country is a provider while the other has not implemented any programmes to enhance the knowledge about HIV and chooses to be a non-providing country. Our analysis starts with the first case.

---

[13]This argumentation can also be applied for country 2. If it chooses to be a non-provider, country 1 will be the single supplier. Therefore, 2 can benefit from an enhanced overall provision level G and thus, is located at the vertical segment of its income expansion path. However, if country 1's maximum income which it is willing to spend on the health-promoting public good $\bar{I}_1$ is also utilised, further increases in and, hence, a vertical income expansion path can only be explained by assuming a third country which provides the public good. If this was not the case, country i's income expansion paths would parallel the horizontal axis until $\bar{I}_1$ was utilised. This results from the definition of an income expansion path: a set of all optima for different incomes. An increasing income only results in an enhanced private consumption in the case of non-providing countries.

[14]The slope of the income expansion paths is also determined by the effective price of a public good. However, marginal cost differentials are not taken into account so far.

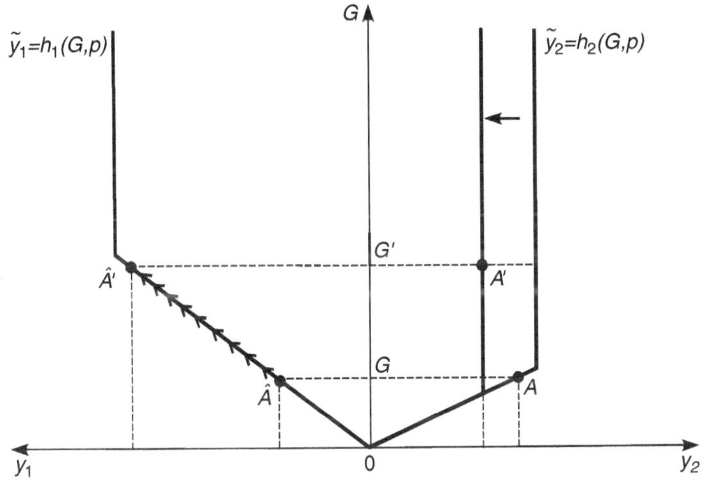

Fig. 4.2 Income transfer and corner solutions (1)

4.1.2.1 Income Redistribution Among Providing Countries

If both countries provide the health-promoting public good, they will be located at the increasing segment on their income expansion paths as depicted in Fig. 4.2.

Our starting point should be $A(\hat{A})$. We consider an income redistribution from country 2 to 1 by assuming that country 2 transfers more financial resources than the value of its original contribution to the public good ($t_2 > g_2$). Therefore, it does not provide the public good afterwards ($g_2 = 0$). It becomes a non-providing country and is located at the vertical segment of its income expansion path. This part of its income expansion path has moved to the left because its income has diminished. As opposed to country 2, country 1's income increases after a redistribution. It augments its contribution to the health-promoting public good "knowledge about HIV". The overall provision level rises, e.g. from point G to point G' because country 2 cannot reduce its effort by the full amount of its cash transfer if $g_2 = 0$ is true. The increased overall provision level can be illustrated by an outward move along country 1's income expansion path. A possible location for country 2 (1) is point $A'(\hat{A}')$.

Let us now consider the second case in which country 2 does not contribute to the health-promoting public good "knowledge about HIV". Therefore, 1 is the single providing country.

4.1.2.2 Income Redistribution Among Providing and Non-providing Countries

Country 2 chooses $y_2 = I_2$ and hence, is located at the vertical segment on its income expansion path as depicted in Fig. 4.3. Country 1 spends its income I_1 on

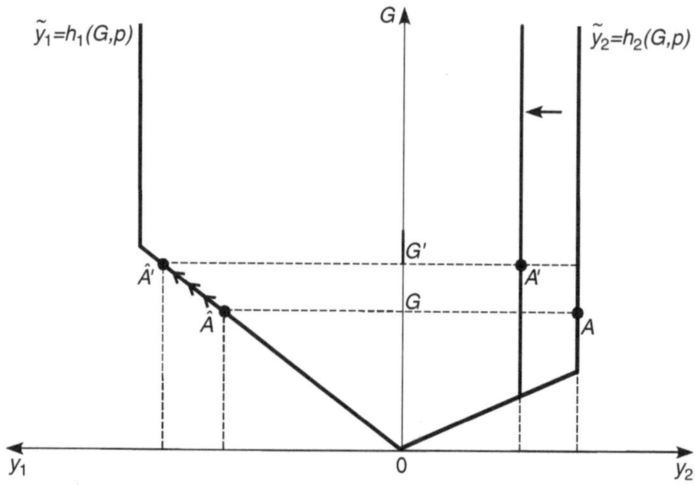

Fig. 4.3 Income transfer and corner solutions (2)

private consumption and on the health-promoting public good. Thus, it is on the increasing segment of its income expansion path. Therefore, possible equilibrium locations are $A(\hat{A})$.

We consider a cash transfer from country 2 (non-contributor) to 1 (contributor). As a result, 2's income falls while 1's income increases. Country 2 cannot reduce its contribution to the public good by the amount of its transfer because it does not contribute anything, $g_2 = 0$. Country 1's effort to provide the public good increases by the full amount of country 2's income transfer. Consequently, the overall public good provision level rises, e.g. from point G to point G'. This can be illustrated by an upward move along 1's income expansion path. Country 2's income expansion path is located further on the left because its income is reduced. However, it also gains from an increased public good provision level. Therefore, ex-post equilibrium allocations can be $A'(\hat{A}')$.

4.1.3 Cost Differentials

In this section, the previous analysis is modified by including differences of marginal costs among countries in producing the public good. Therefore, we assume that countries may have different productivities to provide a health-promoting public good θ_i with $\theta_i \neq \theta_j$ for $i \neq j$. The costs to provide health measures in industrialised countries are lower than in low and middle-income countries.[15]

[15]On the other hand, it is true that countries like India can provide high quality of many health-promoting goods at substantially lower costs than industrialised countries.

If we allow for different productivities in producing a health-promoting public good, country i's contribution g_i will be expressed by $g_i = \theta_i l_g$ where l_g represents its labour inputs for the production of the public good.[16] Thus, the cost of provision is given as

$$c_i = \frac{g_i}{\theta_i} w_i, \quad p_i = c_i = \frac{g_i}{\theta_i} w_i, \tag{4.9}$$

where w_i is country i's wage.

The cost c_i also represents the price of the provided public good p_i. Therefore, (4.9) modifies to

$$p_i = c_i = \frac{g_i}{\theta_i} w_i. \tag{4.10}$$

It implies a negative relationship between country i's price p_i and its productivity θ_i. A low (high) p_i means a high (low) productivity to provide a health-promoting public good. Therefore, marginal cost differentials are reflected by different prices. Country i's price for the public good does not equal country j's price: $p_i \neq p_j$ for $i \neq j$.

Equipped with this observation, the section proceeds by analysing the effects of an income redistribution on the overall public good provision level. In addition, it is determined under which circumstances a donor possesses an incentive to provide income transfers. With respect to allocative implications of unconditional transfers, ex-ante and ex-post equilibrium allocations are compared.[17] Therefore, we employ the technique of Buchholz and Konrad (1995) and sum up the budget constraints of two countries ($n = 2$).[18] We obtain an alternative possibility to characterise an equilibrium allocation:

$$g_1^* + g_2^* = \frac{I_1}{p_1} + \frac{I_2}{p_2} - \frac{y_1}{p_1} - \frac{y_2}{p_2}, \tag{4.11}$$

where the asterisks are standing for the Nash equilibrium. The sum of country 1's and 2's contributions to the public good equals the sum of their incomes minus both countries' private consumption levels.[19] Inserting each country's income expansion

---

[16]For simplicity the factor capital has not been taken into account.

[17]Thus, we follow the model of Buchholz and Konrad (1995).

[18]This restriction seems methodologically useful because a free-rider problem among transfer payers is circumvented (Vicary 1990; Oberender and Fleckenstein 2004, p. 13). By assuming n agents, income transfers are a public good itself from the perspective of the donors. In addition, the assumption of two countries seems plausible when imagining that one region is located in the North while the other one is in the South.

[19]It is important to note that all terms of (4.11) are expressed in real terms and, hence, a nominal exchange rate does not have to be included.

path into the above equation and considering that $G^* = g_1^* + g_2^*$, after rearranging we obtain:

$$G^* + \frac{h_1(G^*, p_1)}{p_1} + \frac{h_2(G^*, p_2)}{p_2} = \frac{I_1}{p_1} + \frac{I_2}{p_2} = I, \tag{4.12}$$

where I represents the maximum level of the public good when all income is spent on it, unless $p_1 = p_2 = 1$. If all terms on the left-hand side of (4.12) are continuous and strictly increasing in G, (4.12) will implicitly determine the Nash equilibrium as a function of both incomes I_1 and I_2.

In order to demonstrate the effects of an income transfer on the public good provision level, we differentiate between several income distributions among countries before a transfer is provided. Our analysis starts with the case that country 2 is endowed with the total income I ($I_2 = I$).[20] It divides its income between private consumption and provision of the health-promoting public good. Since country 1's income equals zero, its private consumption as well as its contribution to the public good are zero. By using (4.12), the equilibrium can be characterised by:

$$G^A + \frac{h_2(G^A, p_2)}{p_2} = \frac{I}{p_2}, \tag{4.13}$$

where G^A represents the public good provision level when country 2 is the single providing country.

Now, we assume that country 2 transfers financial resources to 1. As a result, its income diminishes and, thus, its private consumption and its contribution to the public good reduce. By contrast, country 1's income increases. However, as long as country 1's income I_1 remains sufficiently low, it has no incentive to provide the public good because it uses its whole income for private consumption y_1. Hence, country 1 remains a non-provider. From (4.12) it follows:

$$G^B + \frac{h_1(G^B, p_1)}{p_1} + \frac{h_2(G^B, p_2)}{p_2} = \frac{I_1}{p_1} + \frac{I_2}{p_2} = \frac{h_1(G^B, p_1)}{p_1} + \frac{[I - h_1(G^B, p_1)]}{p_2},$$

where G^B is the amount of the health-promoting public good after a cash transfer has been provided. In addition, it is taken into account that $I_1 = y_1 = h_1(G^B, p_1)$ and $I_2 = I - I_1$. Rearranging leads to:

$$G^B + \frac{h_2(G^B, p_2)}{p_2} + \frac{h_1(G^B, p_1)}{p_2} = \frac{I}{p_2}. \tag{4.14}$$

[20] Even if this assumption seems less plausible because the other country does not possess any income and thus, its private consumption is zero, this case is taken into account because the effects of an income transfer on the public good provision level for all possible income distributions among countries are to be considered.

Combining (4.13) with (4.14), we obtain:

$$G^A + \frac{h_2(G^A,p_2)}{p_2} = G^B + \frac{h_2(G^B,p_2)}{p_2} + \frac{h_1(G^B,p_1)}{p_2}.$$

Rearranging yields:

$$G^A - G^B = \frac{h_2(G^B,p_2)}{p_2} + \frac{h_1(G^B,p_1)}{p_2} - \frac{h_2(G^A,p_2)}{p_2}. \tag{4.15}$$

Proposition 1. *The public good provision level falls after an income redistribution (here: $G^A > G^B$) if $h_1(G,p_1)$ and $h_2(G,p_2)$ are strictly increasing in G.*

Proof. Suppose that an income redistribution increases the public good provision level. This will be the case if $G^A < G^B$ is true. If $G^A < G^B$, the left-hand side of (4.15) will become negative. The right-hand side will be positive because $h_1(G^B,p_1)$ is positive and $h_2(G^A,p_2)$ is increasing in G. Consequently, (4.15) is not fulfilled and, hence, $G^A > G^B$ is true. An income redistribution cannot lead to a Pareto-improvement.

However, if country 2's transfer is large enough to encourage country 1 to contribute to the health-promoting public good, the overall provision level G will increase. The argument runs as follows. As both countries use their endowments for private consumption and for contributions to the public good, an equilibrium allocation can be expressed by (4.12).

Proposition 2. *The public good provision level will rise after an income redistribution if $p_2 > p_1$.*

Proof. Assume that $\Delta G < 0$. Then, private consumption of country i also diminishes (Δy_i for $i = 1, 2$) because its income expansion path $y_i = h_i(G,p_i)$ is monotonically increasing in G. Therefore, the left-hand side of (4.12) falls. However, this reduction cannot restore an equilibrium because country 2's income transfer will increase the right-hand side of (4.12) by $(1/p_1 - 1/p_2)\Delta I$ if $p_2 > p_1$. Thus, the overall public good provision level must increase, $\Delta G > 0$.

The same holds for country 2's private consumption since $y_2^* = h_2(G^*,p_2)$ is strictly increasing in G^*.[21] The increase in its private consumption continues as long as the decrease in its income can result in an interior equilibrium allocation. A critical level of $\tilde{I}_2$ exists where country 2 stops to contribute, $g_2 = 0$. It spends its full income on private consumption $\tilde{I}_2 = y_2 = h_2(G^C,p_2)$ where G^C represents the amount of the public good provision when country 1 becomes the single provider.[22]

---

[21]The same line of reasoning holds for country 1.

[22]Further income transfers reduce country 2's income and, hence, its private consumption y_2.

Its income is a residual of the total income and country 2's income $I_1 = I - \tilde{I}_2$. It uses its income both for providing the health-promoting public good G^C and for private consumption. Thus, the provision level of G is determined by:

$$G^C = \frac{1}{p_1}[I - \tilde{I}_2 - h_1(G^C, p_1)]. \tag{4.16}$$

Inserting $\tilde{I}_2 = h_2(G^C, p_2)$ into the equation above and rearranging, we obtain:

$$G^C + \frac{h_2(G^C, p_2)}{p_1} + \frac{h_1(G^C, p_1)}{p_1} = \frac{I}{p_1}. \tag{4.17}$$

Equating (4.14) and (4.17) yields:

$$G^B + \frac{h_2(G^B, p_2)}{p_2} + \frac{h_1(G^B, p_1)}{p_2} = G^C + \frac{h_2(G^C, p_2)}{p_1} + \frac{h_1(G^C, p_1)}{p_1}.$$

Rearranging, we obtain:

$$G^B - G^C = \frac{h_2(G^C, p_2)}{p_1} + \frac{h_1(G^C, p_1)}{p_1} - \frac{h_2(G^B, p_2)}{p_2} - \frac{h_1(G^B, p_1)}{p_2}. \tag{4.18}$$

Proposition 3. *The public good provision level will rise after an income redistribution (here: $G^C > G^B$) if both income expansion paths are strictly increasing in G and if $p_2 > p_1$.*

Proof. First, we assume that $G^B > G^C$. The left-hand side of (4.18) is positive. The right-hand side will become negative if the income expansion paths are strictly increasing in G and if $p_2 > p_1$. Therefore, (4.18) cannot hold and hence, $G^C > G^B$ is true. Next, it is supposed that $G^B = G^C$. The left-hand side of (4.18) equals zero. Yet, the right-hand side will not equal zero because of price differentials. As a result, (4.18) is also not fulfilled. Consequently, (4.18) will only hold if $G^C > G^B$.

In sum, our analysis indicates that unconditional income transfers can alter the equilibrium allocation of the health-promoting public good "knowledge about HIV" and thus, the neutrality theorem is not valid. Even if there is room for income policies, welfare-reducing cases still exist. Since donors will not possess incentives to give financial resources if they are worse off ex-post, it is identified when there are incentives to provide income transfers.

Proposition 4. *A more cost-efficient country (here: country 1) does not transfer income to a less cost-efficient one (here: country 2).*

Proof. Assume that country 1 redistributes income to country 2. At first, we consider the case in which country 1 provides the health-promoting public good while country 2 chooses to be a non-provider. We consider a marginal reduction of its lump-sum transfer to $t_1 - dt_1$, where $t_1 \geqslant 0$. As its income increases, its private consumption rises in the case of normality.[23] Since lowering financial support enhances country 1's utility, it has no incentive to redistribute income to 2. Next, we assume that country 2 provides the health-promoting public good while country 1 does not contribute to the public good provision.[24] A marginal reduction of country 1's transfer is considered again. As country 1 remains a non-provider, its private consumption increases by $dt_1 = dy_1$. Country 2's private consumption and its contribution to the public good diminish because its income decreases. This can be expressed as follows:

$$- dy_1 = -dt_1 = -dI_2 = -(dy_2 + p_2 dG) < - p_2 dG \tag{4.19}$$

or, equivalently,

$$MRS_1 = dy_1/dG > p_2. \tag{4.20}$$

Since $p_2 > p_1$ and $p_1 = dy_1/dG = MRS_1$ it follows that $p_2 > MRS_1$, which contradicts $dy_1/dG > p_2$. Therefore, the increased utility from the enhanced private consumption will exceed the reduction in utility resulting from the decreased overall provision level G if country 1 lowers its financial support. Hence, it will be better off and has no incentive to transfer income to country 2.

Reconsidering Proposition 3, we analyse under which circumstances the less cost-efficient country (here: country 2) has an incentive to redistribute income. The choice whether country 2 gives financial assistance to the other depends on its own decision to provide the public good or to be a non-provider before the game starts. For example, if both countries contribute to the public good, a cash transfer from the less cost-efficient to the more cost-efficient country will be welfare-enhancing. This can be explained as follows: An income redistribution results in an increased amount of the public good as already demonstrated above (see Proposition 2). In the case of normality, an income expansion path, $y_i = h_i(G, p_i)$ for $i = 1, 2$, is strictly increasing in G and thus, private consumption increases. Therefore, country 2 has an incentive to redistribute income. The same will hold if it does not provide the health-promoting public good while country 1 chooses to be a provider. The argument runs as follows. An income redistribution from country 2 to 1 reduces country 2's private consumption because $I_2 = y_2$ on the one hand. On the other hand, we know from Proposition 2 that the overall public good provision level rises and thus, country 2's utility increases. These effects on its utility can be expressed as:

$$dU_2 = \left(-\frac{\partial U_2}{\partial y_2} + \frac{\partial U_2}{\partial G}\frac{\partial G}{\partial I_2} \right) dI_2, \tag{4.21}$$

[23]Normal goods are goods with a positive income elasticity of demand.

[24]This proof is similar to the one of Proposition 2 in Buchholz and Konrad (1995, p. 498).

with $G = g_1$ since country 1 is the single provider.

Thus, an income transfer will raise country 2's utility if

$$dU_2 = \left(-\frac{\partial U_2}{\partial y_2} + \frac{\partial U_2}{\partial G}\frac{\partial G}{\partial I_2}\right) dI_2 > 0. \tag{4.22}$$

Therefore, country 2 will only have an incentive to support 1 if the increased utility from the raised amount of the health-promoting public good is large enough to compensate its reduction with respect to private consumption. However, country 2 will not redistribute income if it chooses to be a provider. A reduction of its financial support increases its income I_2. Since both goods are normal, its private consumption as well as its contibution to the health-promoting public good rise. Therefore, a decline of its transfer increases its utility, and it will not transfer any financial resources.

In sum, we found that the less cost-efficient country (here: country 2) will have an incentive to support the more cost-efficient one if both have implemented programmes for sexual education or if the more productive one is the single providing country. However, country 2 will not redistribute income if it provides the public good itself. In order to exclude this inefficient solution because country 2 does not possess a cost advantage in providing health measures, we assume that $G^C > G^A$ referring to Buchholz and Konrad (1995, p. 501). The public good provision level will be smaller if the less cost-efficient country provides the public good (G^A) than the provision level if the more productive country is the sole provider (G^C). We know from (4.17) that an equilibrium allocation in point C is determined by:[25]

$$p_1 G^C + h_2(G^C, p_2) + h_1(G^C, p_1) = I.$$

By considering that $G^C > G^A$, we obtain

$$p_1 G^A + h_2(G^A, p_2) + h_1(G^A, p_1) < I.$$

Inserting $h_2(G^A, p_2) = I - p_2 G^A$ from (4.13) and rearranging yields:

$$(p_2 - p_1) G^A > h_1(G^A, p_1), \tag{4.23}$$

where the left-hand side represents the production cost savings if country 1 provides the health-promoting public good instead of country 2. The right-hand side of (4.23) is country 1's private consumption which would be required to encourage it to provide $g_1 = G^A$. The higher the cost differentials among countries are $(p_1 - p_2)$ and the smaller $h_1(G^A, p_1)$ is, the more likely is the condition to be fulfilled. If condition (4.23) holds, the more cost-efficient country will provide health measures

[25] In contrast to (4.17), the variables are not expressed in real terms. However, a nominal exchange rate can be omitted because all terms are expressed in country 1's currency.

to enhance the knowledge about HIV. Subsequent to these observations, the main results are summarised:

1. Even if a summation technology is valid, unconditional income transfers can alter the equilibrium allocations of public goods if there are cost differentials among countries.
2. Only the more productive country provides the health-promoting public good "knowledge about HIV" after an income redistribution. It never supports the other.
3. The less cost-efficient country transfers income to the more efficient one. It does not provide the health-promoting public good in the ex-post equilibrium.

Our results indicate that an income redistribution will be a suitable policy option to overcome suboptimality if transfer-receiving countries are more cost-efficient in providing the public good. Otherwise, income transfers are counterproductive. The question whether or not this conclusion is also valid for the health-promoting public goods "limiting the domain of tuberculosis" and "developing an AIDS vaccine" is investigated in Sect. 4.1.4. This further analysis seems worthwhile because these cases are characterised by a different aggregation technology than the summation technology. As shown below, non-additive technologies are crucial to establish non-neutrality.

4.1.4 *Weakest-Link and Best-Shot Public Goods in the Case of International Assistance*

In this section, all assumptions from the basic model are kept except that the aggregation technology is a minimum technology for the case "limiting the domain of tuberculosis" and a maximum technology for the health-promoting public good "developing an AIDS vaccine". Consequently, country i's demand function is now given by:

$$g_i = f_i(I_i, p) \quad \text{for } i = 1, 2 \ldots, n. \tag{4.24}$$

It is not valid for all countries in the best-shot case, whereas it is valid for all countries in a weakest-link situation. This follows from the assumption that the country with the largest effort will become the single provider if a maximum technology matters. The demand function for non-providing countries can be expressed as $g_j = 0$ for $j \neq i$.

Equation (4.24) reveals that in contrast, to the summation case in which country i's contribution g_i is determined by the full income $I_i + pG_{-i}$, its effort to provide a health-promoting public good only depends on its income I_i. Consequently, the efforts of others G_{-i} are no longer a perfect substitute for country i's income. This indicates that an income redistribution of ΔI_i from country i to country j does not fully compensate country j's effort Δg_j $(i \neq j)$. As a result, neutrality will fail if the weakest-link technology or the best-shot technology prevails. At first, the weakest-link case "limiting the domain of tuberculosis" will be discussed.

4.1.4.1 Weakest-Link Public Goods and International Income Transfers

Income transfers can alter the equilibrium allocation of a public good in a weakest-link case. Jayaraman and Kanbur (1999), for example, show that financial support can increase the public good provision in a Stackelberg framework. This will be the case if a transfer-receiving agent can be encouraged to enhance his contribution in the post-transfer equilibrium. A positive impact of income transfers is also demonstrated by Vicary (1990). Starting from an initial equilibrium involving positive donations, he proves that an income redistribution can affect a public good equilibrium allocation if the set of donors has changed after the financial support. Several theorems in Vicary (1990, p. 386) are parallel to the results of Bergstrom et al. (1986). Among others, he demonstrates that a small redistribution of income among an unchanged set of agents cannot alter the provision level so that neutrality holds. In contrast to Vicary, our analysis will show that suboptimality can be overcome. Our model specifies the one of Vicary (1990) because cash transfers are only given from well to worse endowed agents, while he also considers redistributions among contributors with a low income. In addition to his analysis, it is discussed under which conditions donors have incentives to provide international transfers.

Proposition 5. *The overall provision level of the health-promoting public good "limiting the domain of tuberculosis" cannot decrease if income is redistributed.*

Proof. Suppose that $\Delta G < 0$. If we define G^* as the provision amount of the public good at the Nash equilibrium before an income transfer is provided and G' refers to the ex-post equilibrium, we obtain $G^* > G'$. There is at least one country i so that $\Delta y_i > 0$. Its private consumption increases, $y_i^* < y_i'$, because of the budget constraint. If the equation $y_i = h_i(G)$ determines country i's income expansion path, the reduction of the health-promoting public good G yields:

$$
\begin{aligned}
& h_i^*(G^*, p) > h'_i(G', p) \\
& \text{or} \\
& y_i^* = h_i^*(G^*, p) > h'_i(G', p) = y'_i,
\end{aligned}
\tag{4.25}
$$

because its income expansion path is strictly increasing in G. Equivalently, we can write:

$$y_i^* > y_i',$$

which indicates that country i's ex-ante private consumption is larger than its ex-post private consumption. However, this conclusion contradicts the condition

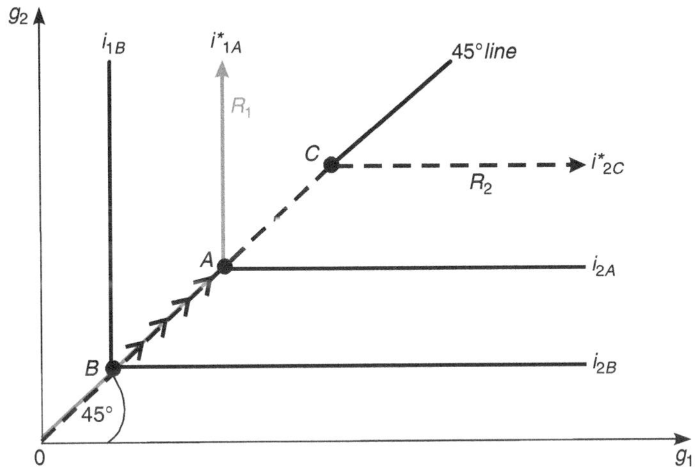

Fig. 4.4 Income redistribution for the weakest-link case "limiting the domain of tuberculosis"

$y_i^* < y_i'$. Hence, the overall public good provision level cannot drop after income is transferred as illustrated for a two-country world in Fig. 4.4. Country 1's effort to limit tuberculosis is measured on the horizontal axis while country 2's contribution to the health-promoting public good is depicted on the vertical axis. As we know from Chap. 3, R_1 and R_2 represent the reaction curves of both countries.

Our analysis starts at point B. We assume that country 2 provides an income transfer to 1. The recipient raises its individual contribution to the health-promoting public good because of its increased income. As a result, country 2 also has to raise its effort to ensure an increased overall prevention level that country 1 desires. Thus, the public good provision G increases. This can be illustrated by an upward move from point B to A which represents the final equilibrium. Following this line of reasoning, it is interesting to investigate under which circumstances donors (here: country 2) have incentives to provide financial assistance and thus, underprovision can be overcome.

As we know from Chap. 3, each country matches the other's efforts in a Nash equilibrium and, hence, the overall public good provision level is determined by $G = g_1 = g_2$. If country 2 wishes to attain a higher level of prevention, it can encourage country 1 to raise its effort by transferring income. It follows that the financial support of the donor influences the quantity of G.

Definition 1. *There is a function $G(t_2)$ that determines the supply of the public good given the amount of income t_2 transferred by the donor.*[26]

[26]A similar function can be found in Vicary (1990). He analyses the effects of an agent i's donation to a charitable organisation distributing these donations to a group of individuals who have the minimum demand for G. Therefore, the function $G(t_i)$ represents the quantity of G given total donations.

$G(t_2)$ is continuous given the fact that country 2's utility function and its demand function are differentiable and strictly continuous. In addition, $G(t_2)$ is strictly increasing because both goods are normal. It follows that

Lemma 1. *The function $G(t_2)$ has an inverse.*

***Proof*[27].** If $dt_2 = dI_1$ and $dI_1 = dG\frac{\partial I_1}{\partial G}$ hold true, it follows that

$$dt_2 = dI_1 = dG\frac{\partial I_1}{\partial G}. \tag{4.26}$$

Or, equivalently, $\frac{dG}{dt_2} = \left(\frac{\partial I_1}{\partial G}\right)^{-1}$, where $\frac{\partial I_1}{\partial G}$ is the inverse of country 1's marginal propensity to provide the public good f_{1I}. Thus, we obtain:

$$\frac{dG}{dt_2} = \left(\frac{\partial I_1}{\partial G}\right)^{-1} = \left(\frac{\partial G}{\partial I_1}\right) = f_{1I}. \tag{4.27}$$

The marginal propensity to contribute to the health-promoting public good represents the slope of the function $G(t_2)$ and measures the increases of G if t_2 is raised by one dollar.

Proposition 6. *In a non-cooperative game with identical countries, a donor (here: country 2) will only have an interest to provide income transfers if the final equilibrium has not been reached.*

Proof. The condition for Pareto-improving transfers is derived as follows:

$$\begin{aligned} &\max_{y_2,t_2} U_2(y_2, \min\{g_1, g_2\}) = U_2(y_2, G) \\ &\text{s.t.} \\ &y_2 + pG(t_2) + t_2 = I_2, \end{aligned} \tag{4.28}$$

where t_2 represents country 2's cash transfer. It divides its endowment into private consumption y_2, health measures to limit tuberculosis g_2 and transferring income.

By inserting its budget constraint into the utility function, we obtain:

$$\max_{y_2,t_2} U_2[I_2 - t_2 - pG(t_2), G(t_2)]. \tag{4.29}$$

The first-order condition can be expressed as:

$$\frac{\partial U_2}{\partial y_2}\left[-1 - p\frac{\partial G(t_2)}{\partial t_2}\right] + \frac{\partial U_2}{\partial G}\frac{\partial G(t_2)}{\partial t_2} \geqslant 0, \tag{4.30}$$

---

[27]A similar proof for n agents can be found in Vicary (1990, p. 382).

where the first term on the left-hand side of condition (4.30) represents the marginal utility with respect to private consumption. The second term expresses the change in utility associated with a small change in the amount of the public good depending on country 2's income transfer.

Rearranging yields:

$$MRS_2 > p + \frac{1}{\frac{\partial G(t_2)}{\partial t_2}}, \tag{4.31}$$

where the left-hand side defines country 2's marginal rate of substitution between the public and the private good. The right-hand side represents the cost of increasing the quantity of the health-promoting public good by one unit. In detail, the first term (p) measures country 2's direct cost of providing one additional unit of the public good. The second expression represents the amount it has to pay to country 1 in order to encourage it to increase its effort by one unit. Due to Lemma 1, the condition for a Pareto-improving transfer is:

$$MRS_2 > p + (f_{1I})^{-1}. \tag{4.32}$$

Country 2 transfers income to 1 up to the level where its marginal rate of substitution between the public and the private good is larger than the price of a unit of the public good p plus the inverse of its demand function (for n countries see Vicary and Sandler 2002, p. 1518). However, it is not interested in giving further income transfers once the final equilibrium has been reached (Vicary and Sandler 2002, p. 1512). In Fig. 4.4, point A represents this equilibrium. Since $MRS_2 = 1$ holds at point A, condition (4.32) is not satisfied. It follows that with an additional transfer, country 2 would be worse off. It has no incentive to redistribute income if the final equilibrium has been reached.

In sum, our analysis indicates that an income transfer is an effective policy option to increase the overall provision level of a weakest-link public good. In contrast to the summation case, the country with the smallest effort to limit tuberculosis has to be provided with financial support. Since the neutrality theorem cannot be extended to a non-additive aggregation technology, we continue by examining the best-shot case "developing an AIDS vaccine".

4.1.4.2 Best-Shot Public Goods and International Transfers

It is well-known that neutrality does not occur when a best-shot public good is provided (Jayaraman and Kanbur 1999, p. 426; Xu 2002a). This fact indicates that income policies are effective to overcome underprovision. Yet, Jarayaman and Kanbur (1999, Proposition 3) show that a Stackelberg equilibrium is characterised by zero lump-sum transfers. A donor does not have an incentive to redistribute income, yet he produces the public good. However, their conclusion does not hold in a more general setting. Xu (2002a) argues that their analysis is only a special case. He extends the model of Jayaraman and Kanbur by considering a Stackelberg leader who chooses to be a non-provider and redistributes income to the Stackelberg follower who will then provide the public good. Since all these studies assume that countries act sequentially, they may not work in the case "developing an AIDS vaccine". Simultaneous behaviour seems generally more appropriate since the efforts of research teams are not noticeable for each other. Furthermore, there is no global authority coordinating national efforts in vaccine research. Consequently, the impact of international transfers on the voluntary provision of vaccine-related activities is investigated in a Nash instead of a Stackelberg framework. In addition, we determine the circumstances under which financial support is given in a best-shot situation. Since only one country produces the best-shot health-promoting public good "developing an AIDS vaccine", we have to examine two cases. First, a donor searches for a vaccine while the recipient is a non-providing country. Second, the donor chooses to be a non-providing country while the recipient is involved in HIV-vaccine research.

We start with a short description of the first case because financial support will not be provided if a donor both contributes to the public good and redistributes income as will be discussed below. Following the analysis in Sonntag (2009b), a more detailed investigation is given for the second case.

4.1.4.3 Income Redistribution from a Donor Searching for a Vaccine to a Non-providing Recipient

We assume that income is transferred from the provider (here: country 1) to the non-provider (here: country 2). Consequently, country 1's income falls. Due to the fact that $g_1 = f_1(I_1, p)$ is true, its contribution to develop a vaccine declines. Since country 1 is the only one who searches for a vaccine, the overall provision level reduces by the same amount ($\Delta g_1 = \Delta G$). Its private consumption y_1 also drops. Its income expansion path $y_1 = h_1(G, p)$ is strictly increasing in G and thus, a diminished G results in a lower y_1. Hence, it is worse off after an income transfer. It follows that country 1 does not have an incentive to give financial support.

4.1.4.4 Income Redistribution from a Non-providing Donor to a Recipient Searching for a Vaccine

We suppose that a non-provider (here: country 2) transfers income to a provider (here: country 1). Furthermore, it is assumed that $I_2 \geqslant I_1$.

Proposition 7. *The overall level of the public good "developing a vaccine against AIDS" cannot drop if a non-contributor provides financial support to a contributor.*

Proof. Suppose that $\Delta G < 0$. If the overall public good provision level decreases, country 1's private consumption will also decrease, $\Delta y_1 < 0$, because of

$y_1 = h_1(G,p)$. However, due to the additional financial resources, its income has increased. Hence, the right-hand side of its budget constraint $pg_1 + y_1 = I_1 + t_2$ also rises. As a result, g_1 has to increase. Equivalently, the overall level of the health-promoting public good rises by the same amount because research is conducted exclusively in country 1 ($\Delta G > 0$). This contradicts the assumption $\Delta G < 0$. Thus, the overall provision level will increase if income is redistributed from a non-provider to a provider.

Such a situation is illustrated in Fig. 4.5.[28] The overall provision level of the health-promoting public good G is measured on the vertical axis. Country 2's private consumption y_2 is depicted on the horizontal axis to the right while country 1's private consumption y_1 is drawn on the left. Furthermore, both countries' income expansion paths $y_1 = h_1(G,p)$ and $y_2 = h_2(G,p)$ are shown. We see that country 1's income expansion path is strictly increasing while country 2's income expansion path parallels the vertical axis. A vertical income expansion path results from the assumption that country 2 is a non-provider and spends its full income I_2 on private consumption y_2. Thus, $y_2 = h_2(G,p) = I_2$ parallels the vertical axis.

Our analysis starts at the initial equilibrium $A(\hat{A})$. Country 1 spends its income on research for an AIDS vaccine and private consumption $y_1 = h_1(G,p)$. Country 2 chooses to be a non-contributor. However, it obtains the same amount of the health-promoting public good as country 1. Its private consumption can be expressed as $y_2 = h_2(G,p) = I_2$. We suppose that country 2 provides an income transfer to country 1. Consequently, its income I_2 falls and I_1 increases. Therefore, country 2's income expansion path moves to the left because its private consumption decreases by the same amount as income is redistributed. Country 1 moves upwards on its income expansion path from point $\hat{A}$ to point $\hat{A}'$. Its contribution to

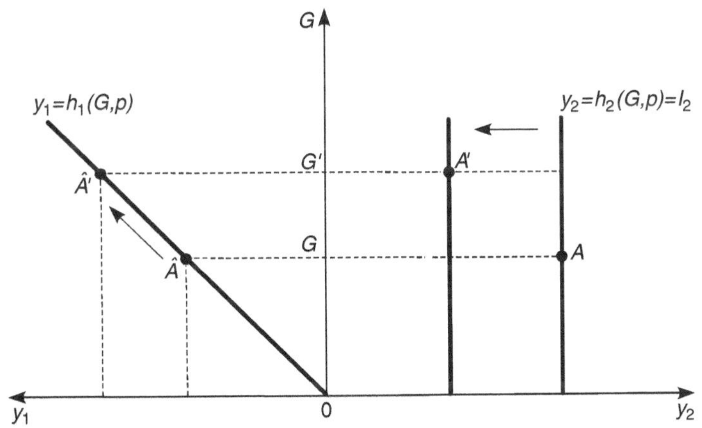

Fig. 4.5 Income redistribution for the best-shot case "developing an AIDS vaccine"

[28]In order to derive Fig. 4.5 we used the diagrammatic method developed by Buchholz (1990). A similar depiction can be found in Sonntag (2009b).

the health-promoting public good rises ($\Delta g_1 > 0$) and, hence, the overall provision level G increases, too. Furthermore, $\Delta y_1 \geqslant 0$, and thus, country 1 is better off after an income redistribution.

Country 2 will only be better off after an income transfer if the increased utility from the higher public good provision is larger than the reduction in utility from the lower private consumption. The argument runs as follows. An income redistribution causes costs for country 2. It has to adjust its private consumption y_2 to its cash transfer. It is a non-provider and, hence, it cannot reduce its effort to develop a vaccine by giving income. Besides, country 2's utility rises due to the higher overall provision level. This increase depends on its income transfer to country 1. The more income is transferred, the higher country 1's contribution to the public good will be. As a consequence, the public good provision level rises. Due to Lemma 1, this relationship can be expressed by f_{1I} which is country 1's marginal propensity to provide the health-promoting public good. Equipped with these observations, country 2 will be better off after an income transfer if the following inequality is satisfied:

$$-\Delta y_2 + \frac{\Delta G}{f_{1I}} > 0. \tag{4.33}$$

The first term on the left-hand side of (4.33) represents country 2's reduction of its private consumption. The second term is the increase of the overall provision level subject to the amount that is transferred by country 2 to encourage country 1 to increase its effort for research.[29] If the reduction of country 2's private consumption is lower than the additional public good provision, the left-hand side will be larger than or equal to zero. It follows that country 2 is better off after an income redistribution.

Following this line of reasoning, we proceed by determining under which circumstances a donor has an incentive to provide a cash transfer. We know that a non-providing country has to give financial resources to a providing country to overcome underprovision (Proposition 7). A country will decide to be a non-contributor if its utility is larger than the utility from contributing:[30]

$$U_2(I_2, g_1) > U_2(I_2 - g_2, g_2). \tag{4.34}$$

If country 2 does not search for a vaccine, country 1 will be the single provider and, hence, $g_1 = G$ is true. Country 2 receives the same amount of the health-promoting public good as country 1. Thus, its utility can be expressed as $U_2(I_2, g_1)$. However, if the public good is only produced by country 2, we obtain $g_2 = G$. Therefore, its private consumption level is reduced by its contribution and its utility is $U_2(I_2 - pg_2, g_2)$. A comparison of $U_2(I_2, g_1)$ and $U_2(I_2 - pg_2, g_2)$ indicates that

[29]For a detailed derivation see Appendix A.

[30]A similar argumentation can be found in Xu (2002a, p. 3).

country 2's utility will be higher if it does not search for a vaccine and rather spends its full income on private consumption.

Yet, the public good provision level will be smaller if country 1 searches for a vaccine. This directly follows from $I_2 \geqslant I_1$ and, hence, $g_1 < g_2$ is true. Since country 2 will only have an incentive to redistribute income if it is better off, condition (4.33) changes to

$$MRS_2 > \frac{1}{f_{1I}}, \qquad (4.35)$$

where MRS_2 is country 2's marginal rate of substitution between the public good "developing an AIDS vaccine" and the private good.[31] The term on the right-hand side represents the inverse of country 1's marginal propensity to provide the public good. If MRS_2 equals the inverse of country 1's marginal propensity to provide the public good, country 2 will have no further incentive to redistribute income. An additional transfer will make it worse off because its reduction in utility resulting from the diminished private consumption ($-\Delta y_2$) will be larger than its increased utility from a rising public good provision level. Consequently, the two conditions (4.34) and (4.35) must be fulfilled for a richer country having an incentive to support the effort of a poorer one.

Summing up, we found that the public good provision level will increase if a donor chooses to be a non-provider and transfers income. However, if a donor contributes to the public good "developing a vaccine against AIDS" and thus, he chooses to be a provider, he will be better off by searching for a vaccine himself rather than redistributing income. Thus, financial resources have to be pooled. This is the case in which an income redistribution is even counterproductive. It follows that financial support should only be given to countries which are more cost-efficient than others in providing the public good. This result is similar to our recommendation in the case of a summation technology.

4.1.5 *Non-neutrality of Unconditional Income Transfers*

In the previous sections, we have analysed the interaction between international health-promoting public goods and financial assistance in a Nash framework. We have identified three reasons for non-neutrality. These conditions are now reviewed:

- Financial support has a positive impact on the international provision level by considering countries that have not implemented programmes to educate people about HIV/AIDS. Hence, the neutrality theorem does no longer hold for *corner*

[31] A similar argumentation can be found in Xu (2002a, p. 3).

solutions. International transfers should be given in the following two cases: First, at least one country does not provide the public good after an income transfer. Second, non-contributors redistribute income to contributing countries.
- If we allow for *marginal cost differentials*, Warr's neutrality theorem fails. We found that countries which are less cost-efficient in producing the public good "knowledge about HIV" have an incentive to redistribute income to countries which are more cost-efficient. The recipients are then encouraged to increase their contributions and, hence, the overall public good provision rises.
- Neutrality cannot be extended to *non-additive aggregation technologies*. If the country with the smallest contribution to the public good "limiting the domain of tuberculosis" is supported financially, the transnational prevention level will rise. This is due to the fact that the actions of countries are matched. In addition, we illustrated that financial support will have a positive impact on the public good provision level if the sole provider is encouraged to increase its vaccine-related activities.

The two former reasons indicate that international income transfers can overcome allocative inefficiency. Hence, they seem to be an effective policy option even in the case of additive aggregation technologies. Thus, a summation technology is crucial but not necessary for the establishment of neutrality. Income policies can be justified in the case of non-additive aggregation technologies.

4.1.6 Discussion and Policy Recommendations

Referring to our analysis, an income redistribution from industrialised to developing countries as carried out today will be an effective policy option if recipients face lower marginal cost than donors in providing health measures increasing the knowledge about HIV.[32] It can straightforward be seen that implemented financing mechanisms may fail because marginal costs in developing countries are often higher than in the industrialised countries.[33] There are several reasons why domestic providers are less cost-efficient in implementing health interventions. The high burden of AIDS and a low level of literacy in general and little expertise in particular are the key determinates of a low productivity. For example, access to schooling is missing or at least restricted in many developing countries. Thus, the education and the training of domestic health professionals to improve their knowledge causes higher costs than exporting health measures to these regions. This does not only indicate that international financial support of developing countries is often

[32]The same line of reasoning holds if donors from developing regions like Asia, Middle East and Eastern Europe provide aid to other low and middle-income countries. A comprehensive overview about donors that are still aid recipients themselves can be found in Browne (2006, pp. 121–134).

[33]A noteworthy exception is India providing high quality of health measures like surgeries at substantially lower costs than high-income countries.

not an efficient policy option. It also shows that a reversed income flow from less to more productive providers is preferable from a global point of view. However, this conclusion is primarily based on the criterion of efficiency whereas additional reasons which justify international assistance, like a recipient's low public budget limiting the ability of a government to intervene, are not taken into account. Moreover, a redistribution of income from developing to industrialised countries contradicts currently implemented financing schemes. Even if such an assistance can improve allocative efficiency as demonstrated in our model, it seems very difficult to justify it because as a consequence, inequality would rise. Since governments of developing countries do not have sufficient financial resources which can be targeted to more cost-efficient providers, it is questionable if such a reversed flow can be carried out. Therefore, a reversed income flow only seems plausible in the case of transition countries like the Russian Federation.

An opposite policy recommendation results from the analysis of the best-shot case "developing an AIDS vaccine". IAVI suggests to build up capacity for large-scale AIDS trials or to establish new trials in developing countries even if the expertise of scientists is currently lower (IAVI 2006, pp. 13–14). Vaccine trials have to be conducted globally and not only in industrialised countries because a variety of several HIV viruses is circulating. The effectiveness of potential vaccines must be validated in different epidemiological settings (IAVI 2006, p. 7). In contrast to IAVI, our analysis indicates that international transfers have to be provided only if scientists from developing countries contribute to vaccine development while the focus of R&D in industrialised countries is shifted to other interests like searching for new anti-retroviral pharmaceuticals, a case we often find in reality. However, it does not seem efficient to concentrate research activities in developing countries while the private industry in industrialised countries choose to be a non-provider.

Vaccine research is primarily conducted in industrialised countries like Canada, Germany, the United States, etc. because providers are more cost-efficient in R&D. Research activities are focused on the HIV subtype B which is predominant in these regions (Ainsworth et al. 2000, p. 8). Yet, in the developing world, different HIV strains are prevalent. In Africa and Asia, for example, the HIV clade C is mainly found (IAVI 2004, p. 18). This is worrying because it is uncertain whether a vaccine which is based on subtype B is effective for other HIV clades as well (Kremer 2007, p. 12). People in developing countries would not gain from such a vaccine if HIV transmission could not be stopped. The initiation of vaccine trials in these countries offers opportunities to halt the spread of HIV from the epidemiological point of view. However, capacities for R&D are often lacking because pre-existing conditions like infrastructure, equipment and expertise are insufficient. Moreover, even if HIV-vaccine trials are established in some countries like in South Africa and Brazil, their capacities need to be scaled up to implement large-scale vaccine trials.

The evaluation of a potential vaccine requires three clinical phases (IAVI 2004, p. 8). However, almost exclusively phase I and II trials are implemented in developing countries. Phase I involves a small number of healthy volunteers (20–50). It aims at obtaining data about safety and immunogenicity. Phase II trials are implemented to receive additional safety information and to improve the dose and the schedule of a vaccine. Therefore, several hundred volunteers are involved. Finally, phase III intends to evaluate the ability of a potential vaccine to prevent HIV. This can be achieved by comparing it with a placebo. Such large-scale trials are conducted among thousands of volunteers. Nowadays, only one large-scale HIV vaccine trial is ongoing in middle-income countries after Thailand's trial has failed in February 2007. This trial, which is supported by the US National Institute of Allergy and Infectious Diseases, was opened in February 2007 in South Africa (Wall Street Journal 2007). It is the largest African vaccine trial since up to 3,000 healthy volunteers are involved, testing whether the vaccine candidate, called MRKAd5, based on the HIV clade B can also prevent the HIV clade C which is prevalent in South Africa (The Kaiser Family Foundation 2007c). Preclinical data have shown reactivity between the vaccine and the HIV subtype C (IAVI 2006).

These observations show that HIV vaccine research is carried out in some low and middle-income countries even if the environment for vaccine-related activities is still weak. Hence, the assumption of our model that transfer-receiving countries are providers is fulfilled.[34] However, the restrictive condition that donors do not contribute to health-related activities does not hold. Although research institutions in industrialised countries are more interested in new therapies which can prolong life, they are still involved in the development of an AIDS vaccine. In addition, their contributions to R&D are more cost-efficient since they are better equipped with laboratories, staff, etc. It follows that R&D carried out in industrialised countries has to be funded rather than promoting research in developing countries.

There are further reasons why financial resources have to be pooled in industrialised countries. First, the model itself recommends a concentration of vaccine research in industrialised countries because their established research institutions are involved in HIV vaccine research and thus, redistributing income may be counterproductive. Yet, monopolising R&D may be less effective than a competitive research for an AIDS vaccine. Second, the willingness of donors to redistribute income diminishes by considering small global benefit spillovers since research on the HIV clade C is not effective for the subtype B. Although a discovery of an AIDS vaccine based on the clade B would result in cross-bordering benefits, these spillovers would be small compared to regional benefits. Third, transfer-payers will not receive public good spillovers if transfer-receiving governments use the financial resources to increase their private consumption instead of spending the funds for the purpose intended by the donors. For example, financial assistance can be used for military or palaces instead of R&D. Thus, donors do not have an incentive to redistribute income because their welfare does not rise. So far, these cases have not been taken into account. Allocative decisions are solved implicitly by a social planner. Therefore, principal-agent problems between donors and recipients, discussed in the public choice literature, have not been explicitly considered. However, the decision whether income is redistributed to a democratic government,

[34]For concreteness, HIV vaccine R&D is primarily carried out by the public sector.

a benevolent or a corrupt autocracy is crucial for determining whether financial support is effective or not.

This issue is not only important in the discussion whether or not income transfers have to be directed to low and middle-income countries in the case "developing an AIDS vaccine"; it is also relevant for the effectiveness of financing policies in general. The idea to assess aid depending on the political environment of a country, e.g. the attitude of governments to the improvement of public services and infrastructure, is quite familiar in the literature. Burnside and Dollar (2000) investigate the impact of fiscal, monetary and trade policies on the opportunity to initiate development by providing aid. Given that institutions and policies influence growth and that aid itself is less effective in poor political environments, the authors test the hypothesis that the effectiveness of donations depends on these institutions and policies. The growth rates of the real per capita GDP in developing countries are defined as variables depending on foreign aid, a policy index which measures policy distortions, etc. (Burnside and Dollar 2000, p. 849). This index weights macroeconomic policies according to their impact on growth. Burnside and Dollar found a significant positive correlation between aid and institutional quality. However, the ensuing literature and a recent meta-analysis of the aid effectiveness literature of Doucouliagos and Paldam (2007) have demonstrated that the results of Burnside and Dollar are not robust. Differences in results arise from the definition of the variables and the composition of the sample (Doucouliagos and Paldam (2009, p. 21), see also Easterly et al. 2003).

These results substantiate the need to to improve the effectiveness and not the quantity of financial assistance. To meet this requirement, donors also have to take into account that, even if governments of developing countries are benevolent, they are often not able to mobilise sufficient domestic resources to facilitate an adequate public health infrastructure. Received financial resources often cannot be used due to a lack of trained staff. Therefore, assistance may be given in form of in-kind transfers. Moreover, a direct supply of health interventions can easily be justified in transfer-giving countries if the awareness exists that weak capacities abroad can influence the own well-being. Following this line of reasoning, we proceed by analysing under which circumstances in-kind transfers are preferable to income transfers.

4.2 In-Kind Transfers

With an additive aggregation technology, neutrality occurs even if aid is provided in kind.[35] Consequently, non-summation technologies are crucial for analysing whether income and in-kind transfers lead to the same allocation or not. There are only a few contributions dealing with the efficiency of the two transfer schemes.

[35]This can be proved in a similar way like in Sect. 4.1.1.

Exceptions are Jayaraman and Kanbur (1999) using a Stackelberg framework to demonstrate that in the best-shot case, transfer-payers are better off by pooling resources to provide the public good themselves instead of redistributing income.[36] For weakest-link public goods it has been argued that an in-kind transfer will be welfare-improving if countries behave simultaneously (Kanbur et al. 1999, p. 68). However, as analytical proofs are missing, these studies do not give a detailed answer to the question whether international support should be given in kind or in the form of income. To our knowledge, only the study of Vicary and Sandler (2002) gives a comprehensive analysis by extending the model of Hirshleifer (1983, 1985). A two-stage game is applied where two countries provide a lump-sum transfer at the first stage. In contrast to Hirshleifer's weakest-link model, countries determine their own contributions to the public good and the transfer in kind to the other country at the second stage. An in-kind transfer shall be given if a donor possesses a cost-advantage in providing the public good (Vicary and Sandler 2002, p. 1516). Otherwise, if countries are equally cost-efficient, an income transfer will Pareto-dominate an in-kind transfer. Yet, they do not analyse the consequences of an in-kind option for the provision level of a best-shot public good.

Against this background, this section aims at investigating the efficiency of the two transfer mechanisms if a best-shot technology prevails.[37] Since our model is based on the analysis of Vicary and Sandler, we outline their analysis for the weakest-link case "limiting the domain of tuberculosis" first.

4.2.1 *Income or In-Kind Transfers in a Weakest-Link Case*

In this section, the model of Vicary and Sandler (2002) is reviewed. Hereinafter donors possess two options to augment the public good provision. First, they can give income transfers to scale up the efforts of recipients as discussed heretofore. A second alternative is to step in poorer regions and provide the weakest-link public good on their behalf. In order to illustrate a comparison between these mechanisms, the following observations are useful (Vicary and Sandler 2002, p. 1516):

- Cost differentials in the provision of the health-promoting public good "limiting the domain of tuberculosis" are explicitly considered.[38] This seems plausible because industrialised countries can possess a technology to control tuberculosis

[36] In-kind versus income transfers for weakest-link public goods are not explicitly investigated. Their analysis is restricted to the effects of unconditional financial support on the public good provision.

[37] An analysis of the health-promoting public good "knowledge about HIV" as an example for the summation technology would show that income transfers and in-kind transfers are equivalent.

[38] An analysis without cost differentials between countries can be found in Vicary and Sandler (2002, pp. 1504–1505). Abandoning differences in marginal costs leads to Pareto-improving income transfers. However, efforts of high-income countries to step in low and middle-income countries and provide health measures do not fit this model.

that is more cost-efficient compared to the technology of developing countries. Consequently, the assumption of equal prices is abandoned. We suppose that the technology of an industrialised country (here: country 2) to control tuberculosis is superior to a developing country's one (here: country 1). If country 2's price of a unit of providing preventive health measures is p_2 and country 1 produces at the price p_1, a cost advantage can be expressed by a lower price per unit, $p_2 < p_1$.

- Countries can influence the overall public good provision level by providing in-kind transfers to the country with the smallest effort to prevent tuberculosis.

Both assumptions modify country i's budget constraint. Subsequently, we want to examine this fact in more detail since this analysis is useful for investigating the efficiency of transfer mechanisms. By considering in-kind transfers, country i's budget constraint changes to:

$$y_i + p_i g_i^i + p_i g_j^i = I_i \quad \text{for } i,\ j = 1, 2, \tag{4.36}$$

where g_i^i represents country i's contribution within its own territory whereas g_j^i is its contribution to country j (in-kind transfer).

By adding country j's contribution on its own territory g_j^j and its contribution on behalf of country i g_i^j to both sides of (4.36), we obtain:

$$y_i + p_i g_i^i + p_i g_j^i + p_j g_j^j + p_j g_i^j = I_i + p_j g_j^j + p_j g_i^j \quad \text{for } i,\ j = 1, 2. \tag{4.37}$$

Equation (4.37) represents an extension of the budget constraint of Hirshleifer $y_i + p_i g_i = I_i$ since it includes in-kind transfers. However, the above budget constraint assumes that both countries give transfers in kind. Against the background that an industrialised country can support a developing country by a resource transfer rather than vice versa, we are interested in cases in which only one country provides an in-kind transfer. Thus, (4.37) has to be further modified. We have to distinguish between the case where country i receives an in-kind transfer and where it provides a transfer. Subsequently, each case and its implications on the budget constraints are examined.

Case 1: Country *i* Receives an In-Kind Transfer

If country i has the lowest effort to limit the transmission of tuberculosis, its contribution g_i^i will determine the overall provision level G. This follows from the weakest-link technology. Consequently, country j receives the same amount of G even if it prefers a higher amount of health measures ($g_j^j \geqslant G$). However, if country i does not have the assets to implement prophylactic health interventions preventing the spread of tuberculosis, country j can support it (g_i^j).[39] For example,

[39] This support is less than country j's effort to limit tuberculosis in its own territory ($g_i^j < g_j^j$). Thus, we restrict our analysis to interior solutions.

an industrialised country assists a developing country to increase its preventive effort against tuberculosis. In such a case, the contribution of the developing country g_i increases and hence, the overall level of prevention G rises. This can be expressed as:

$$g_i^i + g_i^j = g_i = g_j^j = G. \tag{4.38}$$

Equation (4.37) is replaced by:

$$y_i + p_i g_i^i + p_j g_i^j = I_i + p_j g_i^j \quad \text{for } g_j^j \geqslant G \geqslant g_i^j, \tag{4.39}$$

where the in-kind transfer g_i^j from country j is like a gift for country i. Thus, we have added the term $p_j g_i^j$ on the right-hand side of (4.39). Equation (4.39) differs from the expression ($y_i + G = I_i + g_i^j$) used in Vicary and Sandler (2002, p. 1505). In contrast to their analysis, (4.39) includes different prices and thus, the terms $p_i g_i^i + p_j g_i^j$ cannot be summarised to G as expressed by (4.38).

Case 2: Country *i* Provides an In-Kind Transfer

We assume that country j contributes the minimum amount to prevent tuberculosis and does not provide assistance in kind. Its effort within its own territory is represented by g_j^j. Consequently, country i is immediately endowed with g_j^j after providing an amount of prophylactic health measures which equals $(g_j^j - g_i^j)$. This results from the weakest-link technology (Vicary and Sandler 2002, p. 1505). However, if it prefers a higher amount of prophylaxis against tuberculosis than g_j^j, it has to provide preventive health measures within its own region and to country j.

Furthermore, we have to consider that country j's interventions to limit tuberculosis benefit both its own population and the citizens of the other country because tuberculosis is an airborne disease. Efforts in one region to limit its transmission influence the spread of the disease in neighbouring regions. Thus, country j's own prevention is like a gift for country i. Therefore, its income I_i increases. Following these observations, (4.37) is specified as:

$$\begin{aligned} &y_i + p_i g_i^i + p_i g_j^i + p_j g_j^j = I_i - (p_j g_j^j - p_j g_i^j) + 2 p_j g_j^j \quad \text{for} \\ &G \geqslant \max\left\{ g_j^j, g_i^j \right\} = g_j^j. \end{aligned} \tag{4.40}$$

The consideration of cost differentials leads to a different expression than in Vicary and Sandler (2002, p. 1505). By using (4.38), the above equation can be simplified to $y_i + 2G = I_i - (g_j^j - g_i^j) + 2g_j^j$ if cost differentials are omitted.

Equipped with these observations, we proceed by comparing the efficiency of in-kind and income transfers. Following Vicary and Sandler (2002, p. 1516), our starting point is a Nash equilibrium in which one country provides the weakest-link public good to each country.[40] For concreteness, the donor is an industrialised country supplying pharmaceuticals against tuberculosis on behalf of its own and to a developing country.

Proposition 8. *The Nash equilibrium for a given ex-post transfer is unique.*

Proof. Suppose that there are two different equilibrium amounts G^* and G', with $G^* > G'$. At least one country i contributes a larger amount in the equilibrium with G^* than in the equilibrium with the overall provision level G'. Thus, its budget constraint implies $y_i^* < y_i'$. Yet, it holds that $y_i^* = h_i^*(G^*, p_i) > h_i'(G', p_i) = y_i'$ is true since the income expansion paths are strictly increasing in G. This contradicts the condition $y_i^* < y_i'$. Hence, the equilibrium amount is unique.

Given that an unique equilibrium exists, the efficiency of income versus in-kind transfers can be compared at stage 1.

Proposition 9. *An income transfer may not be Pareto-superior to an in-kind transfer if the donor (here: country 2) is more cost-efficient in providing the health-promoting public good "limiting the domain of tuberculosis" than the recipient (here: country 1).*

Proof. We assume that country 2 provides 1 with an income transfer while reducing its in-kind transfer. Therefore, country 2's income diminishes while country 1's income increases by the same amount $\Delta I_1 = -\Delta I_2$. We obtain $-\Delta g_1^2 = -\Delta I_2 = \Delta I_1$. In order to demonstrate the impact of a cash transfer from country 2 to 1, we will follow the reasoning of Buchholz and Konrad (1995) comparing different equilibrium allocations by adding up both budget constraints. From (4.39) for $i = 1$ and $j = 2$ it follows:

$$y_1 + p_1 g_1^1 + p_2 g_1^2 = I_1 + p_2 g_1^2, \tag{4.41}$$

where $p_2 g_1^2$ is country 2's support in kind in terms of its value.

Using (4.40) for $i = 2$ and $j = 1$, we obtain country 2's budget constraint:

$$y_2 + p_2 g_2^2 + p_2 g_1^2 + p_1 g_1^1 = I_2 + p_1 g_1^1, \tag{4.42}$$

where we have neglected the term $p_1 g_2^1$ because country 1 does not give in-kind transfers to country 2.

[40]This follows from the two-stage game which is solved by backward induction. A detailed discussion how in-kind transfers affect Nash equilibria can be found in Gregor (2008, pp. 4–5) as well as Vicary and Sandler (2002, pp. 1506–1510).

Summing up (4.41) and (4.42) and rearranging yields the following necessary feasibility constraint:[41]

$$y_1 + y_2 + 2p_2G + (p_2 - ep_1)g_1^2 = eI_1 + I_2, \tag{4.43}$$

where we have used the fact that $g_1^2 + g_1^1 = G$. In addition, the variable e represents the nominal exchange rate.

Equation (4.43) can be used to analyse the implications of the supposed reduced in-kind transfer for the equilibrium allocation. Therefore, a closer look is taken at the last term on the left-hand side of (4.43), $(p_2 - ep_1)g_1^2$. Since country 2 is more cost-efficient in providing the public good "limiting the domain of tuberculosis", its price of a unit of preventing tuberculosis is lower than country 1's price per unit ($p_2 < p_1$). The expression $p_2 - p_1$ becomes negative. Yet, the last term on the left-hand side of (4.43), $(p_2 - ep_1)g_1^2$, is positive since country 2 has reduced its in-kind transfer. To satisfy the necessary feasibility constraint, country 1's private consumption y_1 has to drop and, hence, it is worse off after an income transfer. Consequently, a Pareto-improvement cannot be achieved by a cash transfer. However, if country 2 is less cost-efficient in providing the weakest-link public good, the expression $p_2 - p_1$ will become positive due to $p_2 > p_1$. Then, (4.43) indicates that country 1's private consumption increases with an income transfer and, hence, it is better off.

4.2.2 *Income or In-Kind Transfers in a Best-Shot Case*

Choosing the optimal policy, i.e. deciding either for income or in-kind transfers, is also relevant in the best-shot case. This analysis is motivated by some observations made by recent initiatives to accelerate the development of an AIDS vaccine. On the one hand, HIV vaccine research and development programmes are funded by research grants. On the other hand, institutions like the U.S. National Institute of Allergy and Infectious Diseases (NIAID), IAVI and others cooperate and pool their R&D efforts to conduct AIDS vaccine trials. Since both mechanisms are implemented, we proceed by discussing whether in-kind or income transfers have to be provided.

There are few theoretical studies discussing whether support in kind is preferable to cash transfers in order to increase the provision level of best-shot public goods. A noteworthy exception is a paper of Sandler and Arce (2002, p. 213) arguing that R&D resources have to concentrate on the research team that is most apt to provide the public good if potential contributors differ in their capabilities. However, their suggestions do not involve a comparison between income and in-kind transfers for the case that research teams are endowed equally and thus, may have an equal

---

[41] A detailed analysis can be found in Appendix B.

likelihood of success. By considering that potential contributors can combine their efforts in HIV vaccine research to increase the probability of success, an analysis of the efficiency of in-kind and income transfers in the case of equal costs among providers remains to be done. We refer to the model of Vicary and Sandler (2002) to verify these recommendations. All assumptions are retained except for the aggregation technology now being a maximum technology. Our analysis starts with a discussion of transfers by abandoning cost differentials between providers.

4.2.2.1 In-Kind Transfers and Identical Costs

Following Vicary and Sandler (2002, p. 1505), we first describe stage 2 where both countries determine their contributions to the health-promoting public good for a given in-kind transfer. Our starting point is country i's budget constraint with an in-kind option. In contrast to the weakest-link case, differences between marginal costs in providing the health-promoting public good are omitted and thus, (4.37) can be simplified to:

$$y_i + pg_i^i + pg_j^i + pg_j^j + pg_i^j = I_i + pg_j^j + pg_i^j \quad \text{for } i, j = 1, 2. \tag{4.44}$$

If we summarise $pg_i^i + pg_i^j = pg_i$ and $pg_j^j + pg_j^i = pg_j$, (4.44) can be expressed as:

$$y_i + pg_i + pg_j = I_i + pg_j^j + pg_i^j, \tag{4.45}$$

where g_i (g_j) represents the total contribution to the public good "developing an AIDS vaccine" in country i's (country j's) territory. Since a best-shot situation is analysed with a single provider being anticipated, (4.45) has to be specified. Either country i chooses being a provider or it is a non-provider and then vaccine-related activities are carried out in country j. Our analysis starts with the first case.

Case 1: Country *i* Chooses Being a Providing Country

If country j's contribution to the development a vaccine equals or is lower than the overall provision level G ($g_j \leqslant G$), its research-related activities are redundant due to the best-shot technology.[42] Thus, it does not search for a vaccine ($g_j^j = 0$) while only country i is involved in R&D. If it prefers a higher amount of the health-promoting public good than country i supplies, it can augment country i's endowment by equipping its laboratory (g_i^j). Consequently, country i's total effort

[42] For concreteness, HIV vaccine research is primarily carried out by the public sector.

increases (g_i) and, hence, the overall public good provision level rises. This follows from the best-shot technology and can be expressed as:

$$g_i^i + g_i^j = g_i = G.$$

Consequently, (4.45) can be written as:

$$y_i + pG = I_i + pg_i^j \quad \text{for } g_j \leqslant G. \tag{4.46}$$

Country i will face a constant price per unit p if it provides the public good for both territories. By contrast, a supplier faces a price of $2p$ in the weakest-link case (Vicary and Sandler 2002, p. 1505).

Case 2: Country *i* Chooses Being a Non-Providing Country

We suppose that country j's effort to find a vaccine exceeds the public good provision level G ($g_j = G$) and hence, it becomes the single provider. Its contribution to the health-promoting public good and thus the overall public good level G can be increased if country i provides an in-kind transfer equaling an amount of $g_j^j + g_j^i$.[43] In addition, if country j has made the discovery, both its own population and people living beyond its national borders can gain from a vaccine.[44] Hence, g_j^j is like a gift for country i.

By using these observations, country i's budget constraint can be written as:

$$y_i = I_i - p(g_j^j + g_j^i) + pg_j^j \quad \text{for } g_j > G. \tag{4.47}$$

Country i's demand function which is associated with these modified budget constraints can be expressed as:

$$\begin{aligned} g^i &= f_i(I_i + pg_i^j, p) - g_i^j \\ &\text{or} \\ g^i &= 0, \end{aligned} \tag{4.48}$$

where g^i represents country i's contribution on behalf of its own (g_i^i) and on country j's behalf (g_j^i).

[43] This follows from $g_j = g_j^j + g_j^i$ and $g_j = G$.

[44] An exception would be if a vaccine was not effective beyond national borders due to different HIV clades.

If country i is the sole provider, its demand function possesses the same analytic form as in a summation case where g_i^j represents the efforts of the others. Its contribution to the public good "developing an AIDS vaccine" is determined by its full income $(I_i + pg_i^j)$. This indicates that an income transfer cannot alter the equilibrium allocation and, hence, the neutrality theorem is valid (Warr 1982, 1983). Financial support does not result in a Pareto-improvement.

Proposition 10. *A cash transfer may not be Pareto-superior to an in-kind transfer if countries are equally cost-efficient in providing the public good "developing an AIDS vaccine".*

Proof. Assume that country 2 transfers income to 1 ($\Delta I_1 = -\Delta I_2$). In addition, we suppose that country 2 reduces its in-kind transfer by the same amount as its endowment diminishes, $-\Delta g_1^2 = -\Delta I_2$. As a consequence, country 1's full income $\Delta I_1 + \Delta g_1^2$ remains unchanged. By applying (4.46) for $i = 1$ and $j = 2$, the implications of an income transfer on country 1's private consumption and its contribution to the public good can be derived. Its budget constraint turns into:

$$y_1 + pG = I_1 + pg_1^2, \tag{4.49}$$

where g_1^2 is country 2's in-kind transfer to 1. The right-hand side of (4.49) becomes zero because the full income has not altered. It follows that country 1 chooses the same amount of the health-promoting public good G as before receiving an income transfer. It uses the financial support to adjust its own contribution (g_1^1) by the exact amount that country 2 reduces its in-kind transfer (g_1^2) and thus, $\Delta g_1^1 = -\Delta g_1^2$ is true. By using the fact that $G = g_1^1 + g_1^2$, the overall public good provision remains unchanged. To satisfy (4.49), country 1's private consumption has also not altered after an income transfer. The same holds for country 2 by (4.47):

$$y_2 + pg_1^2 = I_2, \tag{4.50}$$

where it spends its income on private consumption and on giving support in kind. Due to its reduction in kind, $-\Delta g_1^2$, the left-hand side of (4.50) falls. The right-hand side also declines because $-\Delta I_2$ is true. Therefore, the optimal response for country 2 is to leave its private consumption unchanged ($\Delta y_2 = 0$). As a consequence, neutrality results since the overall public good provision level G and the consumption of the private good do not change. A Pareto-improvement cannot be achieved by giving financial support instead of an in-kind transfer.

Proposition 10 indicates that potential contributors have to pool their R&D efforts. It follows that international approaches facilitating competitive R&D by equipping laboratories in developing countries to increase their own vaccine-related activities are not in line with our result since resources are targeted to less cost-efficient agents. In order to analyse under which conditions such in-kind transfers are preferable, cost differentials between providers have to be taken into account.

4.2.2.2 In-Kind Transfers and Cost Differentials

We follow the procedure of the analysis in the weakest-link situation to define the optimal strategy, i.e. deciding either for income or in-kind transfers in the case of cost differentials. Therefore, we employ the technique of Buchholz and Konrad (1995) and sum up the budget constraints of both countries. As we know from the analysis of the weakest-link case, abandoning the assumption of equal cost leads to modified budget constraints. Equation (4.49) changes to:

$$y_1 + p_1 g_1^1 + p_2 g_1^2 = I_1 + p_2 g_1^2, \tag{4.51}$$

where $p_1 g_1^1 + p_2 g_1^2$ cannot be added up to G because of different prices.

Country 2's budget constraint, which is initially expressed by (4.50), modifies to:

$$y_2 + p_2 g_1^2 = I_2. \tag{4.52}$$

By summing up (4.51) and (4.52), we obtain the following necessary feasibility constraint:[45]

$$y_1 + y_2 + p_1 G + (ep_1 - p_2) g_1^2 = eI_1 + I_2, \tag{4.53}$$

where we have used the fact that $g_1^2 + g_1^1 = G$ and e represents the nominal exchange rate.

If country 1 is less cost-efficient in providing the health-promoting public good, $p_1 > p_2$ is true and, hence, $(ep_1 - p_2)$ is positive. It follows that a reduction of country 2's in-kind transfer results in a decrease of the term $(ep_1 - p_2) g_1^2$. Country 1's private consumption y_1 has to be increased to satisfy (4.53). Consequently, it is better off after an income transfer. Thus, assistance in kind is not preferable to income transfers. However, if country 1 is more cost-efficient, we will obtain $p_1 < p_2$. Equation (4.53) indicates that its private consumption y_1 is reduced after receiving an income transfer and thus, country 1 is worse off. Consequently, in-kind transfers are preferable to cash transfers as suggested by Sandler and Arce (2002).

4.2.3 A Comparison of Income versus In-Kind Transfers

In the previous sections, we have compared the efficiency of income and in-kind transfer mechanisms. The main results are now reviewed:

- Starting with the weakest-link scenario, we replicated the analysis of Sandler and Vicary (2002) for the case that cost differentials between providers are

[45] A detailed derivation of the necessary feasibility constraint can be found in Appendix C.

allowed. We confirm their results that in-kind transfers in comparison to income transfers are welfare-improving if support in kind is supplied by the country possessing a cost advantage.

- In the case of the best-shot health-promoting public good "developing an AIDS vaccine" and no cost differentials, we found that neutrality applies and hence, the equilibrium remains unchanged if a donor, originally giving assistance in kind, now provides a cash transfer. It follows that in-kind transfers seem preferable to financial support because the redistribution of income does not have any positive impact on either the international public good provision level or the private consumption.
- When costs differ between providing countries in the best-shot case, we show that no Pareto-improvement occurs if income is redistributed from the less cost-efficient country previously providing an in-kind transfer to the more cost-efficient country. However, assistance in kind targeted to the country having a cost advantage can be welfare-improving.

These results show that the optimal strategy, i.e. income or in-kind transfers, depends on the relative price of providing a health-promoting public good and thus, they indicate that in-kind transfers are not generally preferable to unconditional cash transfers. Assistance in kind is only preferable to financial support if a donor has a cost advantage in supplying the weakest-link public good "limiting the domain of tuberculosis". Prophylactic health measures have to be supplied directly until a recipient has scaled up his own capacity to provide prevention by himself. By contrast, in-kind transfers will only be welfare-improving in the best-shot case "developing an AIDS vaccine" if they are given to the country which possesses a cost advantage.[46]

4.2.4 Discussion: Transferring Income or Giving in Kind?

Evidence for in-kind transfers in the weakest-link case can be found by considering the variety of initiatives of high-income countries to prevent tuberculosis in low and middle-income countries. In order to give a short overview about implemented policies, we restrict our attention to in-kind transfers provided to countries most affected by tuberculosis. In Nigeria and Senegal, for example, where tuberculosis is a major health problem, USAID has sent medical teams to reinforce the DOTS[47] Strategy and to give technical assistance (USAID 2006a, b). Further examples of assistance in kind are the provision of laboratory equipment and the training of staff. New microscopes and test tubes for diagnosing tuberculosis are supplied to

[46]These opposite policy recommendations can be traced back to the difference between the minimum and the maximum technology.

[47]The Directly Observed Treatment Short-Course (DOTS Strategy is characterised by a supervised treatment of tuberculosis to ensure uninterrupted anti-tuberculosis therapies.

Nigeria, Kenya and the Philippines (USAID 2006a, c, d). In addition, laboratory technicians and microscopists are instructed to strengthen tuberculosis diagnosis and treatment in Nigeria (USAID 2006a). The same holds for Nigerian and Philippine health professionals involved in trainings to improve their skills in treating tuberculosis-infected people (USAID 2006a, d).

Obviously, these observations are linked with some weaknesses since these facts are snapshots. Causal relationships between cost differentials and international assistance have not been tested empirically. In addition, it cannot be explained why donors would be willing to give in-kind transfers. Due to the reduced validity of these facts, we proceed by presenting an economic laboratory experiment allowing a deeper insight into the choice of donors. To our knowledge, the experimental study of Lei et al. (2006) is the first one to investigate differences in efficiency between in-kind and income transfers in a weakest-link case.

The experiment took place at the University of Canterbury (Lei et al. 2006, p. 604). It was conducted with a sample of 140 students from economics and mathematics undergraduate courses. They were separated into groups of two; each person was assigned to a rich or a poor country corresponding to his computer terminal. The experiment aimed at emulating the choice of donors between in-kind and income transfers. The game was structured as follows. In the first stage, participants decided simultaneously which part of their endowment they would like to transfer. They could freely choose between in-kind and cash transfers. As soon as all transfer decisions were finished, participants were made aware of their actual endowment which equalled their initial income minus the cash transfer plus their counterpart's transfer. In the case of in-kind transfers, they were informed about the other's contribution to the public good. Then they decided how much to spend on private consumption and on the public good. Lei et al. (2006, Result 10 and 12) found that donors provided 264 in-kind transfers and 34 cash transfers to recipients. Thus, their study confirms that donors prefer in-kind to income transfers independently from the disparity in endowment between countries. The result is reasoned by the control of an in-kind transfer's utilisation (Lei et al. 2006, p. 618). However, in-kind transfers can also be used for other issues than the donors have intended. Reselling in-kind support like drugs is an alternative. Furthermore, income and in-kind transfers can result in an identical allocation and thus be equivalent if anti-HIV programmes are carried out even without the support of donors. Received transfers are additional financial resources which can be used for private consumption. This line of reasoning indicates that in-kind transfers are not generally preferable to cash transfers. Thus, donors who would ever provide in-kind transfers do not necessarily choose an effective policy tool to increase the public good provision. Finally, the experimental analysis of Lei et al. (2006) indicates why implemented transfer mechanisms may fail by confirming strong preferences to assistance in kind.[48]

[48]However, whether or not implemented policies really fail since donors prefer in-kind transfers exceeds the validity of experimental economics. Consequently, international policy recommendations addressing HIV/AIDS cannot be derived from an experimental study.

Thus, the central argument of this book, reasoning that underprovision can only be overcome if international transfers are implemented in a more efficient way than nowadays, is also substantiated. As we have shown, assistance in kind is only preferable to the provision of financial resources if a donor possessing a cost advantage supplies the weakest-link public good on behalf of its own and to others.

With respect to the best-shot case, our model indicates that R&D efforts have to be monopolised in industrialised rather than in low and middle-income countries where public health infrastructure in general and laboratories to develop an AIDS vaccine in particular are lacking.[49] Even if some countries like South Africa and India may have cost advantages and thus, assistance in kind may be effective to increase R&D efforts, public institutions in most of the low and middle-income countries do not satisfy this condition and, hence, in-kind transfers in the form of equipping laboratories are not effective. By contrast, observations made by ongoing HIV-vaccine trials show that R&D for vaccines in developing countries is encouraged. Vaccine trials often involve both a North American or a European academic institution and research institutes located in developing countries (Hecht et al. 2006, p. 4). Thus, scientists from industrialised countries join in AIDS vaccine trials established in low and middle-income countries and vice versa. In addition, researchers from developing countries are trained in public institutions and universities in the United States, Japan, etc. In these cases, resources in form of knowledge transfers flow in the opposite direction than recommended by the model.

It is clear that cost efficiency is only one criterion for evaluating whether or not in-kind transfers have to be provided. There are further reasons justifying the implementation of HIV-vaccine trials in low and middle-income countries. For example, if these researchers and health professionals are trained in diagnosis and testing of HIV cases in their country, samples of regional HIV clades can be collected. By analysing these samples, specific regional interrelationships can be identified. Endemic diseases like other STIs or tuberculosis possess a potential impact on the transmission of HIV as mentioned in Chap. 2. Since these diseases are linked with a country's HIV/AIDS epidemic, an HIV vaccine may only be effective if these interrelations are also addressed. Thus, the detection of the biological co-factors seems crucial for the design of an effective AIDS vaccine. Moreover, if such a serum was found, worldwide benefits would occur since mutations of HIV clades predominating in industrialised countries would be prevented.

In summary, real observations and the laboratory experiment of Lei et al. (2006) demonstrate that donors prefer in-kind transfers. However, assistance in kind is not in general preferable even if it seems more attractive for transfer-providers because donors have the possibility to control the utilisation of their support. We have

---

[49]Thus, partnerships between U.S. and European scientists to accelerate the development of an HIV vaccine are in line with our result. A 5-year renewal of the "Agreement for Scientific and Technological Cooperation" was signed by the United States and the European Union in October 2004 (U.S. Department of State 2005). Partnerships between the US and the EU were reaffirmed in the U.S.-EU Summit Declaration 2008 (The White House 2008).

identified cases in which income transfers are Pareto-superior. In addition, the in-kind option can only improve the resulting allocation in the case of a non-summation technology.

In the literature, there are also discussions about conditional income transfers in the form of subsidies as an alternative to unconditional income and in-kind transfers (Breyer and Zweifel 1997). Conditionality requires financial support which is restricted to specific purposes such as strengthening infrastructure or health systems. Moreover, recipients pay a share of funding themselves in the case of a subsidy. Financing mechanisms of international organisations, which bundle contributions of donor governments and in turn provide these conditional funds for recipients, are examples for the implementation of conditionality. Since multilateral funding is, besides bilateral assistance, a second key channel to solve underprovision, its effectiveness is analysed and critically discussed in the subsequent section.

4.3 Conditional Income Transfers

Nowadays, there are a variety of international organisations receiving financial assistance from donors like governments, stakeholders, etc. and target it to specific health programmes against AIDS. The main multilateral institutions involved in the field of HIV/AIDS are the World Bank, the Global Fund to fight AIDS, Tuberculosis and Malaria (henceforth, Global Fund) and several legal entities within the United Nations system, e.g. the WHO, the United Nations Children's Fund (UNICEF), the World Food Program (WFP) etc. (The Kaiser Family Foundation 2005, p. 9).

We restrict our attention to the Global Fund since it was the first institution of its kind. Its high prevalence in the field of health in general and in the case of HIV/AIDS in particular results from the fact that the Global Fund is the predominant international funder of programmes addressing concomitant diseases like tuberculosis, and it contributes one-fight of all international HIV/AIDS spending in 2005 (The Global Fund 2006, p. 12). Moreover, the approach of the Global Fund is to provide additional financial resources in the form of grants in order to complement current financial support (The Global Fund 2007, p. 9). Against the background of coordination problems among donors which can result in funding gaps, the provision of additional resources seems important. As we will, the effectiveness of a conditional transfer scheme crucially depends on the question whether funding gaps can be closed or not.

The analysis proceeds as follows. First, we discuss the effects of a conditional subsidy on the overall public good provision if the scheme of the Global Fund works. The implications on efficiency are exemplied for the cases "knowledge about HIV", "limiting the domain of tuberculosis" and "developing an AIDS vaccine". Afterwards, allocative consequences of funding gaps are demonstrated. Additionally, further limits to effectiveness like opportunistic behaviour of recipients are taken into account.

4.3.1 Allocative Consequences of Subsidies in the Case of "Knowledge About HIV"

Conditional transfers in the form of subsidies diminish the effective price per unit that a subsidised country i has to pay for the health-promoting public good "knowledge about HIV".[50] By defining that a subsidy is paid at the rate s with $0 < s < 1$,[51] its price of providing a unit of the public good can be expressed as $\hat{p}_i = (1 - s)p_i$, where $\hat{p}_i$ is the after-subsidy price. Therefore, the budget constraint is now given by:

$$y_i + (1 - s)p_i g_i = I_i. \tag{4.54}$$

Furthermore, the marginal condition for an interior optimum can be expressed by:

$$MRS_i = \hat{p}_i, \tag{4.55}$$

where MRS_i is the marginal rate of substitution between the public and the private good. Country i provides a health-promoting public good up to the level where its marginal rate of substitution MRS_i equals its after-subsidy price $\hat{p}_i$.

The description of the post-transfer Nash equilibrium can be used to illustrate the effects on the public good provision level. Equation (4.55) reveals a reduced right-hand side in contrast to the before-transfer situation, $MRS_i = p_i$. To restore optimality, the left-hand side of (4.55) has to decline. This can be achieved by increasing the amount of the health-promoting public good "knowledge about HIV". Such a positive impact on the public good provision level is depicted in Fig. 4.6.[52] This diagram shows how a subsidy scheme works; the overall provision level G is measured on the vertical axis while country i's private consumption y_i is drawn on the horizontal axis.

Our analysis starts at point A. It represents country i's optimal decision in the before-transfer situation. Its indifference curve i_i is tangent to its budget constraint I_i. In addition, its income expansion path $y_i = h_i(G, p_i)$ is derived by shifting the line I_i outwards. We already know from Chap. 3 that point A does not represent an optimal equilibrium allocation in a world consisting of n countries. To overcome underprovision, a subsidy is paid. The effective price reduction can be illustrated by a rotation of the budget constraint around the horizontal axis from I_i to I_i'. As a result, country i's budget constraint becomes steeper. If this is the case, the indifference curve i_i' which lies above i_i and, hence, represents a higher utility level can be achieved. Point A' represents the new equilibrium allocation because

[50]For this standard result see also Althammer and Buchholz (1993, p. 400) as well as Ihori (1996, p. 147).

[51]A subsidy with $s = 1$ is an in-kind transfer.

[52]A positive impact on the overall public good provision level in the case of bilateral assistance is discussed in Althammer and Buchholz (1993).

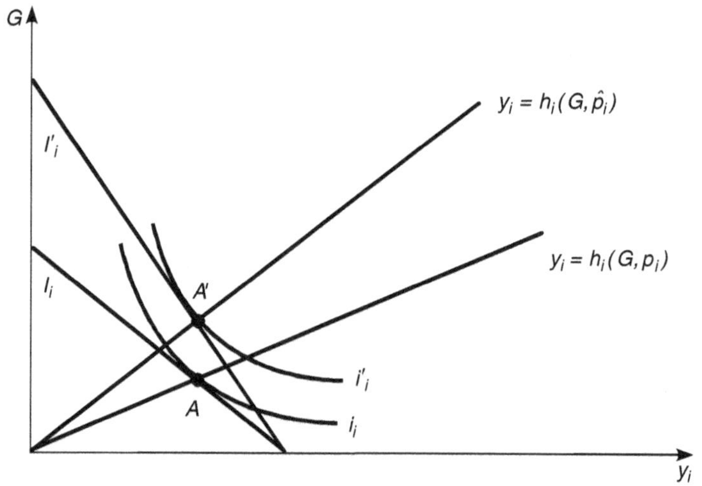

Fig. 4.6 Allocative effects of a subsidy

the indifference curve i_i' is tangent to the new budget constraint I_i'. It is characterised by an increased public good provision level G.

In summary, a conditional transfer seems to be an effective policy tool to overcome underprovision because it has the potential to alter the equilibrium allocation of a health-promoting public good.[53] That indicates that we have found a further reason, besides cost differentials among countries and corner solutions, to circumvent the neutrality theorem even if an additive aggregation technology prevails. In contrast to an income transfer, a subsidy additionally causes a price effect which works in the same direction as the income effect. This results from the reduced marginal cost for the recipient. Therefore, the public good provision is higher than with a cash transfer because of the price effect caused by the subsidy.

4.3.2 Allocative Consequences of Subsidies in the Case of Alternative Aggregation Technologies

The scientific literature pays little attention to the implications of a subsidy on the public good provision level in the case of non-additive aggregation technologies. To our knowledge, only Xu (2002b) exemplifies the allocative consequences of a subsidy on the development of software which is characterised by a best-shot technology. He shows that depending on the distribution of the valuation of the benefits resulting from an innovation, a reduction of development costs caused by a

[53]The same holds if subsidies are analysed in a framework of privately provided public goods. A detailed analysis about conditional transfers which are funded by another country can be found in Appendix D.

subsidy may hamper the development of new software programmes. If all programmers have the same development cost, yet, the benefits are not identically distributed, a decline in costs does not accelerate the research-related activities (Xu 2002b, Proposition 4). Our analysis contributes to this strand of literature. In contrast to the analysis of Xu (2002b) which is restricted to an interior equilibrium, we discuss corner solutions where only one provider is involved in R&D.

In order to evaluate the allocative consequences of conditional income transfers in the case of non-additive aggregation technologies, all assumptions from the analysis of the summation case are kept except that the aggregation technology is a minimum technology for the case "limiting the domain of tuberculosis" and a maximum technology for the health-promoting public good "developing an AIDS vaccine". Consequently, the marginal conditions for an interior equilibrium in the weakest-link case can be expressed by:

$$\begin{aligned} MRS_i &= \hat{p}_i, \quad \text{for some } i \in R, R = \{i | g_i \leqslant g_j\}, \\ MRS_j &\geqslant \hat{p}_i, \quad \text{for all } j \neq i, j = 1, 2, \ldots, n, \end{aligned} \tag{4.56}$$

where country i is the first one that achieves an equality between the marginal rate of substitution between the public good "limiting the domain of tuberculosis" and the private good MRS_i and its after-subsidy price $\hat{p}_i$.

Equation (4.56) reveals a reduced right-hand side compared to the situation before a subsidy has been paid.[54] This can be reasoned by the fact that the price per unit for providing the health-promoting public good has declined by s. In order to restore an equilibrium, the left-hand side of (4.56) has also declined by the same amount. Therefore, similar to the summation case, the provision of the public good G increases. However, unlike the summation case, a conditional income transfer has to be targeted to the country providing the lowest amount of prevention since the overall public good provision level is determined by the smallest contribution. As we know from Chap. 3, individual contributions to the health-promoting public good "limiting the domain of tuberculosis" g_i are perfect complements. The overall public good provision level cannot be raised if a subsidy is given to other countries preferring a higher level of prevention and which are therefore interested to increase their contributions to the public good while the country which is the least involved in anti-tuberculosis policies does not match the behaviour of other countries.

Now, let us turn to the allocative implications of a subsidy in the case of developing an AIDS vaccine. From the analysis in Chap. 3 we already know that the optimal provision level of country i which is the first one making the discovery can be expressed by:

$$MRS_i(\widehat{g}_i) = p_i, \quad \text{for some } i \in S, S = \{i | g_i > \max\{g_j\}\}, j = 1, 2, \ldots, n, \tag{4.57}$$

[54]As shown in Chap. 3, the marginal conditions for an interior solution in a weakest-link situation are $MRS_i = p_i$ for $i \in R, R = \{i | (g_i \leqslant g_j)\}$ and $MRS_j \geqslant p_i$ for all $j \neq i$.

where $\hat{g}_i$ is the largest effort to find a vaccine and p_i represents the price per unit of a public good before a subsidy has been paid. In the case of a subsidy, (4.57) modifies to:

$$MRS_i(\hat{g}_i) = \hat{p}_i, \quad \text{for some } i \in S, S = \{i | g_i > \max\{g_j\}\}, j = 1, 2, ..., n, \quad (4.58)$$

where $\hat{p}_i$ represents the after-subsidy price with $\hat{p}_i < p_i$.

A comparison of (4.57) and (4.58) reveals that the new equilibrium can be restored by an increasing amount of the health-promoting public good "developing an AIDS vaccine". This observation is similar to the summation and the weakest-link case. However, unlike to these two previous cases, the public good provision level can only be raised if the country providing the largest amount of the public good is subsidised and thus, its willingness to produce the public good increases as a result of the reduced marginal costs.[55] This is because it provides the entire amount of the health-promoting public good.

In summary, a conditional transfer in the form of a subsidy will also be effective if non-additive aggregation technologies are taken into consideration. Similar to the case "knowledge about HIV", the willingness of transfer-receiving countries to implement health programmes against tuberculosis and to participate in vaccine-related activities increases because their effective prices decline. Moreover, our findings indicate that the price effect cannot be abolished in the case of non-additive aggregation technologies. In contrast to the summation case, the single contributing country only has to be subsidised to result in an increased public good provision level. The price effect is working for country i's contribution which equals the whole provided amount of the health-promoting public good.

4.3.3 Limits of a Subsidy Mechanism

Conditional transfers will only work in the described way if a pivotal condition is fulfilled. It is implicitly supposed that the full amount of costs is covered by a multilateral organisation and, hence, funding gaps do not exist.[56] The financial support has to be large enough to subsidise each country i's contribution to the health-promoting public good g_i.[57] However, if country i's effort is subsidised

[55]The opposite results from weakest-link and best-shot aggregation technologies can be traced back to differences between the minimum and the maximum technology.

[56]If the costs of the public good G are funded by another country, $\sum_i sp_ig_i = \sum_j L_j$ must also hold, where L_j represents the amount of lump-sum transfers, i are the recipients and j are the contributing countries ($i \neq j$).

[57]This requirement is particularly crucial in the case of a summation technology because the overall public good provision level is not only determined by a single contribution as in weakest-link and best-shot situations, but by the sum of all individual contributions. Therefore, we restrict our analysis to the case "knowledge about HIV".

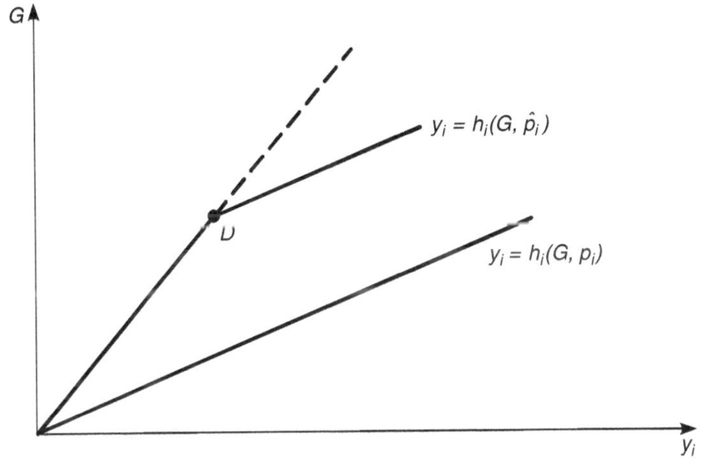

Fig. 4.7 The income effect of a subsidy

partially, a conditional transfer will only result in an income effect as depicted in Fig. 4.7.[58]

In Fig. 4.7 the line $y_i = h_i(G, p_i)$ represents country i's income expansion path before a subsidy has been received whereas the line $y_i = h_i(G, \hat{p}_i)$ is country i's income expansion path after a subsidy. In contrast to Fig. 4.6, country i's expansion path $y_i = h_i(G, \hat{p}_i)$ is not always steeper than $y_i = h_i(G, p_i)$. It is kinked at point D. The slope of the line $y_i = h_i(G, \hat{p}_i)$ is larger up to that point D and then becomes the same as the slope of $y_i = h_i(G, p_i)$. This follows from the fact that the price reduction is effective for the subsidised contributions g_i. However, if the financial support is utilised as in point D, the effective price per unit of further contributions to a health-promoting public good will not reduce. Therefore, only an income effect occurs while the price effect disappears.

As we have shown in the last section, the price effect of conditional transfers is the reason why the neutrality theorem (Warr 1982, 1983) does not hold here. It follows that those transfers become de facto unconditional in the absence of the price effect. The resulting implications on the public good provision level are particularly unfavourable in cases in which countries do not differ in productivity as shown by Buchholz and Konrad (1995, p. 495), Ihori (1996, p. 142), and others. The equilibrium allocation cannot be altered and, hence, the neutrality result applies.[59]

[58]Nevertheless, a partial subsidisation can be intended if solutions like point D are to be implemented. For example, the EU subsidises projects to improve infrastructure in which a maximum amount of donations is determined ex-ante. The remaining costs have to be paid by the transfer-receiving government.

[59]The neutrality theorem is not valid for non-additive aggregation technologies like weakest link and best shot. Both are characterised by a single contributor. If country i's individual contribution is subsidised, the resulting price effect will be effective for the full amount of the provided public good.

Underprovision of a health-promoting public good cannot be solved because insufficient incentives for contributing cannot be overcome. Even though productivity differentials among countries exist, subsidies do not seem preferable in comparison to lump-sum transfers. As a result of the disappearing price effect, the willingness of countries to provide the health-promoting public good "knowledge about HIV" falls because their effective prices are not reduced any further. As can be seen from Fig. 4.7, $y_i = h_i(G, p_i)$ is parallel to $y_i = h_i(G, \hat{p}_i)$ after point D has been reached. Therefore, a subsidy does not result in a higher utility level than an income transfer.

Against this background, coordination problems of donors, i.e. an overlap of funding between organisations, are fatal. In the field of HIV/AIDS, multilateral organisations like the WHO, the World Bank and UNICEF often support the same projects or programmes like several other agencies including the UNDP (Riddell 2007, p. 87). Since funding is duplicated on the one hand whereas the finance of other projects is not ensured on the other hand, the approach of the Global Fund to close funding gaps by financing costs which cannot be covered without its support seems attractive. If the total costs for the implementation of anti-HIV programmes are funded, subsidies will result in an income and a price effect. Therefore, conditional transfers do not become de facto unconditional. However, the attractiveness of this financing mechanism depends on the ability to close funding gaps. A main weakness results from the fact that additional funding depends on the current financial contributions of recipient countries. It is well-known that transfer-receiving countries have incentives to behave strategically and demonstrate a low or even no willingness to provide a health-promoting public good.[60] If the Global Fund gives a larger amount of grants than necessary to close funding gaps, recipient countries can use these additional resources to increase their private consumption instead of transforming it into public good provision. Subsidies become de facto unconditional income transfers because the price effect disappears. Then, we are back in the situation of unconditionality as depicted in Fig. 4.7. In order to restrict opportunistic behaviour of recipient countries and, hence, to ensure the higher effectiveness of grants compared with cash transfers, an alternative conditional mechanism is subsequently developed.

4.3.4 An Alternative Subsidy Mechanism

In this section, all assumptions are kept as above. However, a subsidy is now contingent on some minimum level of provision. One can imagine that recipients have to cover the fixed costs of an anti-HIV programme, e.g., costs for operating donor assistance, before financial support is given by a multilateral organisation. The contributions to the health-promoting public good "knowledge about HIV" will

[60] Incentives to behave strategically will be limited if several rounds of financial support exist. If transfer-receiving countries use grants for other purposes than intended, donors can reduce their financial commitments at the next round.

only be subsidised if a threshold has been surpassed. Otherwise, no conditional transfer will be paid. Such a mechanism seems attractive because a critical value limits the incentives of countries to act as free riders. Insufficient incentives in providing the public good are reasons for underprovision. Conditional transfers in the form of subsidies are defined as:

$$s = \begin{cases} \tilde{s} & \text{if } g_i \geqslant \tilde{g}_i \\ 0 & \text{if } g_i < \tilde{g}_i \end{cases}, \tag{4.59}$$

where g_i is country i's contribution to the public good and $\tilde{g}_i$ represents a threshold. In addition, $\tilde{s}$ can be interpreted as the subsidy rate. Both $\tilde{s}$ and $\tilde{g}_i$ are announced by a transfer-paying organisation.

Equation (4.59) states that a subsidy $\tilde{s}$ is paid if country i's contribution g_i is larger or equal to a threshold $\tilde{g}_i$; otherwise, $s = 0$ holds. Hence, conditionality has been achieved by introducing a threshold. In contrast to the financing scheme described above, a minimum contribution level has to be met or surpassed before a subsidy is paid. This pivotal difference is illustrated in Fig. 4.8.

Figure 4.8 reveals that country i's new budget constraint I_i' has not turned to the left in the origin of the ordinate as in the previous model. It is kinked at point E which follows from (4.59). More precisely, I_i' possesses the same slope as the budget constraint I_i if contributions to a health-promoting public good are lower than $\tilde{g}_i$. This follows from the fact that no financial support is given if $g_i < \tilde{g}_i$. Country i's budget constraint I_i' is steeper from point E due to the price effect. As a further consequence, its income expansion path after a subsidy $y_i = h_i(G, \hat{p}_i)$ lies above $y_i = h_i(G, p_i)$ after a threshold has been surpassed.

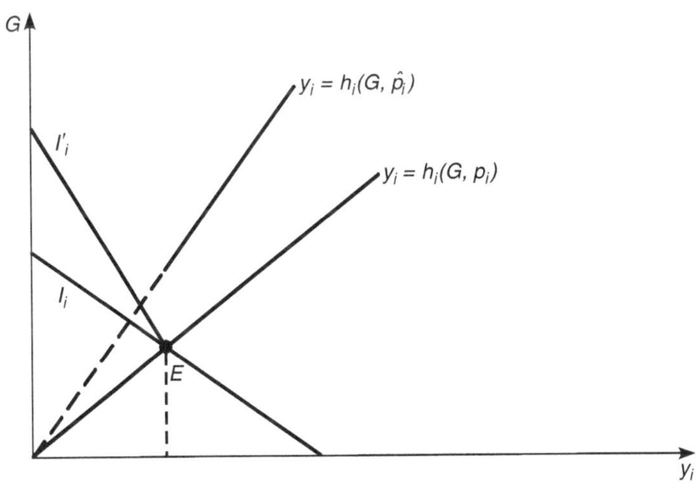

Fig. 4.8 An alternative subsidy mechanism

The efficiency of the mechanism depends on the critical value $\tilde{g}_i$. In order to determine $\tilde{g}_i$, the subsidy scheme is characterised as a two-stage game. Starting from a certain income distribution among the countries, a multilateral organisation sets the subsidy rate equal for all, and one threshold for each country at stage 1. Country i will only receive a subsidy if its contribution is larger or equal to the minimum contribution level at stage 2. Otherwise, a subsidy will not be funded by the multilateral organisation. Solving backwards, country i's maximisation problem is analysed at first.

Stage 2: Country *i's* Decision Problem

Whether a recipient is willing to provide at least $\tilde{g}_i$ depends on the comparison between its utility received if a threshold has been met and its utility if this is not the case. If a minimum provision level has not been surpassed, country i has to obtain at least the same utility level as before a financing scheme was implemented. Otherwise, conditional transfers would be welfare-reducing.

If no subsidy is paid ($s = 0$), its contribution to a health-promoting public good is $g_i^* = \text{argmax}(I_i - p_i g_i, g_i)$. Therefore, the utility in the initial Nash equilibrium can be expressed by $U_i^N = U_i(I_i - p_i g_i^*, g_i^*)$.

Stage 1: A Multilateral Organisation Selects a Threshold

First, we consider $\tilde{g}_i = 0$. An introduction of a threshold does not have any impact because the financial support is not contingent on a minimum contribution level. Therefore, $(g_1^*, g_2^*, ..., g_n^*)$ represents the Nash equilibrium. The same holds if $\tilde{g}_i < g_i^*$. Such a threshold does not influence the equilibrium allocation as it is too low. Next, we consider the case $\tilde{g}_i \geqslant \max\{g_i\}$, where $\max\{g_i\}$ represents the largest feasible provision level of a health-promoting public good among all countries. Due to the fact that the threshold is too large, the new Nash equilibrium can be represented by $(g_1^*, g_2^*, ..., g_n^*)$.

Proposition 11. *If there is a vector* $(\tilde{g}_1, \tilde{g}_2, ..., \tilde{g}_n)$ *such that* $\max\{g_i\} > \tilde{g}_i \geqslant g_i^*$ *for each country i, then* $(\tilde{g}_1, \tilde{g}_2, ..., \tilde{g}_n)$ *is a Nash equilibrium.*

Proof[61]**.** First, no country i provides less than the threshold. If g_i is reduced below the threshold, a country will not receive any subsidy and obtain its utility in the initial Nash equilibrium U_i^N. Such a situation is represented by its indifference curve i_i as depicted in Fig. 4.6. Yet, country i can increase its welfare by providing

[61]The proof is similar to one of Proposition 3 in Andreoni (1998, pp. 1194 ff.).

$g_i \geqslant \tilde{g}_i$ and thus, it obtains a subsidy $\tilde{s}$. A higher indifference curve, e.g. i_i', will be attainable as illustrated in Fig. 4.6. Second, no country i provides more than the threshold. By assuming that both goods are normal, no country can increase its utility by providing more than a threshold. This follows from the summation technology. The single contributions to a health-promoting public good are perfect substitutes. Consequently, $\tilde{g}_i$ is the best response for each country i.

Moreover, this Nash equilibrium is Pareto-efficient. The following Lagrange function is considered:

$$L = U_j(I_j - p_j g_j - sp_i g_i, G) + \lambda[U_i(I_i - (1-s)p_i g_i, G) - U_i^N], \tag{4.60}$$

where λ is the Lagrange multiplier on the utility constraint and $sp_i g_i$ determines the amount that a multilateral organisation has to pay to country i. By using the fact that $g_j + g_i = G$ with $j \neq i$, the first-order conditions are

$$\frac{\partial U_j}{\partial G} - p_j \frac{\partial U_j}{\partial y_j} + \lambda \frac{\partial U_i}{\partial G} = 0, \tag{4.61}$$

$$\frac{\partial U_j}{\partial G} - sp_i \frac{\partial U_j}{\partial y_j} + \lambda \left[\frac{\partial U_i}{\partial G} + (s-1)p_i \frac{\partial U_i}{\partial y_i} \right] = 0. \tag{4.62}$$

Equating (4.61) and (4.62) yields[62]:

$$\frac{\partial U_j / \partial G}{\partial U_j / \partial y_j} + \frac{s - \frac{p_j}{p_i}}{s-1} \frac{\partial U_i / \partial G}{\partial U_i / \partial y_i} = p_j. \tag{4.63}$$

Financial support is provided until the sum of the marginal rates of substitution between a health-promoting public and a private good equals the price per unit p_j. Equation (4.63) is just a modified Samuelson condition (Samuelson 1954, p. 387, 1955, p. 354). The term $\left(s - \frac{p_j}{p_i}\right)(s-1)^{-1}$ corresponds to the Samuelson condition for any $p_j = p_i$. By contrast, (4.63) is dependent both on the subsidy rate and on the real exchange rate $\frac{p_j}{p_i}$. It determines the international exchange of a health-promoting public good between two regions and thus, it is the rate at which a public good of one agent can be traded for that of another.

Equation (4.63) indicates that financial support which depends on a minimum provision level can result in Pareto-optimality. This follows from the fact that the recipient country does not have an incentive to reduce its effort because its own contribution to the public good determines whether or not a subsidy will be paid by the multilateral organisation.

[62] A detailed derivation can be found in Appendix E.

4.3.5 *Discussion: Strengths and Weaknesses of the Subsidy Mechanism*

The idea to link financial support to a threshold or a baseline is not new. However, it is pioneering to apply it to the field of health. This approach is comparable to the subsidy scheme of the Global Environmental Facility (henceforth, GEF) which was established by the United Nations Development Programme (UNDP), the United Nations Environment Programme (UNEP) and the World Bank as a financing mechanism in the context of global environmental concerns (UNDP 2007b). Weaknesses compared to our subsidy scheme result from the assumption that the threshold is based on current efforts and not on a minimum provision level. As a consequence, the financing mechanism of the GEF is not incentive-compatible. Transfer-receiving countries are willing to behave strategically (Ruebbelke 2005, pp. 72–73). To circumvent this behaviour, we have assumed that the baseline is contingent on a minimum level of provision. Financial support will only be given if a threshold has been surpassed. In contrast to the GEF's financing mechanism, the implementation of a threshold $\tilde{g}_i$ prevents a multilateral organisation from becoming de facto the single financing institution while transfer-receiving countries act as free riders. A minimum provision level has to be met to receive financial assistance.

It is obvious that the implementation of this subsidy scheme is linked with some problems. The effectiveness of the mechanism depends on the ability to determine a threshold. After that, it has to be monitored whether or not a minimum provision level has been surpassed. With respect to the height of a threshold, it seems plausible to equate $\tilde{g}_i$ with the fixed costs in producing a health-promoting public good. Based on the experiences of the past, it is easy to calculate costs for technical assistance and administration. More difficulties will arise if recipients do not meet a minimum provision level because of missing capacity. It is hard to decide whether it is politically justifiable to reject financial support if countries cannot fulfill this prerequisite. Refusing international assistance may not be an adequate penalty. Therefore, the introduction of several levels of sanctions is more appropriate.

4.4 Conclusions

In this chapter, there are several international transfer mechanisms discussed as a means to overcome underprovision. First, we have investigated unconditional transfer schemes. This analysis indicates that unconditional financial support to developing countries will only be effective if:

- The supply of health-promoting public goods is more cost-efficient in developing than in industrialised countries and the aggregate public good provision level equals the sum of all individual contributions

or

- The lowest quantity of health interventions is supplied in developing countries.

Otherwise, redistributing income to developing countries will not raise the overall provision level of health interventions. That indicates that unconditional income transfers are not generally an effective funding mechanism. This argument is strengthened by considering that their effectiveness is small because transferring income is an expensive way to overcome underprovision (Vicary 1990, p. 393). If transfer-receiving governments cannot be forced to use donations for health interventions, donors have to bear high costs of control.

Nevertheless, there are motives for donors to give cash transfers. Additional private benefits can encourage them to provide financial support for low and middle-income countries. Nigeria, for example, has the largest reserves of oil in Africa and is the tenth largest exporter of oil worldwide (CIA 2008). In addition, it has large resources of natural gas. Since it is an important raw material supplier, industrialised countries are willing to support Nigeria financially without any altruistic background.[63] The United States, for example, is the biggest importer of Nigerian oil and is therefore interested in a frequent supply of oil. However, the rate of violence is high in the Niger Delta, the epicenter of the petroleum industry. This region is one of the poorest in Nigeria. Revenues of oil supply flow primarily to oil companies and the Nigerian government whereas the population does not gain from the oil exports. Therefore, oil companies like Exxon assist Nigeria with the implementation of social and health programmes to improve the living standards of the Nigerian people and thus to reduce the violence. This argument is strengthened by the current situation. As a result of the restricted hauling of oil since about 2005 on the one hand and the growing demand based on the economic development, particularly in countries like China and India, on the other hand, the price of oil has risen lately. If the OPEC does not increase the delivered amounts, the current rise of the oil price as well as the augmentation of the price of natural gas which adapts to the oil price after 6 months (so-called oil price maintenance) will continue.[64]

Since unconditional transfers are less stimulative, the chapter highlighted further kinds of assistance like in-kind transfers and subsidies. A direct provision is preferable to unconditional income transfers if the incentives of transfer-receiving governments to spend support for their own interests like increasing expenditures for the military are thereby reduced. International transfers remain effective in the sense that principal-agent problems between donors and recipients are at least mitigated. As shown, in-kind transfers to developing countries facilitate a more efficient use of resources than financial support if donors possess a cost advantage. In general, support in kind is a means to raise provision levels in the short run. In the long run, the capability of providers in developing countries has to be scaled up to avoid a never-ending aid dependence. Moreover, we have identified cases in which in-kind transfers are not welfare-enhancing, for example, if knowledge is

---

[63] Further reasons, besides oil security, are discussed in Browne (2006, pp. 109 ff).

[64] The oil price maintenance was constructed in the 1960s. The idea was an adaptation of the price of natural gas to the price of oil to avoid competition between both resources.

transferred from researchers of industrialised to developing countries. In the second part of this chapter, we have critically discussed multilateral support in the form of subsidies. It has been shown that the effectiveness of subsidy schemes is influenced by the ability of donors to coordinate their funding. If they can coordinate their funding with each other in a way that the full amount of costs is covered, subsidy mechanisms will be more effective than lump-sum transfers. However, if costs are partially covered due to lacks in donor coordination or opportunistic behaviour of recipients, conditional funding will become de facto unconditional because the price effect disappears. Moreover, we have shown that the introduction of a baseline which depends on a minimum provision level is an effective tool to keep the price mechanism. The incentives of transfer receivers to behave strategically are thereby reduced.

These findings indicate that the difficulty to cope with underprovision of health interventions is not based on missing instruments, but on the choice of the most appropriate one from the large variety of mechanisms. Particularly the fact that there are cases in which a reversed financial support has a welfare-increasing effect is currently rarely taken into account. Therefore, international assistance can no longer be interpreted conventionally as foreign aid.

We cannot ignore that the results of this chapter are based on restrictive assumptions and thus, the analysis should be understand as a benchmark. First, aspects of equity have been neglected because they are linked to normative aspects. Our policy recommendations are primarily based on the criterion of effectiveness. Second, the pooling of resources by research teams that are most likely to find an AIDS vaccine results from the best-shot technology implying one provider. Multiple institutions that are engaged in HIV vaccine research have been neglected. By allowing R&D by more than one provider, the better-shot technology seems more precise to describe competition in vaccine research. Moreover, monopolising HIV vaccine research may be less effective than competitive R&D. Additional efforts to find a vaccine arise from the pressure of competition and thus research can be fostered. Third, the discussion about aid effectiveness indicates that decisions of donations cannot be detached from the specific economic, political and social circumstances in a country. For example, the situation within Africa is quite diverse. Uganda and Nigeria, for example, are both most affected by HIV/AIDS, but the political environment facilitates different anti-HIV policies. The government of Uganda has supported a frank and honest communication about HIV/AIDS by implementing anti-HIV programmes since 1986. By contrast, the HIV/AIDS epidemic in Nigeria results primarily from a lack of sexual health information because the government has repudiated the consequences of HIV/AIDS (Office of the United States Global AIDS Coordinator 2006, p. 1; UNGASS 2008, p. 15).[65] This brief consideration of several economic and political circumstances shows that policy responses which focus on allocative aspects, while the situation in recipient

[65]Empirical evidence of the impact of education campaigns on the HIV prevalence can be found in de Walque (2007).

countries has been neglected, may fail. In order to demonstrate the limits of previous analyses, attention is drawn to an issue which is little recognised in the aid effectiveness literature as well as in anti-HIV programmes: HIV-related regional constraints like malnutrition or missing access to safe water.[66] Therefore, some of these regional shortcomings and their consequences for international transfer mechanisms are outlined in Chap. 5.

[66]Exceptions are Stillwaggon (2005, 2006a) explaining the spread of HIV in the context of malnutrition and parasitic diseases.

Chapter 5
Regional Constraints and HIV/AIDS

We shall not finally defeat AIDS, tuberculosis, malaria, or any of the other infectious diseases that plague the developing world until we have also won the battle for safe drinking water, sanitation and basic health care.
Kofi Annan (2001)

HIV did not develop in a vacuum, and it will not be stopped in isolation.
Eileen Stillwaggon (2006b)

It seems that the global AIDS concern is embedded in several regional crises. HIV/AIDS is most widely spread in regions where basic human needs such as safe drinking water, sanitation, nutrition and schooling cannot be secured. For example, in parts of Southern, Eastern and Central Africa which are seriously affected by AIDS, access to clean water is at the lowest level all over the world (WHO and UNICEF 2000, p. 11). In high-endemic countries like Chad and Ethiopia the coverage of the safe water supply constituted approximately 30% or less compared to 56% in Sub-Saharan Africa in 2006 (African Development Fund 2006, pp. 2–3), the World Bank Group (2007). The same line of reasoning holds for the geographical distribution between HIV prevalence and a lack of schooling. Access to primary education is at its lowest in Sub-Saharan Africa, the epicentre of HIV/AIDS. While 93% of the children at the age of entering school are enrolled in Latin America and the Caribbean, 69% have entered the first grade of primary schooling in Sub-Saharan Africa in 2006 (World Bank 2008b). The same holds for the participation of children in secondary and higher education. About 70% of pupils receive a higher literacy in Latin America and the Caribbean compared to 25% in Sub-Saharan Africa in 2004 (World Bank 2008b).[1]

Against this background, this chapter shows why effective policy responses to HIV/AIDS also require solutions that address regional constraints. The analysis proceeds as follows: Starting from a short overview about the impacts of regional deficiencies on HIV/AIDS, we take the role of official development assistance (henceforth, ODA) into account as a supplement to international transfer schemes

[1]An overview of the progress towards universal enrollment corresponding with goal 2 of the MDGs can be found in United Nations (2007, p. 10).

D. Sonntag, *AIDS and Aid*, Contributions to Economics,
DOI 10.1007/978-3-7908-2419-3_5, © Springer-Verlag Berlin Heidelberg 2010

which were discussed in Chap. 4. Subsequently, institutional considerations are presented. The conclusion summarises the main results and gives a couple of policy recommendations.

5.1 The Impact of Regional Constraints on HIV/AIDS

In order to give an insight into how HIV/AIDS is influenced by regional concerns, the interrelationships between HIV/AIDS and a lack of nutrition, of access to safe water as well as sanitation, are discussed in-depth. This restriction seems useful because nutrition and water are two of the physiological human needs and, hence, essential for the life of people. A further rationale results from the fact that little attention is paid to these regional constraints and their impacts by international negotiations. For example, the HIV programme of USAID which was designed to meet the targets set by the UN General Assembly Session on HIV/AIDS does not include any reference to ensure access to safe water and sanitation (USAID 2002). However, since 1995 evidence exists that inadequate sanitary facilities have a negative influence on the transmission of HIV (Feldmeier et al. 1995a). A similar situation can be found for the relationship between malnutrition and HIV which is only partially recognised by anti-HIV programmes. The interests are focused on the impact of HIV on nutrition. We proceed by discussing first the impact of missing sanitation and unsafe drinking water on HIV/AIDS.

5.1.1 The Relationship Between Missing Access to Water, Sanitation and HIV/AIDS

Missing sanitary facilities are conducive to the transmission of parasitic infections like schistosomiasis and soil-transmitted helminths. Nowadays, around two billion people are suffering from these diseases, more than one third of the worldwide population (WHO 2007b). Schistosomiasis, for example, is the most prevalent parasitic disease all over the world besides malaria (Stillwaggon 2006b, p. 174; Harms and Feldmeier 2002, p. 482). For instance, people become infected by swimming or washing clothes in water with snails that harbour the worms (WHO 2007c, p. 1). These penetrate the skin and leave eggs inside the body. In contrast, the worm eggs of soil-transmitted helminths can be distributed by eating vegetables which are not carefully washed or cooked (WHO 2007c, p. 3). Moreover, helminths can be directly transmitted by unwashed hands. Therefore, young children who crawl around on the ground are at high risk (WHO 2007c, p. 4).

Since lacks of sanitation and of safe water are common concerns in the developing world, the majority of parasitic diseases can be found there as depicted in Fig. 5.1.

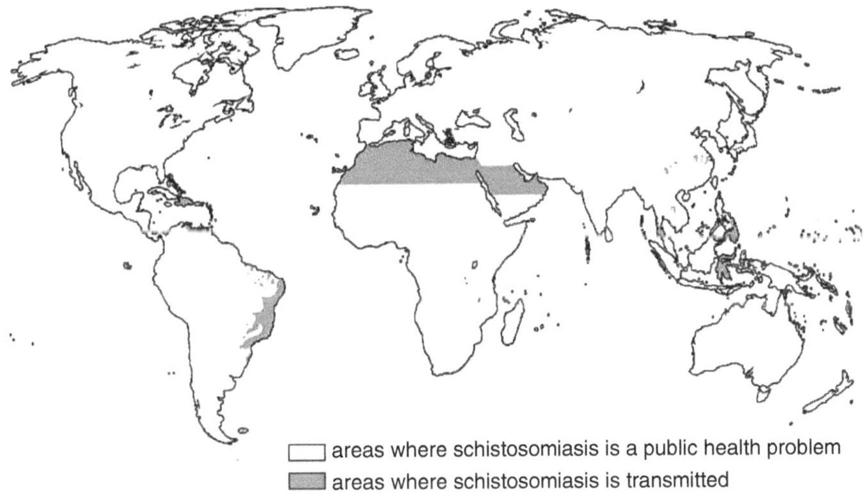

Fig. 5.1 The distribution of schistosomiasis
Source: WHO (2007b)

Comparing this illustrated epidemiological distribution to that of HIV/AIDS, a striking feature is the similarity in geographic incidence. These snapshots indicate links between parasitic and infectious diseases. Clinical characteristics of schistosomiasis imply that it could be one of the most significant parasite co-factors of HIV (Stillwaggon 2006b, p. 174). This follows from its biological effects on the immune system of infected people. Schistosomiasis disrupts genital epithelium which is an effective barrier to viral transmission (Feldmeier et al. 1994, p. 368, 1995b, p. 9). As a result, the likelihood to transmit HIV enhances (Poggensee et al. 1999, p. 380, 2000, pp. 1212–1213; Poggensee and Feldmeier 2001, p. 204). In addition, genital schistosomiasis does not only increase the spread of HIV, it also raises the susceptibility to the virus for HIV-negative people because genital lesions bleed easily (Feldmeier et al. 1994, pp. 368–369). In contrast to other STIs, which are also co-factors of HIV, lesions from schistosomiasis can already be found in children before their first sexual intercourse (Feldmeier et al. 1995a, p. 237, 1995b, p. 9). Consequently, a high prevalence of schistosomiasis within this age-group is worrying because it possesses the potential to drive HIV/AIDS epidemics once those people start to be sexually active.

Prospective studies that confirm this observation are not available because of lacking data. The analysis of biological mechanisms between parasitic diseases and HIV/AIDS is also complicated as comparison groups are often missing. This results from the fact that this kind of infection is ubiquitous in the developing world. Thus, it is almost impossible to detect populations who are not infected with parasites. Therefore, the hypothesis of interrelationships has to be derived from snapshots as illustrated in Fig. 5.1.

In contrast to schistosomiasis, the impact of soil-transmitted helminths on HIV is evidenced. The recent immigration of Ethiopian Jews to Israel at the beginning of the

1990s offered an unique possibility to identify the synergy between a parasitic disease and HIV/AIDS since some of them were HIV-positive. The majority of these immigrants was infected with helminth parasites. Thus, the capability of their immune system to respond was diminished, even if they were not infected with HIV (Borkow et al. 2000, pp. 1053, 1058; Bentwich et al. 2000, p. 2075). To test the interrelationship between helminth infections and HIV, Ethiopian immigrants received anti-helminthic treatment after their arrival in Israel. It was found that HIV-negative individuals were highly susceptible to HIV before they received any therapy (Bentwich et al. 1999, pp. 188, 190). People who were infected with HIV and had at least one parasitic disease suffered from an enhanced HIV replication to full-blown AIDS before their illness was treated (Bentwich et al. 1999, p. 189). However, after treatment, these effects could be mitigated (Wolday et al. 2002, p. 58).

These explanations do not only reinforce the hypothesis about a linkage between parasites and HIV, but also indicates the importance of deworming in anti-HIV programmes. As we know from the survey of immigrated Ethiopians, treatment is conducive to prevent soil-transmitted helminths and, thus, reduces the susceptibility to a HIV-infection. In addition, curing parasitic diseases can be realised at low costs and thus, it is preferable in developing countries those governments face scarce financial resources. For example, costs for deworming are about US $ 0.20 per capita per year (WHO 2005b, p. 1). The need to implement such a treatment is also strengthened by considering its possible positive spillovers on the nutrition status which is a co-factor for HIV itself as will be discussed below.

5.1.2 The Relationship Between Malnutrition and HIV/AIDS

The implications of malnutrition on the transmission of infectious diseases have been recognised before the first AIDS cases were reported. In the late 1960s, the WHO acknowledged the importance of food security for prevention in its monograph “Interactions of nutrition and infections” (Scrimshaw et al. 1968). In the course of time, the specific mechanisms between poor nutrition and infectious diseases have been detected. In the following, malnutrition is defined as deficiencies in macronutrients like a low protein and energy consumption and vitamin malnutrition (micronutrition).

Macronutrient deficiencies, for example, increase the vulnerability to other infections like other STIs or tuberculosis because of a weakened immune system. Since these diseases are co-factors of HIV, susceptibility to HIV increases (Stillwaggon 2006b, p. 171). Moreover, the progression from HIV to AIDS will be accelerated (Stillwaggon 2005, p. 12). A comparable impact results from deficiencies in micronutrients. Numerous case studies have shown that a low intake of vitamins A, B and E is associated with an increased HIV progression (Semba and Tang 1999, p. 185; Tang et al. 1993, p. 945). Particularly, a deficiency of vitamin A possesses a negative impact on HIV/AIDS (Tang et al. 1993, p. 945; Semba et al. 1994, p. 1593). Studies have indicated that a low level may increase the risk of

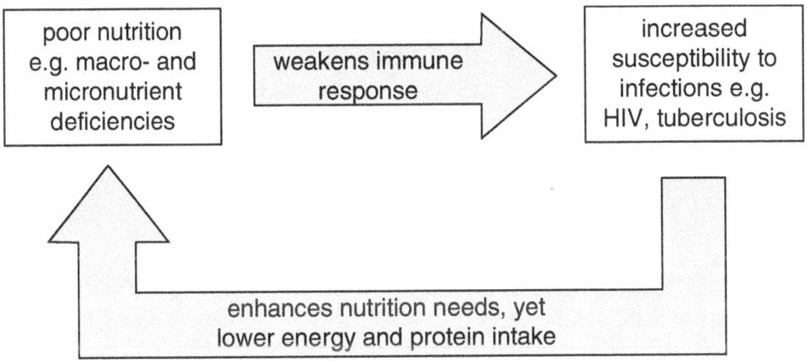

Fig. 5.2 The relationship between malnutrition and HIV/AIDS

a mother-to-child transmission because of an impaired placental integrity (Semba et al. 1994, p. 1596; WHO 2004b, p. 3; Dreyfuss and Fawzi 2002, p. 965; Greenberg[2] et al. 1997). Moreover, children can be infected through breastfeeding because breast milk can contain the virus (Semba et al. 1994, p. 1596, 1999, p. 96; Semba 2000, p. 158; Dreyfuss and Fawzi 2002, p. 965).

To sum up, deficiencies in malnutrition and micronutrition weaken the immune system and, hence, people are more vulnerable to any infectious disease like tuberculosis or even HIV. In addition, these infections have repercussions on nutrition. HIV, for example, reduces the food intake due to a loss of appetite (Mcallan et al. 1995, p. 87; Marston and de Cock 2004, p. 79). Therefore, a biological interrelationship as depicted in Fig. 5.2 exists.

However, in contrast to other infectious diseases, the occurrence of HIV/AIDS has increased the number of incidences and the severity of pre-existing malnutrition. Several studies have shown that households affected by HIV/AIDS need to substitute labour-intensive, but nutritious crops for less nutritious crops like roots and tubers if family members become sick (Food and Agriculture Organization (FAO) 2001, p. 7; 2002a, p. 8; Hamusimbi et al. 2006, p. 30). Productivity will additionally be reduced through the loss of knowledge about farming methods if parents die before their agricultural skills can be transferred to their children (FAO 2002a, p. 8, 2002b). In this case, food intake can diminish and, if so, nutritional deficiencies will worsen.

5.1.3 *Discussion: The Role of ODA*

Regional shortcomings such as missing access to safe drinking water and sanitation as well as deficiencies in nutrition have a negative impact on the global AIDS

[2] The study of Greenberg et al. (1997) determines whether or not deficiencies in vitamin A are associated with an increased mother-to-child-transmission. The analysis is carried out in two areas in the U.S., Baltimore and the Bronx.

problem. Since the discussed international transfer mechanisms from Chap. 4 do not address these constraints, traditional development assistance should be supplied to reduce these consequences. However, recent studies indicate that the share of ODA allocated to transnational public goods has increased whereas regional shortcomings were neglected (te Velde et al. 2002; Anand 2004).

One of the first studies that estimated the extent of aid diversion was conducted by Raffer (1999). By using the Credit Reporting System (CRS) which was implemented by the Organisation of Economic Cooperation and Development (OECD), Raffer observes that the share of funding for transnational public goods has been increased in the 1990s (from 12% in 1991 to 26% in 1997) (Raffer 1999, Table 1 and p. 15). Moreover, the analysis infers that the share of public goods in ODA started to move up to 40% (Raffer 1999, p. 12). Similar results were found by te Velde et al. (2002, p. 128). They estimate that aid for providing transnational public goods has more than doubled from 16.22% in 1980–1982 up to 38.19 in 1996–1998. The same was found for the interaction between ODA and the finance of health-promoting public goods. The steepest increase in the share of funding was found from 4.10% in 1980–1982 to 11.40% in 1996–1998 (te Velde et al. 2002, p. 133, 135).

Such a crowding out is serious because shortcomings in nutrition and sanitation have the potential to drive HIV/AIDS epidemics. Furthermore, if aid declines which is supposed to reduce poverty or to build up the infrastructure of developing countries, the benefits from an increased transnational public good provision level will diminish (Sandler and Arce 2007, p. 528).[3] For example, the supply of health-promoting public goods like measures to limit tuberculosis or care for sick people is complicated in an environment where hygienic standards cannot be ensured. The treatment of people like the intake of drugs requires water. In addition, behaviour-changing interventions like school-based education or public awareness campaigns will not make sense if people do not understand it. For example, illiterate men and women cannot read newspapers and thus cannot adopt preventive activities. The same line of reasoning holds if children are not enrolled in school. Hence, their vulnerability to HIV cannot be reduced by schooling.

This brief presentation of some consequences of aid diversion does not only indicate that regional constraints remain an issue if ODA declines. Moreover, the effectiveness of international transfer schemes can decline if regional shortcomings are not addressed. If this is the case, these mechanisms cannot move closer to a Pareto-optimal allocation of health-promoting public goods and thus do not fulfill the criterion of efficiency. However, donors are less interested in financing regional programmes because their benefits seem modest compared to the gains of transnational health-promoting public goods like an AIDS vaccine (Sandler and Arce 2007, p. 541). Therefore, the question of institutional considerations is relevant.

---

[3]A more general discussion can be found in Guillaumont (2002). In addition, Guillaumont takes the impact of the provision of public goods on the effectiveness of ODA into account.

5.2 Institutional Considerations

The principle of subsidiarity states that institutions should coincide with the geographical scope of the externalities of an activity. This coincidence of political jurisdiction and economical consequences means that those who gain from the provision of a public good finance its supply. Choosing the most localised organisation diminishes transaction costs by limiting the number of participants and thus reasons subsidiarity (North 1990, p. 63). Regional institutions can intervene more flexibly than multilaterals with a complex administration and long organisational communication lines. In addition, the fact of integrating less participants increases incentives to keep commitments because identifying and punishing those who do not respect agreements is relatively easy. If this is the case, enforcement costs fall since the willingness to cooperate is fostered in a smaller group of agents. Following the principle of subsidiarity and applying it to the health sector, regional institutions have to address localised shortcomings like deficiencies in nutrition or missing sanitary facilities.

However, it seems that this recommendation is not plausible when considering the variety of international organisations and multilaterals that finance regional interventions. The Food and Agriculture Organisation (FAO) or the World Bank, for example, intervene if regional institutions do not exist or at least do not have sufficient financial capacities to cover the costs. If multilaterals are more suited to resolve regional shortcomings, the subsidiarity principle should not be applied. The same holds if economies of scale are relevant (Sandler 2006, p. 159). With respect to the health sector, a centralised supply of health interventions is preferable if the diminished unit cost exceeds the loss of efficiency in the case of abandoned subsidiarity. Another rationale to supply health measures beyond the most localised organisation results from economies of scope (Sandler 2006, p. 159). These effects result if supplying two or more regional programmes by a single organisation yields lower total costs than providing them separately by different institutions. Therefore, expenditures can be reduced if inputs like staff can be used jointly. If these cost savings are larger than the loss of efficiency from non-coincidence between political and economical domains, turning away from the principle of subsidarity is justified. This line of reasoning can be applied to international non-governmental organizations (NGOs[4]) such as "Action against Hunger" (AAH). The AAH works in regions where malnutrition and HIV are highly prevalent and where access to safe water is missing as well. Although its primary goal is to address malnutrition, interventions are not only focussed on improving the nutritional status (AAH 2008). In contrast to other donors like the Consultative Group on International Agricultural Research (CGIAR), support in the field of water supply and sanitation is additionally carried out (AAH 2008). Therefore, health-related activities in the fields of malnutrition and water supply can be better coordinated and financed because the same resources like staff, knowledge and equipment can be used for different

[4]A NGO is a non-profit, voluntary citizens group.

projects. Consequently, interventions are more efficient because the same programmes do not have multiple support by different donors.

In sum, the presentation of the detracting factors on subsidiarity indicates that this principle is counterproductive whenever missing financial capacity becomes an issue and, hence, localised organisations cannot cover the whole amount of costs. In addition, the principle of subsidarity may not be useful if economies of scale and scope occur. Multilaterals have to finance interventions of regional governments.

5.3 Conclusions

Based on the observation that a policy response cannot be given in isolation from the economic, political and social situation of a country, this chapter serves two purposes. First, it deals with the impact of regional shortcomings like malnutrition and a missing access to safe water and sanitation on the global AIDS concern. Second, it discusses how these interrelationships can be mitigated to ensure effective policy responses.

With respect to the implications of regional constraints on HIV/AIDS, a number of main results and some policy recommendations arise. At first, we find that these pre-existing conditions are linked with HIV/AIDS. The presentation of some biological mechanisms indicates that HIV/AIDS is not an isolated problem and thus cannot be dealt with as such. Therefore, it seems less plausible why deficiencies in nutrition and sanitation which are conducive to the transmission of HIV have rarely been addressed by current anti-HIV-programmes. There are several reasons to explain this failure. Parasitic diseases are ubiquitous in the developing world and, hence its implications on the HIV/AIDS crisis have been considered to a lesser extent or have been even overlooked. A further cause results from the fact that HIV/AIDS has become a global issue and thus too much attention on the importance of transnational interventions exists in recent years. However, even if HIV/AIDS is spread globally and the provision of international health-promoting public goods is justified, it cannot be neglected that HIV remains an infectious disease. As a result, it is influenced by the same regional conditions like any other infection. Therefore, the second basic message of the chapter is that effective policy responses require more than addressing HIV from the transnational perspective. Interventions which focus on regional issues should be fostered as a part of an international response.

This argument is strengthened by considering the impact of regional shortcomings on the effectiveness of international transfers in the second part of this chapter. Our analysis indicates that these deficiencies hamper governments to benefit from an increased transnational public good provision level. An adequate health infrastructure is a prerequisite to absorb health-promoting public goods. Since international transfers only aim at overcoming the underprovision at the transnational level while regional shortcomings are not addressed, the third key recommendation is to supplement other forms of assistance. Furthermore, the discussion by whom these regional interventions have to be financed indicates that the identity of a donor – multilaterals, international NGOs, bilateral donors, etc. – has not only be based on the geographical spillovers of a public good. A centralised organization is preferable if economies of scale or scope exist. Therefore, the decision whether financing institutions should mirror the scope of externalities of an intervention has to be made on a case-by-case basis. For a better understanding of institutional agreements and how best practices can be applied, a more detailed discussion of the interrelationship between multilaterals, governments and NGOs is required.

Chapter 6
Summary and Concluding Remarks

More than 25 years after the first cases of AIDS were reported in Los Angeles, AIDS became one of the major health concerns. Moreover, the prospects graduating from the HIV/AIDS crisis are bleak; it seems that MDG 6 cannot be achieved in most developing countries by 2015. Experiences from the past indicate that the establishment of new financing mechanisms which are initiated to close funding gaps is not entirely effective. Repeated pledges at international conferences to finance the implementation of anti-HIV programmes are not sufficiently binding. Governments that acquit themselves of their promises are not sanctioned since no enforcing authority exists. Motivated by these observations, this book has discussed an alternative approach, advocating the use of existing but ameliorated financing mechanisms to facilitate effective solutions.

The necessity to intervene successfully at the transnational level has been pointed out by the description of the geographical extent of HIV/AIDS and its cross-border externalities in Chap. 2. The concept of international public goods is recommended for analyses with the aim of deriving effective transnational policies. The characterisation of several health interventions from the demand as well as from the supply side shows that activities can vary according to their aggregation technology even if the characteristics on the demand side do not differ. It follows that a simple transformation of preventive and curative measures into health-promoting public goods as currently practised fails and can lead to ineffective provision policies if supply-side characteristics are not explicitly considered. Therefore, it seems useful to analyse the allocative implications of several aggregation technologies in Chap. 3. As a main result of this investigation, we have found that underprovision is not an inherent problem linked with international public goods. The opposite line of reasoning of the academic literature on AIDS results primarily from the standard argument of the public goods literature that the characteristics of non-rivalry and non-excludability result in suboptimality. Modeling allocative aspects of several health interventions like "developing an AIDS vaccine", "knowledge about HIV" and "limiting the domain of tuberculosis" reveals that the efficiency of provision policies is mainly influenced by supply-side characteristics. Based on these analyses we have also identified several causes of

D. Sonntag, *AIDS and Aid,* Contributions to Economics,
DOI 10.1007/978-3-7908-2419-3_6, © Springer-Verlag Berlin Heidelberg 2010

underprovision. In contrast to the economic literature with respect to HIV/AIDS explaining existing shortcomings as an outcome of insufficient incentives, our analysis indicates that missing capacity becomes a concern in the case of non-additive aggregation technologies. As a consequence, incentive-compatible mechanisms to overcome weak or missing willingness to provide health interventions as suggested by parts of the academic literature on AIDS are less suitable to address capacity problems.

By contrast, we have proceeded by discussing several international bi- and multilateral transfers as a means to solve underprovision. Starting with unconditional income transfers, our analysis identifies several reasons why the neutrality theorem fails and thus, income policies are justified. We have found that financial support has a positive impact on the provision level by considering corner solutions. For example, some governments have not implemented programmes to educate people about HIV. The same holds by allowing for cost differentials in providing the public good "knowledge about HIV". We show that unconditional financial support can only increase the overall provision level if income is redistributed from less to more cost-efficient agents. This outcome indicates that financial assistance given to build up educational campaigns in developing countries raises concerns if these governments do not have a cost advantage in supplying them. A completely new line of policy recommendations arises because reversing the direction of international assistance is effective. However, this result also indicates the limits of our model because a reversed financial support seems problematic from an equity point of view. Therefore, it remains uncertain whether or not this recommendation is politically feasible. Furthermore, we find that the neutrality theorem does not hold in the cases of limiting the domain of tuberculosis and developing an AIDS vaccine. This reinforces the argument of the literature that non-additive aggregation technologies are crucial for the establishment of non-neutrality. In detail, we demonstrate that the capacity of developing countries has to be scaled up in the weakest-link case because the transnational prevention level is determined by the smallest contribution. In contrast to the weakest-link, the overall provision of the best-shot public good "developing an AIDS vaccine" will increase if financial resources are transferred to the research team that is most cost-efficient in R&D. It follows that targeting financial resources to R&D institutions in low and middle-income countries is not effective. This contradicts recommendations which are based on the epidemiology of HIV/AIDS. IAVI, for example, advises to strengthen the establishment of vaccine trials in low and middle-income countries.

Acknowledging the criticism that the effectiveness of lump-sum transfers diminishes since recipients often cannot mobilise domestic resources to use financial support, we have analysed under which circumstances in-kind transfers are preferable. This investigation casts new light on the discussion of efficiency of transfer schemes because the central assumption of a summation technology has impeded such a comparison. The main findings of this analysis are as follows. First, both the investigation of the weakest-link and the best-shot case reveal that the relative price of providing a health intervention determines which strategy, in-kind or income transfers has to be chosen. Second, we have replicated the results of the literature for the weakest-link case arguing that donors have to step in developing countries and provide preventive health measures themselves only if they have cost advantages. An economic laboratory experiment has confirmed that implemented policies are not effective since donors have strong incentives to provide in-kind transfers even in cases in which financial support is preferable. Third, especially the analysis in the best-shot case "developing an AIDS vaccine", which has not been modeled so far, challenges several policy responses practised today. Referring to our model, in-kind transfers will be less stimulative to increase transnational efforts in R&D if transfer-recipients do not possess a cost advantage. However, assistance like equipping laboratories in low and middle-income countries or knowledge transfers is carried out although HIV vaccine research is done at higher cost in most of these countries.

The analysis has proceeded by discussing international support given by multilateral organisations. Our attention focuses on the financing mechanism of the Global Fund. We have found that matching grants have a positive impact on the overall public good provision. In addition, it has been demonstrated that the public good provision level in the case of subsidies is higher than with lump-sum transfers because of the price effect generated by a subsidy. However, a subsidy scheme will result in an equivalent allocation to unconditional financial support if the Global Fund fails and thus, funding gaps cannot be closed. Conditional support becomes de facto unconditional. The same line of reasoning results from opportunistic behaviour of recipient countries. To ensure the higher effectiveness of subsidies compared to lump-sum transfers, an alternative approach has been suggested. We have assumed that financial support has to be paid if a minimum provision level has been surpassed. By modeling a two-stage game we have not only shown that a Pareto-efficient outcome can be achieved. Our analyses also revealed why other subsidy mechanisms linking financial support with a threshold have failed. By contrast, the incentives of a transfer-receiving country to behave strategically are reduced in our case because financial support depends on the behaviour of this country.

Although these analyses show that bi- and multilateral transfer mechanisms have a positive impact on the allocation of health-promoting public goods or might even yield a Pareto-efficient outcome, the discussion in Chap. 5 indicates that the effectiveness of these solutions cannot be evaluated isolated from regional problems. We find that shortcomings like deficiencies in nutrition and missing access to water as well as sanitary facilities do not only have biological implications. These constraints also prevent governments gaining from an increased provision of international health-promoting public goods. Thus, the impacts of regional concerns mitigate the effectiveness of international transfer mechanisms.

The results of this book have revealed some weaknesses of implemented anti-HIV policies. Building on these findings, three major implications for international financing policies arise. First, increasing the quantity of funding which is targeted to developing countries is not efficient. Even though HIV/AIDS has originated in the developing world and these governments bear a high financial burden of AIDS, transnational impacts of HIV can no longer be met with policies that are focused on scaling up the capacity of the poor. Interventions which are tailored to the epidemiology of HIV confine the cause of global underprovision to developing countries. By contrast, our analysis has shown that a concentration of R&D resources in industrialised countries is efficient while the epidemiology of HIV reasons that vaccine trials have to be conducted in the developing world. Second, international assistance has to be linked to domestic anti-HIV efforts of recipients. Motivated by the fact that transfer-receiving governments have incentives to behave opportunistically, the dependence of disbursements on the own provision level of transfer-recipients has to be strengthened. Moreover, international financing policies would be more effective if the global HIV/AIDS problem was no longer isolated from regional issues. International support cannot be used effectively in transfer-receiving countries if a health infrastructure is lacking. As a third policy recommendation it follows that regional concerns have to be a priority of anti-HIV policies.

These findings provide some scope for further empirical and theoretical research. Since regional concerns are crucial to ensure best practices of international financing mechanisms and to reduce also aid dependence in the long run, further empirical research has to examine these interrelationships in more detail.[1] A further research direction results from the criticism that our policy recommendations are primarily based on welfare-economic considerations whereas the public choice perspective has not been explicitly considered and thus, it is assumed that benevolent dictators intervene. However, decentralisation processes in the health sector, i.e. the shift of authority and resources from the central Ministry of Health to local institutions, has been observed in low- and middle-income countries (Bossert and Beauvais 2002). In order to analyse the consequences on the effectiveness of national anti-HIV programmes if established vertical health programmes have to be integrated into health services supplied by NGOs or the private sector, institutional determinates of AIDS have to be discussed.[2] Further research is also required in theoretical work since the interests of policymakers and organised pressure groups in industrialised countries as well as the interests of international aid organisations have not been considered so far.

Finally, this book provides a first step to a proper understanding of the functioning of implemented financing mechanisms and their effective refinement. The effective design of international transfers is crucial to overcome shortcomings in anti-HIV programmes and urgently needed against the background of a possible missing of MDG 6.

[1]An empirical analysis of biological and social determinates of AIDS in Central and Eastern Europe can be found in Buehn and Sonntag (2009).

[2]For further discussions about how varying institutional arrangements in the health sector can influence the behaviour of individuals and thus the spread of HIV see Persson and Sjoestedt (2008).

Appendices

Appendix A: Providing Unconditional Income Transfers in a Best-Shot Case

Country 2's maximisation problem can be set as follows:

$$\max_{y_2,t_2} U_2(y_2, G) \quad \text{s.t.} \quad y_2 = I_2 - t_2, \tag{A.1}$$

where t_2 represents country 2's income transfer to country 1.

The overall public good provision level G is influenced by the amount of income that is redistributed from country 2 to 1 because country 1 is the single provider of the best-shot health-promoting public good. It follows $G = G(t_2)$. Consequently, country 2's maximisation problem modifies to:

$$\max_{y_2,t_2} U_2[I_2 - t_2, G(t_2)] \quad \text{s.t.} \quad y_2 = I_2 - t_2. \tag{A.2}$$

Solving leads to:

$$-\frac{\partial U_2}{\partial y_2} + \frac{\partial U_2}{\partial G}\underbrace{\frac{\partial G(t_2)}{\partial t_2}}_{(f_{il})} > 0, \tag{A.3}$$

where f_{1l} is country 1's marginal propensity to provide the health-promoting public good.

Country 2 has an incentive to redistribute income to country 1 as long as its increased utility from a raised public good provision level more than offsets its reduction in utility with respect to its private consumption.

Appendix B: Necessary Feasibility Constraint in a Weakest-Link Case

The necessary feasibility constraint can be obtained if we employ the reasoning of Buchholz and Konrad (1995) to compare different equilibrium allocations of a public good by adding up both budget constraints.

1. Country 1's budget constraint can be expressed as:

$$y_1 + p_1 g_1^1 + p_2 g_1^2 = I_1 + p_2 g_1^2. \tag{B.1}$$

2. Country 2's budget constraint corresponds to:

$$y_2 + p_2 g_2^2 + p_2 g_1^2 + p_1 g_1^1 = I_2 + p_1 g_1^1. \tag{B.2}$$

Summing up (B.1) and (B.2) leads to:

$$y_1 + y_2 + ep_1 g_1^1 + p_2 g_1^2 + p_2 g_2^2 + p_2 g_1^2 + ep_1 g_1^1 - p_2 g_1^2 - ep_1 g_1^1 = eI_1 + I_2. \tag{B.3}$$

Rearranging yields:

$$y_1 + y_2 + ep_1 g_1^1 + p_2 g_1^2 + p_2 g_2^2 = eI_1 + I_2, \tag{B.4}$$

which includes, in contrast to Vicary and Sandler (2002, p. 1516), a nominal exchange rate e because interdependences between countries are taken into account.

By using the fact that $p_1 g_1^1 = 2p_1 g_1^1 - p_1 g_1^1$, the above equation modifies to:

$$y_1 + y_2 + 2ep_1 g_1^1 - ep_1 g_1^1 + p_2 g_1^2 + p_2 g_2^2 = eI_1 + I_2. \tag{B.5}$$

If $G = g_1^2 + g_1^1 = g_2^2$ is true, we obtain:

$$y_1 + y_2 + 2ep_1 g_1^1 - ep_1 g_2^2 + ep_1 g_1^2 + p_2 g_1^2 + p_2 g_2^2 = eI_1 + I_2 \tag{B.6}$$

or, equivalently

$$y_1 + y_2 + 2ep_1 g_1^1 + ep_1 g_1^2 + p_2 g_1^2 = eI_1 + I_2, \tag{B.7}$$

where the term $p_1 g_2^2$ can be expressed as $p_2 g_2^2$ because country 2's per-unit price is p_2.

By considering that $p_1 g_1^2 = 2p_1 g_1^2 - p_1 g_1^2$, (B.7) modifies to:

$$y_1 + y_2 + 2ep_1 g_1^1 + 2ep_1 g_1^2 - ep_1 g_1^2 + p_2 g_1^2 = eI_1 + I_2. \tag{B.8}$$

Rearranging leads to:

$$y_1 + y_2 + 2ep_1 G + (p_2 - ep_1)g_1^2 = eI_1 + I_2, \tag{B.9}$$

where $2ep_1 g_1^1 + 2ep_1 g_1^2 = 2ep_1 g_2^2 = 2ep_1 G$.

In contrast to Vicary and Sandler (2002, p. 1516), (B.9) includes the nominal exchange rate e.

Appendix C: Necessary Feasibility Constraint in a Best-Shot Case

Country 1's and 2's budget constraints are added together to receive the necessary feasibility constraints for the best-shot case.

1. Country 1's budget constraint can be expressed as:

$$y_1 + p_1 g_1^1 + p_2 g_1^2 = I_1 + p_2 g_1^2. \tag{C.1}$$

2. Country 2's budget constraint is:

$$y_2 + p_2 g_1^2 = I_2. \tag{C.2}$$

Summing up (C.1) and (C.2) leads to:

$$y_1 + y_2 + ep_1 g_1^1 + p_2 g_1^2 - p_2 g_1^2 + p_2 g_1^2 = eI_1 + I_2, \tag{C.3}$$

where e represents the nominal exchange rate.

By using the fact that $G = g_1^2 + g_1^1 = g_2^2$, (C.3) can be expressed as:

$$y_1 + y_2 + ep_1 g_2^2 - ep_1 g_1^2 + p_2 g_1^2 = eI_1 + I_2. \tag{C.4}$$

Rearranging yields the necessary feasibility constraint for a best-shot case:

$$y_1 + y_2 + ep_1 G + (ep_1 - p_2)g_1^2 = eI_1 + I_2. \tag{C.5}$$

Appendix D: The Effects of a Subsidy in a Framework of Private Provided Public Goods

A Pareto-improving effect of a subsidy also occurs if interrelations between a subsidised country i and others are taken into account. In order to illustrate such a positive impact on the public good provision level, a case of two groups of countries ($n = 2$) is supposed. The following proposition holds.

Proposition 1. *The provision level of the health-promoting public good "knowledge about HIV" cannot fall if a subsidy has been paid.*

Proof: Assume that $\Delta G<0$. If we define G^* as the public good provision level at the Nash equilibrium before a subsidy is paid and G' refers to the ex-post equilibrium, we obtain $G^*>G'$. Moreover, private consumption has also decreased ($\Delta y_i<0$ for $i = 1,2$) because country i's income expansion path $y_i = h_i(G,p_i)$ is strictly increasing in G.

In order to demonstrate that this case does not exist, we employ Buchholz' and Konrad's reasoning (1995) and add up the budget constraints of both country groups to compare different equilibrium allocations of a health-promoting public good. An equilibrium allocation before a subsidy has been paid can be expressed as:

$$ep_1g_1^* + p_2g_2^* + y_1 + y_2 = eI_1 + I_2, \tag{D.1}$$

where the asterisks are standing for the Nash equilibrium. The variable e represents the nominal exchange rate, i.e., the price of one currency in terms of another (here: country 1's currency is expressed in terms of country 2's currency).[1] The sum of country group 1's and country group 2's contribution to a health-promoting public good and their private consumption must be equal to the sum of both country group's income. Inserting $y_i = h_i(G,p_i)$ into the above equation and considering that $G^* = g_1^* + g_2^*$, we obtain:

$$G^* + \frac{1}{p_1}h_1(G^*,p_1) + \frac{1}{p_2}h_2(G^*,p_2) = \frac{1}{p_1}I_1 + \frac{1}{p_2}I_2. \tag{D.2}$$

If all terms on the left-hand side of (D.2) are continuous and strictly increasing in G^*, (D.2) implicitly determines the Nash equilibrium as a function of both incomes I_1 and I_2 (Buchholz and Konrad (1995, p. 495)).[2]

The equilibrium allocation after a subsidy has been paid can be expressed by

$$G' + \frac{1}{p_1}h_1(G',p_1) + \frac{1}{\hat{p}_2}h_2(G',\hat{p}_2) = \frac{1}{p_1}I_1' - \frac{1}{p_1}sp_2g_2' + \frac{1}{\hat{p}_2}I_2, \tag{D.3}$$

where $\hat{p}_2$ represents the after-subsidy price of country 2. Accordingly, the income of country 1 has been reduced by the subsidy granted to country 2, $I_1' = I_1 - sp_2g_2'$.

[1] Since private consumption y_i represents the numeraire, the nominal exchange rate e can be left.

[2] The nominal exchange rate e can be omitted because all variables are expressed in real terms in (D.2).

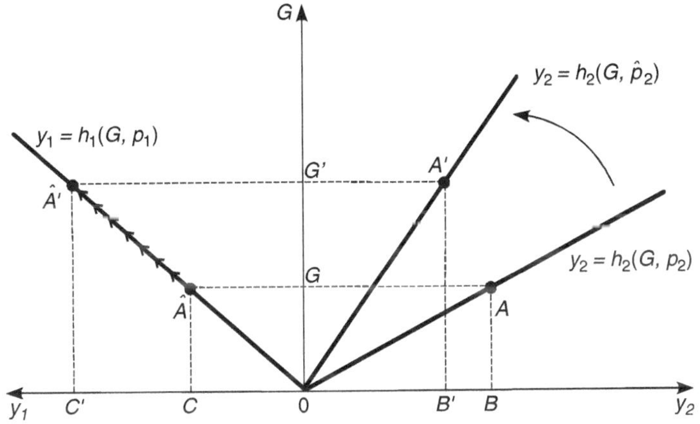

Fig. A1 A subsidy's impact by considering interrelations between countries

Equating (D.2) and (D.3), we obtain:

$$G^* - G' = \frac{1}{p_1} h_1(G', p_1) + \frac{1}{\hat{p}_2}(G', \hat{p}_2) - \left[\frac{1}{p_1} h_1(G^*, p_1) + \frac{1}{p_2} h_2(G^*, p_2)\right]. \quad \text{(D.4)}$$

If $G^* > G'$ the left-hand side will become positive. The right-hand side will be negative if the income expansion paths are strictly increasing in G and if $p_1 > p_2 > \hat{p}_2$. Therefore, (D.4) cannot hold, and, hence, $G^* < G'$ is true.

Such a positive impact of a subsidy on the overall public good provision level is depicted in Fig. A1 that is a more detailed illustration than Fig. 4.6.[3] We have added a second quadrant at the left which represents the subsidising countries's behaviour. Our starting point is at point $A(\hat{A})$ which represents the pre-transfer equilibrium.[4] It is assumed that country group 2 which should be more cost-efficient in providing a health-promoting public good than country group 1 ($p_2 < p_1$) receives a subsidy at stage 1. As a result, its effective per-unit price declines. This can be illustrated by an inward move of its income expansion path as already discussed in Fig. 4.6.

By contrast, country group 1's income expansion path remains unchanged because its effective price has not changed. Yet, it moves outwards to point $\hat{A}'$ due to the increased overall provision level of the health-promoting public good.

---

[3] This depiction follows the figures in Buchholz and Konrad (1995, p. 503) as well as Althammer and Buchholz (1993, p. 402).

[4] If productivity differentials are omitted the overall provision level can be measured by BA and the sum of both country groups´ private consumption can be represented by $OC + OB$, the sum of both country groups´ incomes equals the half of the length of the rectangle's $A\hat{A}BC$ perimeter (Buchholz 1990, p. 103).

In addition, its private consumption y_1 has been raised and thus, it is better off. Country group 2's private consumption y_2 has been reduced as illustrated in Fig. A1. This results from the fact that the slope of its budget line ($\tan\alpha = -1/\hat{p}_2$) becomes steeper after a subsidy has been paid. Consequently, its new indifference curve which would pass through the point A' would be lying below its indifference curve depicting the situation before a transfer has been received. In this case, country group 2 would be worse off and thus is reluctant to accept assistance in the form of a subsidy.[5] Yet, both utilities are growing as long as countries move on their new income expansion paths. If country group 1 finds a voluntary income transfer to country group 2 which is high enough, country 2 is willing to accept the subsidy.[6]

Appendix E: A Modified Samuelson Condition

A multilateral organisation´s maximisation problem can be expressed as follows:

$$\max\left[U_j(y_j, G) + U_i(y_i, G)\right] \tag{E.1}$$

subject to the following constraints:

$$\begin{aligned}
&I_j = y_j + p_j g_j + s p_i g_i,\\
&I_i = y_i + (1-s) p_i g_i,\\
&G = g_j + g_i,\\
&s = \begin{cases} \tilde{s} & \text{if } g_i \geqslant \tilde{g}_i \\ 0 & \text{if } g_i < \tilde{g}_i, \end{cases}\\
&U_i = U_i^N,\\
&y_j, y_i, g_j, g_i \geqslant 0.
\end{aligned} \tag{E.2}$$

It follows from (E.1) and (E.2) that

$$L = U_j(I_j - p_j g_j - s p_i g_i, g_j + g_i) + \lambda\left[U_i(I_i - (1-s) p_i g_i, g_j + g_i) - U_i^N\right], \tag{E.3}$$

where λ is the Lagrange multiplier on the utility constraint.

5 Welfare-reducing subsidies are well-known in the literature (Bergstrom 1989; Buchholz 1990; Ihori 1992).

6 A simulation using CES utility functions confirms this observation. Data are available after request.

The first-order conditions are:

$$\underbrace{\frac{\partial U_j}{\partial g_j}}_{U_G} - \underbrace{p_j \frac{\partial U_j}{\partial y_j}}_{p_j U_{yj}} + \underbrace{\lambda \frac{\partial U_i}{\partial g_j}}_{\lambda V_G} = 0, \tag{E.4}$$

which can also be expressed as:

$$\lambda_j = \frac{-U_G + p_j U_{y_j}}{V_G} \tag{E.5}$$

and

$$\underbrace{\frac{\partial U_j}{\partial g_i}}_{U_G} - \underbrace{s p_i \frac{\partial U_j}{\partial y_j}}_{s p_i U_{yj}} + \lambda \left[\underbrace{\frac{\partial U_i}{\partial g_i}}_{V_G} + \underbrace{(s-1) p_i \frac{\partial U_i}{\partial y_i}}_{(s-1) p_i U_{yi}} \right] = 0, \tag{E.6}$$

which is correspondingly:

$$\lambda_i = \frac{-U_G + s p_i U_{y_j}}{V_G + (s-1) p_i V_{y_i}}. \tag{E.7}$$

By equating λ_1 with λ_2, yields:

$$\frac{-U_G + p_j U_{y_j}}{V_G} = \frac{-U_G + s p_i U_{y_j}}{V_G + (s-1) p_i V_{y_i}}. \tag{E.8}$$

Solving leads to:

$$\begin{aligned} &- U_G V_G - (s-1) p_i V_{y_i} U_G + p_j U_{y_j} V_G + (s-1) p_i p_j U_{y_j} V_{y_i} \\ &= -U_G V_G + s p_i U_{y_j} V_G. \end{aligned} \tag{E.9}$$

Rearranging and we obtain:

$$-(s-1) p_i V_{y_i} U_G + (p_j - s p_i) U_{y_j} V_G + (s-1) p_i p_j U_{y_j} V_{y_i} = 0, \tag{E.10}$$

or, alternatively

$$\frac{\partial U_j / \partial G}{\partial U_j / \partial y_j} + \frac{s - \frac{p_j}{p_i}}{s-1} \frac{\partial U_i / \partial G}{\partial U_i / \partial y_i} = p_j. \tag{E.11}$$

where $\frac{p_j}{p_i}$ represents a real exchange rate. Equation (E.11) reveals that financial support is provided until the sum of the marginal rates of substitution between a health-promoting and a private good equals its per-unit price p_j. Therefore, (E.11) is simple a modified Samuelson condition (Samuelson (1954, p. 387; 1955, p. 354)).

References

Action Against Hunger (AAH). (2008). *Action against hunger's 2008 institutional booklet.* New York: AAH.

African Development Fund. (2006). *Chad. National rural drinking water supply and sanitation programme (PNEAR).* Abidjan: African Development Group.

Ainsworth, M., & Over, M. (1999). *Confronting AIDS: Public priorities in a global epidemic* (2nd ed.). Oxford: Oxford University Press.

Ainsworth, M., et al. (2000). *Accelerating an AIDS vaccine for developing countries: Recommendations for the World Bank.* Washington DC: World Bank.

Althammer, W., & Buchholz, W. (1993). Lindahl-equilibria as the outcome of a non-cooperative game. A reconsideration. *European Journal of Political Economy, 9*, 399–405.

Altman, L. (1982, June 06). Clue found on homosexuals´ precancer syndrome. *The New York Times.*

Anand, P. B. (2004). Financing the provision of global public goods. *World Economy, 27*, 215–237.

Andreoni, J. (1990). Impure alturism and donations to public goods: A theory of warm-glow giving. *The Economic Journal, 100*, 464–477.

Andreoni, J. (1998). Toward a theory of charitable fund-raising. *Journal of Political Economy, 106*, 1186–1213.

Annan, K. (2001). *Speech of Kofi Annan to the fifty-fourth World Health Assembly in Geneva.* The speech is contained in the following volume: Document WHA54/2001/REC/2 a verbatim records of the plenary sessions of the fifty-fourth World Health Assembly.

Arce, D. (2001). Leadership and the aggregation of international collective action. *Oxford Economic Papers, 53*, 114–137.

Arce, D., & Sandler, T. (2001). Transnational public goods: Strategies and institutions. *European Journal of Political Economy, 17*, 493–516.

Arce, D., & Sandler, T. (2002a). Regional public goods: Typologies, provision, financing, and development assistance. *EGDI Studies in Brief, 1*, 1–3.

Arce, D., & Sandler, T. (2002b). *Regional public goods: Typologies, provision, financing, and development assistance.* Stockholm: Almkvist and Wiksell.

Archibugi, D., & Bizzarri, K. (2004). Committing to vaccine R&D: A global science policy priority. *Research Policy, 33*, 1657–1671.

Arhin-Tenkorang, D., & Conceicão, P. (2003). Beyond communicable disease control: Health in the age of globalization. In I. Kaul et al. (Eds.), *Providing global public goods. Managing globalization.* New York: Oxford University Press.

Axelrod, R. (1980a). The effective choice in the Prisoner's Dilemma. *The Journal of Conflict Resolution, 24*, 3–25.

Axelrod, R. (1980b). More effective choice in the Prisoner's Dilemma. *The Journal of Conflict Resolution, 24*, 379–403.

Barrett, S. (2006). Critical factors for providing transnational public goods. In Secretariat of the International Task Force on Global Public Goods (Ed.), *Expert paper series seven: Cross-cutting issues*. Stockholm: International Task Force on Global Public Goods.

Becker, G. (1974). A theory of social interactions. *Journal of Political Economy, 82*, 1063–1093.

Bentwich, Z., Kalinkovich, A., & Weisman, Z. (1999). Immune activation is a dominant factor in the pathogenesis of African AIDS. *Immunology Today, 16*, 187–191.

Bentwich, Z., et al. (2000). Concurrent infections and HIV pathogenesis. *AIDS, 14*, 2071–2081.

Bergstrom, T. (1989). Love and spaghetti, the opportunity cost of virtue. *Journal of Economic Perspectives, 3*, 165–173.

Bergstrom, T., Blume, L., & Varian, H. (1986). On the private provision of public goods. *Journal of Public Economics, 29*, 25–49.

Borkow, G., et al. (2000). Chronic immune activation associated with intestinal helminth infections results in impaired signal transduction and anergy. *The Journal of Clinical Investigation, 106*, 1053–1060.

Bossert, T. J., & Beauvais, J. C. (2002). Decentralisation of health systems in Ghana, Zambia, Uganda and the Philippines: A comparative analysis of decision space. *Health Policy and Planning, 17*, 14–31.

Boulton, I. C., & Gray-Owen, S. D. (2002). Neisserial binding to CEACAM1 arrests the activation and proliferation of CD4+T lymphocytes. *Nature Immunology, 3*, 229–236.

Breyer, F., & Zweifel, P. (1997). *Gesundheitsökonomie* (2nd ed.). Berlin: Springer.

Brown, T., et al. (2001). *Effective prevention strategies in low HIV prevalence settings, U.S. Agency for International Development (USAID), implementing aids prevention and care project (Impact).* Arlington, VA: Family Health International (FHI).

Browne, S. (2006). *Aid and influence. Do donors help or hinder?* London: Cromwell Press.

Buchholz, W. (1990). Gleichgewichtige Allokation öffentlicher Güter. *Finanzarchiv, 48*, 97–126.

Buchholz, W., & Konrad, K. (1995). Strategic transfers and private provision of public goods. *Journal of Public Economics, 57*, 489–505.

Buehn, A., & Sonntag, D. (2009). What expenditure the AIDS epidemics in Central and Eastern Europe? An empirical analysis of biological, institutional and social determinates (mimeo).

Burnside, G., & Dollar, D. (2000). Aid, policies, and growth. *American Economic Review, 90*, 847–868.

Centers for Disease Control and Prevention (CDC). (1981). Pneumocystis pneumonia – Los Angeles. *Morbidity and Mortality Weekly Report, 30*, 1–3.

Centers for Disease Control and Prevention (CDC). (1982a). Opportunistic infections and Kaposi's Sarcoma among Haitians in the United States. *Morbidity and Mortality Weekly Report, 31*, 353–354, 360–361.

Centers for Disease Control and Prevention (CDC). (1982b). Epidemiologic notes and reports pneumocystis carinii pneumonia among persons with Hemophilia A. *Morbidity and Mortality Weekly Report, 31*, 365–367.

Centers for Disease Control and Prevention (CDC). (1982c). Current trends update on Acquired Immune Deficiency Syndrome (AIDS) – United States. *Morbidity and Mortality Weekly Report, 31*, 507–508. 513–514.

Central Intelligence Agency (CIA). (2008). *The 2008 Worldfact book*. Washington DC: CIA. CIA Website: https://www.cia.gov/library/publications/the-world-factbook/index.html.

Chen, L., Evans, T., & Cash, R. (1999). Health as a global public good. In I. Kaul, I. Grunberg, & M. Stern (Eds.), *Global public goods: International cooperation in the 21st century*. New York: Oxford University Press.

Commission of the European Communities (2007) Financing for development – from Monterrey 2002 to Doha 2008. Progress report. (2007). *Is the European Union on track to meet its commitments by 2010?* Brussels: EU.

Commission on Macroeconomics and Health (CMH). (2001). *Macroeconomics and health: Investing in health for economic development*. Geneva: WHO.

Congress of the United States of America. (2008). *Tom Lantos and Henry J. Hyde United States global leadership against HIV/AIDS, tuberculosis, and malaria reauthorization act of 2008*. Washington, DC: Congress of the United States of America.

Conybeare, J., Murdoch, J., & Sandler, T. (1994). Alternative collective-goods models of military alliances: Theory and empirics. *Economic Inquiry, 32*, 525–542.

Corbett, E., et al. (2002). HIV-1/AIDS and the control of other infectious diseases in Africa. *The Lancet, 359*, 2177–2187.

Corbett, E., et al. (2003). The growing burden of tuberculosis. Global trends and interactions with the HIV epidemic. *Archives of Internal Medicine, 163*, 1009–1021.

Cornes, R. (1993). Dyke maintenance and other stories: Some neglected types of public goods. *Quarterly Journal of Economics, 108*, 259–271.

Cornes, R., & Hartley, R. (2006). *Weak links, good shots and other public good games: Building on BBV* (Discussion Paper EDP-0624). Manchester

Cornes, R., & Hartley, R. (2007a). Weak links, good shots and other public good games: building on BBV. *Journal of Public Economics, 91*, 1684–1707.

Cornes, R., & Hartley, R. (2007b). Aggregative public good games. *Journal of Public Economic Theory, 9*, 201–219.

Cornes, R., & Sandler, T. (1984a). Easy riders, joint production, and public goods. *The Economic Journal, 94*, 580–598.

Cornes, R., & Sandler, T. (1984b). The theory of public goods: Non-Nash behaviour. *Journal of Public Economic, 23*, 367–379.

Cornes, R., & Sandler, T. (1985). The simple analytics of pure public good provision. *Economica, 52*, 103–116.

Cornes, R., & Sandler, T. (1996). *The theory of externalities, public goods, and club goods* (2nd ed.). Cambridge: Cambridge University Press.

Dasgupta, P., & Stiglitz, J. (1980). Uncertainty, industrial structure, and the spreed of R&D. *Bell Journal of Economics, 11*, 1–28.

de Walque, D. (2007). How does the impact of an HIV/AIDS information campaign vary with educational attainment? Evidence from rural Uganda. *Journal of Development Economics, 84*, 686–714.

Department for International Development (DFID). (2001). *HIV/AIDS Strategy 2001*. London: DFID.

Department of HIV/AIDS Family and Community Health. (2003). *Global health-sector strategy for HIV/AIDS: 2003–2007. Providing a framework for partnership and action*. Geneva: WHO.

Dikhanov, Y. (2005). *Trends in global income distribution, 1970–2000, and scenarios for 2015. Human Development Report Office – Occasional paper*. New York: UNDP.

Divisions of HIV/AIDS Prevention (DHAP). (2005). *Living with HIV/AIDS*. Atlanta: CDC.

Doucouliagos, H., & Paldam, M. (2009). The aid effectiveness literature: The sad results of 40 years of research. *Journal of Economic Surveys, 23*, 433–461.

Doucouliagos, H., & Paldam, M. (2007). *Conditional aid effectiveness. A meta-study* (Working Paper 2005-14).

Dreher, A., & Gaston, N. (2008). Has globalization increased inequality? *Review of International Economics, 16*, 516–536.

Dreyfuss, M. L., & Fawzi, W. W. (2002). Micronutrients and vertical transmission of HIV-1. *The American Journal of Clinical Nutrition, 75*, 959–970.

Easterly, W., Levine, R., & Roodman, D. (2003). New data, new doubts: A comment on Burnside and Dollar's aid. *American Economic Review, 94*, 774–780.

Engqvist, L. (2001). Final EU statement at UNGASS on HIV/AIDS. *Statement by Mr. Lars Engqvist, Swedish Minister for Health and Social Affairs*. UN Website: http://www.un.int/sweden/pages/eu/state_eu/stjune25.htm. Accessed on 2009, January 26.

European Centre for Epidemiological Monitoring of HIV/AIDS (EuroHIV) et al. (2007). *HIV/AIDS Surveillance in Europe* (Mid-year report 2007). Saint-Maurice: Institut de Veille Sanitaire.

Evans, D. (2004). Communicable diseases: Perspective paper. In B. Lomborg (Ed.), *Global crisis, global solutions*. Cambridge: Cambridge University Press.

Feldmeier, H., Krantz, I., & Poggensee, G. (1994). Female genital schistosomiasis as a risk-factor for the transmission of HIV. *International Journal of STD and AIDS, 5*, 368–372.

Feldmeier, H., Krantz, I., & Poggensee, G. (1995). Female genital schistosomiasis: A neglected risk factor for the transmission of HIV? *Transactions of the Royal Society of Tropical Medicine and Hygiene, 89*, 237.

Feldmeier, H., et al. (1995). Female genital schistosomiasis. *New challenges from a gender perspective. Tropical and geographical medicine, 47*, 2–15.

Fleming, D., & Wasserheit, J. (1999). From epidemiological synergy to public health policy and practice: The contribution of other sexually transmitted diseases to sexual transmission of HIV infection. *Sexually Transmitted Infections, 75*, 3–17.

Food and Agriculture Organization (FAO) (2001). The impact of HIV/AIDS on food security. FAO Website: http://www.fao.org/DOCREP/MEETING/003/Y0310E.HTM. Accessed on 2009, January 26.

Food and Agriculture Organization (FAO) (2002a). HIV/AIDS, agriculture and food security in mainland and small island countries of Africa. FAO Website: http://www.fao.org/DOCREP/MEETING/004/Y6059E.HTM. Accessed on 2009, January 26.

Food and Agriculture Organization (FAO). (2002b). *HIV/AIDS, food security and rural livelihoods*. Rome: FAO.

Greenberg, B., et al. (1997). Vitamin A deficiency and maternal-infant transmission of HIV in two metropolitan areas in the United States. *AIDS, 11*, 325–332.

Gregor, M. (2008). On the strategic non-complementarity of complements. *Economics Bulletin, 8*, 1–7.

Guillaumont, P. (2002). Linkages between official development assistance and global public goods. In I. Kaul, K. L. Goulven, & M. Schnupf (Eds.), *Global public goods financing: new tools for new challenges. A policy dialogue*. New York: United Nations Development Programme (UNDP).

Hamers, F., et al. (2006). HIV/AIDS in Europe: Trends and EU-wide priorities. *Eurosurveillance Weekly Release, 11*, 3083.

Hamusimbi, C., Mataa, M., & Jere, G. (2006). *Impact of HIV and AIDS on agriculture and food security in SADC. The case of Zambia* (FANRPAN working document No. NAT ZAM002). Pretoria: FANRPAN.

Harms, G., & Feldmeier, H. (2002). HIV infection and tropical parasitic diseases – Deleterious interactions in both directions? *Tropical Medicine and International Health, 7*, 479–488.

Harrison, G., & Hirshleifer, J. (1989). An experimental evaluation of weakest link/best shot models of public goods. *Journal of Political Economy, 97*, 201–225.

Health Protection Agency (HPA). (2006). *A complex picture. HIV and other sexually transmitted infections in the United Kingdom: 2006*. London: HPA.

Health Protection Agency (HPA). (2007). *Testing times: HIV and other sexually transmitted infections in the United Kingdom: 2007*. London: HPA.

Health Protection Agency (HPA). (2008). *HIV in the United Kingdom: 2008 Report*. London: HPA.

Hecht, R., Becker, J., & Roca, E. (2006). AIDS vaccine research today. A deeper partnership between countries. *The New Magazine of the Global Health Council, 138*(4–5), 16.

Hirshleifer, J. (1983). From weakest-link to best-shot: The voluntary provision of public goods. *Public Choice, 41*, 371–386.

Hirshleifer, J. (1985). From weakest-link to best-shot: Correction. *Public Choice, 46*, 221–223.

HIV Vaccines and Microbicides Resource Tracking. (2008). *Sustaining the HIV prevention research agenda: Funding for research and development of HIV vaccines, microbicides and other new prevention options 2000 to 2007*. New York: AVAC.

HM Treasury, Department for International Development (DFID). (2004). *International finance facility proposal*. London: HM Treasury.

Ihori, T. (1992). Impure public goods and transfers in a three-agent model. *Journal of Public Economics, 48*, 385–401.
Ihori, T. (1996). International public goods and contribution productivity differentials. *Journal of Public Economics, 61*, 139–154.
Ihori, T. (2005). Weakest link and best shots. (mimeo).
International AIDS Vaccine Initiative (IAVI). (2004). *Scientific blueprint 2004: Accelerating global efforts in AIDS vaccine research and development*. New York: IAVI.
International AIDS Vaccine Initiative (IAVI). (2006). *AIDS vaccine blueprint 2006: Actions to strengthen global research and development*. New York: IAVI.
International AIDS Vaccine Initiative (IAVI). (2008). *Ongoing trials of preventive AIDS vaccines*. New York: IAVI.
International Bank for Reconstruction and Development (IBRD), World Bank. (2004). *Global monitoring report 2004. Policies and actions for achieving the millennium development goals and related outcomes*. Washington DC: World Bank.
International Organization for Migration (IOM). (2008). *World migration 2008: Managing labour mobility in the evolving global economy*. Geneva: IOM.
Jacquet, P., & Marniesse, S. (2006). Financing global public goods: Issues and prospects. In Secretariat of the International Task Force on Global Public Goods (Ed.), *Expert paper series seven: Cross-cutting issues*. Stockholm: International Task Force on Global Public Goods.
Jamison, D., Frenk, J., & Kaul, F. (1998). International collective action in health: Objectives, functions, and rationale. *Lancet, 351*, 514–517.
Jayaraman, R., & Kanbur, R. (1999). International public goods and the case for foreign aid. In I. Kaul, I. Grunberg, & M. Stern (Eds.), *Global public goods: International cooperation in the 21st century*. New York: Oxford University Press.
John, K. D., & Ruebbelke, D. (2007). *Development aid and environmental protection*. Frankfurt am Main: Peter Lang Verlag.
Kanbur, R., Sandler, T., & Morrison, K. (1999). *The future of development assistance: Common pools and international public goods*. (Essay No. 25). Washington DC: Overseas Development Council.
Kaul, I. (2002). *Profiling the provision status of global public goods*. New York: UNDP.
Kaul, I. (2005). *Global public goods: A key to achieving the millennium development goals*. New York: UNDP.
Kaul, I., & Faust, M. (2001). Global public goods and health: Taking the agenda forward. *Bulletin of the World Health Organisation, 79*, 869–874.
Kaul, I., Grunberg, I., & Stern, M. (1999). *Global Public Goods: International co-operation in the 21st century*. New York: Oxford University Press.
Kemp, M. (1984). A note of the theory of international transfers. *Economics Letters, 14*, 259–262.
Killick, T. (2005). Don´t throw money to Africa. *IDS Bulletin, 26*, 14–19.
Kremer, M. (1998). AIDS: The economic rationale for public intervention. In M. Ainsworth, L. Fransen, & M. Over (Eds.), *Confronting AIDS: Evidence from the developing world*. Brussels: European Commission.
Kremer, M. (2006). Global public goods in communicable disease control. In Secretariat of the International Task Force on Global Public Goods (Ed.), *Expert paper series one: Infectious disease*. Stockholm: International Task Force on Global Public Goods.
Kremer, M. (2007). *Creating markets for new vaccines. Part I: Rationales* (Working Paper).
Lamptey, P., Zeitz, P., & Larivee, C. (2001). *Strategies for an expanded and comprehensive response (ECR) to a national HIV/AIDS epidemic: A handbook for designing and implementing HIV/AIDS programs*. Arlington, VA: FHI.
Lei, V., Tucker, S., & Vesely, F. (2006). Foreign aid and weakest-link international public goods: An experimental study. *European Economic Review, 51*, 599–623.
Lewis, M. (2005). A war chest for fighting HIV/AIDS. *Finance and Development, 42*, 38–41.
Loewenson, R., & Whiteside, A. (2002). *HIV/AIDS: Implications for poverty reduction* (UNDP policy paper). New York.

Marston, B., & de Cock, K. (2004). Multivitamins, nutrition, and antiretroviral therapy for HIV disease in Africa. *The New England Journal of Medicine, 1*, 78–80.

Marx, J. (1982). New disease baffle medical community. *Science, 13*, 618–621.

Mathers, C., et al. (2005). *Uncertainty and data availability for the global burden of disease estimates 2000–2002. Evidence and information for Policy* (Working Paper). Geneva: WHO.

Mcallan, D., et al. (1995). Energy expenditure and wasting in human immunodeficiency virus infection. *The New England Journal of Medicine, 2*, 83–88.

Milanovic, B. (2005). *World apart: Global and international inequality, 1950–2000*. Princeton, NJ: Princeton University Press.

Milanovic, B. (2007). *An even higher global inequality than previously thought. A note on global inequality calculations using the 2005 ICP results* (Policy Research Working Paper). Washington DC: World Bank.

Mills, A. (2001). *Technology and science as global public goods: Tackling priority diseases of poor countries*. Washington DC: World Bank.

Mills, A., & Shillcutt, S. (2004). Communicable diseases. In B. Lomborg (Ed.), *Global crisis, global solutions*. Cambridge: Cambrigde University Press.

Ministry of Health China. (2006). *2005 update on the HIV/AIDS epidemic and response in China*. Beijing: Ministry of Health, UNAIDS and WHO.

Murray, C. (1996). Rethinking DALYs. In C. Murray & A. Lopez (Eds.), *The global burden of disease*. Havard: Havard University Press.

Murray, C., & Lopez, A. (1996). *Global Burden of Disease. A comprehensive assessment of mortality and disability from diseases, injuries, and risk factors in 1990 and projected to 2020*. Harvard: Harvard University Press.

Musgrave, R. A., Musgrave, P. B., & Kullmer, L. (1994). *Die öffentlichen Finanzen in Theorie und Praxis* (6th ed.). Tübingen: J.C.B Mohr Verlag.

National AIDS Manual (NAM) (2002). Impact of immigration and international travel on HIV in UK. NAM Website: http://www.aidsmap.com/cms1007180.asp?type=preview. Accessed on 2009, January 26.

Nicoll, A., & Godfrey-Faussett, P. (1999). HIV and tuberculosis in the Commonwealth. *BMJ, 319*, 1086.

North, D. C. (1990). *Institutions, institutional change and economic performance*. Cambridge: Cambridge University Press.

Oberender, P., & Fleckenstein, J. (2004). *HIV/AIDS-PrŠvention als globale Herausforderung: Eine institutionenǒkonomische Analyse* (discussion paper 01-04). Bayreuth.

Office of the United States Global AIDS Coordinator. (2006). *Country profile – Uganda*. Washington DC: PEPFAR.

Office of the United States Global AIDS Coordinator. (2007). *Country profile – Uganda*. Washington DC: PEPFAR.

Olsen, M. (1965). *The logic of collective action*. Cambridge: Harvard University Press.

Organisation for Economic Cooperation and Development (OECD) (2008). Aid activities in support of HIV/AIDS control. Aid Activities (CRS) database:http://stats.oecd.org/WBOS/Index.aspx?DatasetCode=CRSNEW. Accessed on 2009, January 26.

Organisation for Economic Cooperation and Development (OECD), The Joint United Nations Programme on HIV/AIDS (UNAIDS). (2004). *Analysis of aid in support of HIV/AIDS control, 2000-2002*. Paris: OECD.

Pallangyo, K. J. (2001). Clinical features of tuberculosis among adults in Sub-saharan Africa in the 21st century. *Scandinavian Journal of Infectious Diseases, 33*, 488–493.

Pareto, V. (1906). *Manuale di economia politica*. New York: Augustus M Kelley. Revised and 1971 translated into English as Manual of political economy.

Persson, A., & Sjoestedt, M. (2008). *Government structures and behavior change in the politics of HIV/AIDS* (QoG Working Paper No. 10). Gothenburg.

Piot, P. (2005). *Speech of Dr. Peter Piot in New Delhi, India, 21th November 2005*. Geneva: UNAIDS.

Poggensee, G., & Feldmeier, H. (2001). Female genital schistosomiasis: Facts and hypotheses. *Acta Tropica, 79*, 193–210.

Poggensee, G., Feldmeier, H., & Krantz, I. (1999). Schistosomiasis of the female genital tract: Public health aspects. *Parasitology Today, 15*, 378–381.

Poggensee, G., et al. (2000). Female genital schistosomiasis of the lower genital tract: Prevalence and disease-associated morbidity in Northern Tanzania. *Journal of Infectious Diseases, 181*, 1210–1213.

Population Reference Bureau. (2007a). *2007 World population data sheet.* Washington DC: Population Reference Bureau.

Population Reference Bureau. (2007b). World population highlights. Key findings from PRB's 2007. World population data sheet. *Population Bulletin, 62*, 1–12.

Raffer, K. (1999). *ODA and global public goods: A trend analysis of past and present spending patters.* New York: Office of Development Studies, United Nations Development Programme (UNDP).

Ramachandran, V., Shah, M. K., & Turner, G. (2006). *Does the private sector care about AIDS? Evidence from Investment Climate Surveys in East Africa* (Working paper No. 76). Washington DC.

Riddell, R. C. (2007). *Does foreign aid really work?* Oxford: Oxford University Press.

Rojanapithayakorn, W., & Hanenberg, R. (1996). The 100% condom program in Thailand. *AIDS, 10*, 1–7.

Rotchford, K., et al. (2000). Effect of coinfection with STDs and of STD treatment on HIV shedding in genital-tract secretions: Systematic review and data synthesis. *Sexually Transmitted Diseases, 27*, 243–248.

Ruebbelke, D. (2005). Der Schutz globaler Umweltgüter und internationale Transfers. *Zeitschrift für Umweltpolitik und Umweltrecht, 1*, 65–78.

Sala-i-Martin, X. (2002). *The disturbing "rise" of world income inequality* (NBER Working Paper 8904). Cambridge: National Bureau of Economic Research.

Samuelson, P. (1954). The pure theory of public expenditure. *The Review of Economics and Statistics, 36*, 387–389.

Samuelson, P. (1955). A diagrammatic exposition of a theory of public expenditure. *The Review of Economics and Statistics, 37*, 350–356.

Sandler, T. (1978). Interregional and intergenerational spillover awareness. *Scottish Journal of Political Economy, 25*, 273–284.

Sandler, T. (1992). *Collective action: Theory and applications.* Ann Arbor, MI: University of Michigan Press.

Sandler, T. (1997). *Global Challenges: An approach to environmental, political, and economic problems.* Cambridge: Cambridge University Press.

Sandler, T. (2001a). Understanding global public goods. *OECD Observer, 228*, 15–18.

Sandler, T. (2001b). Financing international public goods. In M. Ferroni & A. Mody (Eds.), *International public goods: Incentives, measurement, and financing.* Dordrecht: Kluwer.

Sandler, T. (2002). On financing global and international public goods. In M. Ferroni & A. Mody (Eds.), *International public goods: Incentives, measurement, and financing.* Boston: Kluwer.

Sandler, T. (2003). Assessing the optimal provision of public goods. In search of the Holy Grail. In I. Kaul et al. (Eds.), *Providing global public goods.* Oxford: Oxford University Press.

Sandler, T. (2004). Regional public goods: Demand and institutions. In A. Estevadeordal, B. Frantz, & T. R. Nguyen (Eds.), *Regional public goods. From theory to practise.* Washington, DC: IDB.

Sandler, T. (2006). Regional public goods and regional cooperation. In Secretariat of the International Task Force on Global Public Goods (Ed.), *Meeting global challenges: International cooperation in the national interest: Cross-cutting issues.* Stockholm: Secretariat.

Sandler, T., & Arce, D. (2002). A conceptual framework for understanding global and transnational public goods for health. *Fiscal Studies, 23*, 195–222.

Sandler, T., & Arce, D. (2007). New face of development assistance: Public goods and changing ethics. *Journal of International Development, 19*, 527–544.

Sandler, T., & Sargent, K. (1995). Management of transnational commons: Coordination, publicness, and treaty formation. *Land Economics, 71*, 145–162.

Scrimshaw, N., Taylor, C., & Gordon, J. (1968). *Interactions of nutrition and infections*. Geneva: WHO.

Semba, R. (2000). Mastitis and transmission of human immunodeficiency virus through breast milk. *Annals of the New York Academy of Sciences, 918*, 156–162.

Semba, R., & Tang, A. (1999). Micronutrients and the pathogenesis of human immunodeficiency virus infection. *British Journal of Nutrition, 81*, 181–189.

Semba, R., et al. (1994). Maternal vitamin A deficiency and mother-to-child transmission of HIV-1. *Lancet, 343*, 1593–1597.

Semba, R., et al. (1999). Human Immunodeficiency Virus load in breast milk, mastitis, and mother-to-child transmission in Human Immunodeficiency Virus Type 1. *Journal of Infectious Diseases, 180*, 93–98.

Shibata, H. (1971). A bargaining model of pure theory of public expenditure. *Journal of Political Economy, 79*, 1–29.

Sinka, K., et al. (2003). Impact of HIV epidemic in Sub-Saharan Africa on the pattern of HIV in the UK. *AIDS, 17*, 1683–1690.

Smith, R., & MacKellar, L. (2007). Global public goods and the global health agenda: Problems, priorities and potential. *Globalization and Health, 3*, 9.

Smith, R., et al. (2003). *Global public goods for health. Health economic and public health perspectives*. New York: Oxford University Press.

Smith, R., et al. (2004). Communicable disease control: A 'global public good' perspective. *Health Policy and Planning, 19*, 271–278.

Sonntag, D. (2009a). Providing global public goods against AIDS – A public good approach. In D. Duffy & E. Shinnick (Eds.), *Public goods, public policy and taxation: An European perspective*. Berlin: LIT.

Sonntag, D. (2009b). Financing vaccine research in developing countries – A public good approach. In D. Duffy & E. Shinnick (Eds.), *Public goods, public policy and taxation: An European perspective*. Berlin: LIT.

Stansfield, S. K., et al. (2002). *Innovative financing of international public goods for health* (CMH Working Group 2, Working Paper 22).

Stiglitz, J. E. (1999). Knowledge as a global public good. In I. Kaul, I. Grunberg, & M. Stern (Eds.), *Global Public Goods: International co-operation in the 21st century*. New York: Oxford University Press.

Stillwaggon, E. (2005). Impacts of food and nutrition insecurity on the spread of HIV. In S. Gillespie & S. Kadiyala (Eds.), *HIV/AIDS and food and nutrition security. From evidence to action*. Washington DC: IFPRI.

Stillwaggon, E. (2006a). *AIDS and the ecology of poverty*. Oxford: Oxford University Press.

Stillwaggon, E. (2006b). The ecology of poverty: Nutrition, parasites, and vulnerability to HIV/AIDS. In S. Gillespie (Ed.), *AIDS, poverty, and hunger*. Washington DC: International Food Policy Research Institute.

Tang, A., et al. (1993). Dietary micronutrient intake and risk of progression to Acquired Immunodeficiency Syndrome (AIDS) in Human Immunodeficiency Virus Type 1 (HIV-1)-infected homosexual men. *American Journal of Epidemiology, 138*, 937–951.

te Velde, D., Morrissey, O., & Hewitt, A. (2002). Allocating aid to international public goods. In M. Ferroni & A. Mody (Eds.), *International public goods: Incentives, measurement, and financing*. Boston, MA: Kluwer.

Teixeira, L. (2006). Evaluation of the United Nations Declaration on HIV/AIDS resource targets. *Rev Saúde Pública, 40*, 52–59.

The Economist (2005, July 30). AIDS – No carnival.

The Forum for Collaborative HIV research, TB/HIV working group. (2007). *HIV-TB Co-infections: Meeting the challenge*. Washington DC: The Forum for Collaborative HIV Research.

The Global Fund to Fight AIDS, Tuberculosis and Malaria. (2006). *Funding the global fight against HIV/AIDS, tuberculosis and malaria. Resource needs for the Global Fund 2006–2007 and 2008–2010*. Geneva: The Global Fund to Fight AIDS, Tuberculosis and Malaria.

The Global Fund to Fight AIDS, Tuberculosis and Malaria. (2007). *The Global Fund: Who we are, what we do*. Geneva: The Global Fund to Fight AIDS, Tuberculosis and Malaria.
The Henry J. Kaiser Family Foundation. (2005). *Financing the response to HIV/AIDS in low and middle income countries: Funding for HIV/AIDS from G7 and the European Commission, July 2005*. Washington DC: The Henry J. Kaiser Family Foundation.
The Henry J. Kaiser Family Foundation. (2007a). *HIV/AIDS policy fact sheet: The global HIV/AIDS epidemic*. Washington DC: The Henry J. Kaiser Family Foundation.
The Henry J. Kaiser Family Foundation. (2007b). *HIV/AIDS policy fact sheet: The HIV/AIDS epidemic in the Caribbean*. Washington DC. The Henry J. Kaiser Family Foundation.
The Henry J. Kaiser Family Foundation. (2007c). *Large-scale trial of Merck's experimental HIV vaccine to begin in South Africa*. Washington DC: The Henry J. Kaiser Family Foundation.
The Henry J. Kaiser Family Foundation. (2008). *HIV/AIDS policy fact sheet: Understanding the new UNAIDS estimates*. Washington DC: The Henry J. Kaiser Family Foundation.
The Henry J. Kaiser Family Foundation Website: http://www.kaisernetwork.org/daily_reports/print_report.cfm?DR_ID=42828&dr_cat=1. Accessed on 2009, January 26.
The Joint United Nations Programme on HIV/AIDS (UNAIDS). (2006c). *Fact sheet: Sub-Saharan Africa*. Geneva: UNAIDS.
The Joint United Nations Programme on HIV/AIDS (UNAIDS). (2007a). *Fact sheet: China*. Geneva: UNAIDS.
The Joint United Nations Programme on HIV/AIDS (UNAIDS). (2007b). *Fact sheet: Key facts by region – 2007 AIDS epidemic update*. Geneva: UNAIDS.
The Joint United Nations Programme on HIV/AIDS (UNAIDS). (1998). *HIV-related opportunistic diseases: UNAIDS technical update*. Geneva: UNAIDS.
The Joint United Nations Programme on HIV/AIDS (UNAIDS). (2000). *Voluntary counselling and testing (VCT): Technical update*. Geneva: UNAIDS.
The Joint United Nations Programme on HIV/AIDS (UNAIDS). (2001). *The global strategy framework on HIV/AIDS*. Geneva: UNAIDS.
The Joint United Nations Programme on HIV/AIDS (UNAIDS). (2004). *Report on the global AIDS epidemic 2004*. Geneva: UNAIDS.
The Joint United Nations Programme on HIV/AIDS (UNAIDS). (2006a). *Fact sheet: Asia 06*. Geneva: UNAIDS.
The Joint United Nations Programme on HIV/AIDS (UNAIDS). (2006b). *Report on the global AIDS epidemic 2006*. Geneva: UNAIDS.
The Joint United Nations Programme on HIV/AIDS (UNAIDS). (2008). *Report on the global AIDS epidemic 2008*. Geneva: UNAIDS.
The Joint United Nations Programme on HIV/AIDS (UNAIDS), World Health Organization (WHO). (2004). *AIDS epidemic update – December 2004*. Geneva: UNAIDS.
The Joint United Nations Programme on HIV/AIDS (UNAIDS), World Health Organization (WHO). (2005). *AIDS epidemic update – December 2005*. Geneva: UNAIDS.
The Joint United Nations Programme on HIV/AIDS (UNAIDS), World Health Organization (WHO). (2006). *AIDS epidemic update – December 2006*. Geneva: UNAIDS.
The Joint United Nations Programme on HIV/AIDS (UNAIDS), World Health Organization (WHO). (2007). *AIDS epidemic update – December 2007*. Geneva: UNAIDS.
The Wall Street Journal (2007, February 9). South Africa plans AIDS vaccine trial.
The White House (2008, 6, October 2008) *2008 U.S.-EU Summit Declaration* (Press release)
The World Bank Group (2007). Ethiopia at the glance. The Africa Life Database (LDB). World Bank Website: http://www4.worldbank.org/afr/stats/ldb.cfm. Accessed on 2009, January 26.
U.S. Agency for International Development (USAID). (2006a). *Country profile: Nigeria*. Washington DC: USAID.
U.S. Agency for International Development (USAID). (2006b). *Country profile: Senegal*. Washington DC: USAID.
U.S. Agency for International Development (USAID). (2006c). *Country profile: Kenya*. Washington DC: USAID.
U.S. Agency for International Development (USAID). (2006d). *Country profile: Philippines*. Washington DC: USAID.

U.S. Agency for International Development (USAID). (1998). *USAID responds to HIV/AIDS: A strategy for the future. To increase the use of improved, effective and sustainable responses to reduce HIV transmission and to mitigate the impact of the HIV/AIDS pandemic*. Washington DC: USAID.

U.S. Agency for International Development (USAID). (2002). *USAID's expanded response to HIV/AIDS*. Washington DC: USAID.

U.S. Agency for International Development (USAID). (2004). *HIV/AIDS: A guide for nutritional care and support 2004* (2nd ed.). Washington DC: Food and Nutrition Technical Assistance (FANTA).

U.S. Agency for International Development (USAID). (2005). *Health profile: East Africa*. Washington DC: USAID.

U.S. Agency for International Development (USAID), U.S. Department of Commerce. (1998). *World population profile: 1998*. Washington DC: U.S. Government Printing Office.

U.S. Agency for International Development (USAID), U.S. Department of Commerce. (2002). *Global population profile: 2002*. Washington DC: U.S. Government Printing Office.

U.S. Department of State. (2005). *U.S., EU cooperate on science and technology, fact sheet*. Brussels: U.S. Mission to the European Union.

Uganda AIDS Commission. (2003). *The HIV/AIDS epidemic: Prevalence and impact, June 2003*. Kampala: Uganda AIDS Commission.

UN Millennium Project. (2005). *Investing in development. a practical plan to achieve the millennium development goals*. London: Earthscan.

United Nations (UN). (2000). *Resolution 55/2 United Nations Millennium Declaration*. New York: UN.

United Nations (UN). (2001). *Resolution 26/2 Declaration of Commitment on HIV/AIDS*. New York: UN.

United Nations (UN) (2006). *World migrant stock: The 2005 Revision*. Population Database.

United Nations (UN). (2007). *The millenium development goals report 2007*. New York: UN.

United Nations (UN), Department of Economic and Social Affairs, Population Division. (2007a). *Population and HIV/AIDS 2007*. New York: UN.

United Nations (UN), Department of Economic and Social Affairs, Population Division. (2007b). *World population prospects: The 2006 Revision*. UN, New York: Highlights.

United Nations Development Programme (UNDP). (2007a). *Human development report 2007/08. Fighting climate change: Human solidarity in a divided world*. UNDP, New York.

United Nations Development Programme (UNDP) (2007b). The Global Environmental Facility (GEF). UNDP Website: http://www.undp.org/gef/05/about/gefsec.html. Accessed on 2009, January 26.

United Nations General Assembly Special Session (UNGASS). (2008). *Nigeria UNGASS Report 2007*. Geneva: UNAIDS.

United Nations Population Fund (UNFPA) (2002). *HIV prevention now* (Programme brief No. 8). New York: Author.

Varian, H. (2004). *System reliability and free riding* (Working Paper). Berkeley.

Vicary, S. (1990). Transfers and the weakest-link: An extension of Hirshleifer's analysis. *Journal of Public Economics, 43*, 375–394.

Vicary, S., & Sandler, T. (2002). Weakest-link public goods: Giving in-kind or transferring money. *European Economic Review, 46*, 1501–1520.

Warr, P. (1982). Pareto optimal redistribution and private charity. *Journal of Public Economics, 19*, 131–138.

Warr, P. (1983). The private provision of a public good is independent of the distribution of income. *Economics Letters, 13*, 207–211.

Wasserheit, J. (1992). Epidemiological synergy. *Interrelationships between human immunodeficiency virus infection and other sexually transmitted diseases. Sexually Transmitted Diseases, 19*, 61–77.

Wines, M. (2007, 28 January 2007). Virulent TB in South Africa may imperil millions. *The New York Times*.

Wolday, M., et al. (2002). Treatment of intestinal worms is associated with decreased HIV plasma viral load. *Journal of Acquired Immune Deficiency Syndromes, 31*, 56–62.

Woodward, D., & Smith, R. (2003). Global public goods and health: Concepts and issues. In R. Smith et al. (Eds.), *Global public goods for health*. New York: Health economic and public health perspectives. Oxford University Press.

Working group 5 of the Commission on Macroeconomics and Health. (2002). *Improving health outcomes of the poor*. Geneva: WHO.

World Bank. (1993). *World Development Report 1993: Investing in health*. New York: Oxford University Press.

World Bank. (2000). *Poverty reduction and global public goods: Issues for the World Bank in supporting global collective action*. Washington DC: World Bank.

World Bank (2007). Country classification. World Bank Website:http://web.worldbank.org/WBSITE/EXTERNAL/DATASTATISTICS/0,contentMDK:20487070~menuPK:64133156~pageK:64133150~piPK:64133175~theSitePK:239419,00.html. Accessed on 2009, January 26.

World Bank (2008a). The 2005 International Comparison Program. Background document. World Bank Website: http://go.worldbank.org/VMCB80AB40. Accessed on 2009, January 26.

World Bank (2008b). Education trends and comparison. World Bank Website: http://go.worldbank.org/JVXVANWYY0. Accessed on 2009, January 26.

World Bank, International Bank for Reconstruction and Development. (2008). *Global purchasing power, parities and real expenditures. 2005 International Comparison Program*. Washington DC: World Bank.

World Health Organization (WHO). (2003a). *Regional strategic plan on HIV/TB*. Geneva: WHO.

World Health Organization (WHO). (2003b). *HIV/TB – Report of the third working group meeting, Montreux*. Geneva: WHO.

World Health Organization (WHO). (2004a). *The World Health Report 2004: Changing History*. Geneva: WHO.

World Health Organization (WHO). (2004b). *Nutrition counselling, care and support for HIV-infected women. Guidelines on HIV-related care, treatment and support for HIV-infected women and their children in resource-constrained settings*. Geneva: WHO.

World Health Organization (WHO). (2005a). *The "3 by 5" target*. Geneva: WHO.

World Health Organization (WHO). (2005b). *The Millennium Development Goals*. Geneva: WHO.

World Health Organization (WHO). (2007a). *Quarterly report comparing the transaction prices paid in the last 3 months for antiretroviral drugs by low and middle income countries to the price paid the previous years. A summary report from the global price reporting mechanism on antiretroviral drugs, March 2007*. Geneva: WHO.

World Health Organization (WHO) (2007b). Geographical distribution and useful facts and stats, Geneva. WHO Website: http://www.who.int/wormcontrol/statistics/geographical/en/index.html. Accessed on 2009, January 26

World Health Organization (WHO) (2007c). Useful information on schistosomiasis and STH, Geneva. WHO Website: http://www.who.int/wormcontrol/statistics/useful_info/en/index.html. Accessed on 2009, January 26.

World Health Organization (WHO). (2008). *Global tuberculosis control 2008. Surveillance planning financing*. Geneva: WHO.

World Health Organization (WHO), United Nations International Children's Emergency Fund (UNICEF) (2000). (2000). *Global water supply and sanitation assessment. 2000 report*. New York: UNICEF.

World Health Organization (WHO) et al. (2006). Epidemiological fact sheets on HIV/AIDS and other sexually transmitted diseases. WHO Website: http://www.who.int/globalatlas/default.asp. Accessed on 2009, January 26.

Xu, X. (2002a). International best-shot public goods and foreign aid. *Economics Bulletin, 3*, 1–4.

Xu, X. (2002b). Development costs and open source software (Discussionpaper). Berkeley.

Zhu, T., et al. (1998). An African HIV-1 sequence from 1959 and implications for the origin of the epidemic. *Nature, 391*, 594–597.

Index

FSC
www.fsc.org
MIX
Papier | Fördert
gute Waldnutzung
FSC® C083411

Kolibri 360 GmbH
Ferdinand-Jühlke-Straße 7
99095 Erfurt, Deutschland
produktsicherheit@kolibri360.de